BL
11101-

THE HOLLOW MEN

To Becky, Laurie and Andy

THE HOLLOW MEN

An Examination of
British Foreign Policy Between
the Years 1933 and 1939

Margaret George

With a Foreword by A L Rowse

LESLIE FREWIN : LONDON

© Margaret George, 1965 and 1967

First published in Great Britain by
Leslie Frewin Publishers Limited,
15 Hay's Mews, Berkeley Square, London W1

This book is set in Baskerville,
printed by Anchor Press and
bound by William Brendon,
both of Tiptree, Essex

Contents

Foreword

By A L Rowse

WHEN MY LITTLE book *Appeasement: A Study in Political Decline* (American title, and the American edition is the fuller) came out, C P Snow had the kindness to say, 'This is exactly as it was.' I can now hand on the compliment to Professor George. My short book was in no sense a history of Appeasement, merely a personal contribution to its history from a fairly close-up view of some of the leading Appeasers. Professor Margaret George's book is a more extended and impersonal account of the matter, looking at it from a distance and with no axe to grind. Her book is history: though she did not have the bitter experience of going through it at the time. I do not differ very much from her view of it all: she has got it essentially right.

One correction of perspective at the outset. It is a mistake to blame what happened upon the Treaty of Versailles – that is a mistake the Appeasers made. The Treaty of Versailles was essentially just in its territorial provisions – if you want to know what kind of treaty the Germans would have imposed on Europe had they won their First World War you have only to look at the Treaty of Brest-Litovsk they imposed on Russia in 1917. They took, or imposed their domination on, practically all Eastern Europe: Hitler's demand for *Lebensraum* was simply continuous with it.

L S Amery was one of the few Conservative leaders not infected with Appeasement, and was therefore kept out during the whole of that decade 1931–40; he was also partly Central European and knew what he was talking about when it was a question of Germany. He summed it up to me once: 'Germany came so near to bringing it off the first time that it was only to be expected that she should have another try.' This is the long

7

and the short of the matter. Ludwig Dehio, the leading German historian today – like Friedrich Meinecke before him – practically alone among German academics has the candour and courage to admit that the war was but the first crest in the two great waves of German aggression, the attempt to achieve ascendancy in Europe in double-quick time before it was too late. What really irked the Germans was not so much the Treaty of Versailles as the fact that they lost the war. They could not believe that they had been defeated; they certainly did not accept it (hence the 'stab-in-the-back' legend they propagated so effectively); the occult forces in the background, the General Staff, the Army, the Right, were determined to have another try.

Nor were the economic clauses of the Treaty of Versailles really inoperable. The simple fact was that the Germans never intended to work them or to pay for the damage they had done to others. Keynes's *Economic Consequences of the Peace* did untold damage in undermining the authority of the Treaty and, Liberal intellectual that he was, he was completely wrong. Etienne Mantoux showed in his book *The Carthaginian Peace* that in the 1930s the Germans were able to pay twice as much on armaments than ever they were asked to pay in reparations. Even for what they did pay in reparations, they borrowed more from Wall Street and the City – only too eager to lend, as Professor George tells us, by 1929 'the German national income rose to a level seventy-seven per cent higher than in 1913', while claiming all the time that they couldn't pay.

It is certainly true, as Professor George says – and as anyone who knew anything of Montagu Norman's circle can corroborate – that the City was strongly pro-German and anti-French. We are certainly being made to pay for that today.

These people, the Appeasers, from Neville Chamberlain downwards and outwards, were also anti-Foreign Office, which had a far better grasp of the situation, a more trained and educated knowledge of Europe, and knew far better what the Germans were up to. The awful thing about these people was their sheer, smug ignorance: not one of them knew Germany or German, or Germany's malign record in modern history; not one of them ever bothered to read *Mein Kampf*, in which Hitler practically told them beforehand what he intended to do.

Professor George addresses herself to the question: Why? How can these people have been so terribly, so obviously, wrong?

They were not malign; they were well-meaning enough. As the late Lord Astor insisted in defending them against my strictures upon them in my book: 'My father and his friends were Christian gentlemen, bent on peace – and imbued with a distrust of the Foreign Office.' They were, it is true, mostly Christians and mostly gentlemen; it was hard luck that they should have come up against thugs of genius in Hitler and his crew. As for peace—commonsense should have told them that, if you want peace from such people, it is no use giving way all along the line: that is precisely what brought the war down on us. Only a grand alliance against the aggressors would have stopped them. As for their attitude toward the Foreign Office – which was largely right and had an instructed view of events – these meddling amateurs, Lord Lothian and the rest of them, did nothing but damage. His greatest friend, Lionel Curtis, said of him: 'Philip died in the knowledge that he had been wrong.'

There is a joker in the pack: there was an element in the situation of which they were too fly to speak openly. They were confused and befoozled by their anti-Red attitude, their anti-Communism. Nothing wrong in being anti-Communist – none of them was more anti-Bolshevik than Churchill was. But this did not confuse his mind as to the real interests of his country. He saw that Hitler's Germany was a more immediate danger to Britain and everybody else, the Russians a remoter one. The Appeasers were confused: at the back of their minds they thought of Hitler as a bulwark against Communism. The result was that they brought the war down upon themselves, let the Russians into the centre of Europe, and practically ruined their country.

What a record for those well-meaning Christian gentlemen, bent on peace, and with a distrust of the Foreign Office! When I look back on my own little book, I do not think that it erred on the side of harshness. No responsible historian can condemn too strongly the conduct of affairs that led us to that pass.

This is not merely my judgment, it was also Churchill's: the 'unnecessary war,' he called it. It should never have been necessary, if the proper steps had been taken to stop these things at almost any point before, say, 1938. The proper steps were perfectly clear: keeping the alliance against them firm, instead of giving way, plus a proper modicum of armaments, enough to do the job, so that if the break came it would be an internal bursting of the abscess within Germany.

But those in control of our affairs *would* not look at the situation in these terms – they were Churchill's terms. They constantly 'preferred their own sources of information' within Germany, which meant listening to what Hitler told them; what they really were after was an accommodation with Hitler – as if any accommodation were possible except on his terms. And these stooges on the Right played bat and ball with the lunatic fringe on the Left, while the sensible men in both Parties were forced to watch their country piloted on to the rocks. That is not a misrepresentation of what Neville Chamberlain did, with the full consent of the bulk of the Conservatives in that unspeakable Parliament. As one of our ambassadors to the United States said to me recently: 'Poor Neville! He didn't know *what* he was doing. He hadn't a clue.' I replied: 'You didn't say that at the time: you left that to me to say.'

One can only conclude, sadly, with the great Oxenstierna: 'You see, my son, with what little wisdom the world is governed.'

But the fact that the Appeasers brought the war down upon themselves does not mean that they made it, or that they were equally to blame with Hitler and Germany. There is no intellectual confusion more gratuitous and silly than to say that we were all equally to blame. There is nothing crazier than the view put forward by irresponsible historians that Hitler was no more to blame, or not much more, than we were for the war. Of course, Hitler was an opportunist, making the most of all opportunities that were given him. But no national leader ever told people beforehand what he intended to do more clearly than he did in *Mein Kampf*. It was a programme: 'settlement' of the Jewish 'question', *Lebensraum* for the Germans in Eastern Europe (what about *Lebensraum* for other peoples whose lands they were?), hatred of the Slavs, Germany's 'historic mission', the glorification of war, destruction of liberty, contempt for democracy. No leader was ever more explicit about his objectives; it was only with regard to means that he was flexible, varied according to circumstances. To confuse means with ends – tactical variation and flexibility with fixed aims and objectives – is simply second-rate thinking. It is astonishing that this mixed-up state of mind should ever have been taken seriously; but I suppose it is too much to expect people to be able to think straight. It is merely shocking that their supposed intellectual leaders, from whom they take their cue, should start the rot – one more sign of decadence and decline.

For one has only to look to see all round the results of failure to think straight, of the lack of moral and political courage for which we are paying and shall continue to pay. During the past two or three centuries our ancestors achieved an astonishing position for the small island-power in the world; the old British governing class was the ablest, the most responsible, the most creative in Europe. Out of a small people and a small island it created the greatest empire in the world; even its record in India alone is one of the most extraordinary in human history – that a small handful of Anglo-Indian civil servants, with the minimum exertion of power, should have licked a sub-continent into shape and order.

Look at it now! Look at the picture Britain presents, having muddled itself into an unnecessary war, thrown away an Empire, drifted into near-bankruptcy as a nation, a pathetic suppliant to be admitted into the comity of Europe, on her knees to France – after her record in the Second German war! – and to Germany who made it! I hope those people on both sides, for both political parties are to blame, who are responsible for the decline of their country, will take the picture home to themselves and recognise where the responsibility historically lies.

And Professor George's sensible and reliable book – as against the irresponsible views of more publicised historians, forever playing to the gallery – will help to keep the record straight.

Author's Preface

IN THE YEARS since World War II, interest in the story of the appeasement era has rarely lagged, especially in British studies, where the details of the 'fine mess of things' the government made before the war continue a matter of often hot debate. In part, this interest is the natural result of the ugly memory that the appeasement story is for British participants – whom it worries like a sore tooth; in part, it is because, as documents and memoirs appear, the facts behind the fact of the dismal decade become ever more plain. It well may be, as Kingsley Martin observes (*New Statesman*, 26th April 1963), that it is still 'too soon to write authentically or authoritatively about the thirties', that 'personal and party emotions are too close', and that 'an accumulation of myths obscures the whole', but people persist in trying – not the least of them Mr Martin himself.

The work which follows is offered as an addition to the continuing exploration of the appeasement period. I have attempted, not primarily to tell the story – for that is now well known – but to understand it, to probe deeper into the motives of the appeasers, to explain why they behaved as they did, what they were trying to do with their policy; therefore, my emphasis is different from that of books concentrating on the 'what' rather than the 'why' of appeasement. Furthermore, my study is not without certain bases of preconception – the identification of the main actors of appeasement, for one thing. I have started with the proposition that, although a nation of varied groups and individuals followed the course of appeasement for a multiplicity of reasons, the Conservative governing group constructed it, administered it (often in total secrecy), and bore for it the prime responsibility; thus, I have not been concerned in any depth with the (sometimes very real) involvement of others, Liberals, Socialists, or whatever. And, from the start, I have proposed a certain content to the motives of the appeasers, special attitudes of Conservative politicans which emerged in their response to threatening forces within the interwar world; defensive reactions were, I think, at the root of the choices, as well as the vacillation and inadequacies of the appeasement policy.

In this way I have tried to build: first, to trace the origin and development of the complex of ideas and attitudes which, I submit, lay behind the Conservative response of appeasement and, second, having proposed this part of a Conservative 'mind', to observe its operation within the diplomacy of appeasement.

MG

Introduction

In even the Tory view of the matter there is broad consensus that British foreign policy in the 1930s was an unqualified disaster. Led by the governments of Stanley Baldwin and Neville Chamberlain, the British nation pursued the will-o'-the-wisp of peace with Fascism, peace at any price, peace – as one Conservative put it – 'at any cost in humiliation'.[1] The story of the decade is its series of dramatic retreats, of British acquiescence in Nazi aggression, in designs of domination that became reality in staccato bursts of German activity: there was the public announcement of German rearmament in 1935; Hitler's march into the Rhineland in 1936; Fascist subjugation of Spain from 1936; and – in quickening tempo – the disappearance into the German gullet of Austria and Czechoslovakia in 1938 and 1939. By the end of the decade, when even Conservatives sickened of the humiliating cost, Britain had lost not only the great goal of peace but in the judgment of the world, and in the shamed awareness of her own citizens, she had lost an incalculable amount of prestige and respect.

It was a baffling age. Why, basically, did it happen? Why did the British follow a course which so isolated their nation? Why were they blind to the challenge of Fascist expansionism —inevitably aimed at the sitting target of imperial Britain and its century-long domination of world affairs? What pushed a proud man like Neville Chamberlain, who had called Adolf Hitler 'the commonest little dog he had ever seen', to plead hat in hand before Hitler? What blunted British perception to the unparalleled barbarism of the Nazi system; why did so few say clearly that it was 'absolutely immoral' to give Germany

[1] Thomas Jones, *A Diary with Letters, 1931–1950*, p 411.

15

'a free hand to annex other people's property in central or Eastern Europe'?[1]

Perhaps the chief problem in the puzzle of appeasement is that, on one level, there has seemed to be no problem at all. Few commentators – journalists, historians, postwar politicians – would excuse it, this policy that made war inevitable and 'well-nigh ruined' the country,[2] but they understand it. Appeasement happened because it happened; the British Government and the British people longed too desperately for peace and, for both, judgment about peace-preserving methods was impaired by the supreme value placed upon the goal.

No doubt it is the very obviousness of this answer that has made it suffice for so many people who remember vividly the climate of opinion in interwar Britain. The horror of war was the main thing: the memory of total war, after 1918, was a living force, an ineradicable consciousness that made pacifism a passionate creed with millions, that brought a mass denial of any issue being worth another international conflict. Then, too, there spread in Britain of the 1920s a special regard for Germany, directly attributable to the half-shamed awareness that the 'guilt clause' of the Versailles Treaty, and the postwar punishment of Germany, had been less than fair – grossly unjust, in fact, to a German people who assuredly could not be stigmatised with criminal responsibility for the Great War. Appeasement, then, was the political and diplomatic expression of these two factors – the aversion to war and sympathy for the Germans. The British started with the proposition that another war was unthinkable, and that in any case war with Germany was unnecessary; from that point they were bound to yield before aggressively aggrieved German spokesmen in the 1930s, bound to concede that Hitler's complaints of 'legal inequalities' had basis in fact, bound to attempt the accommodating gesture that would soothe the resentful leaders of the New Germany.

There is no question about this account of reality in inter-

[1] Sir Robert Vansittart, quoted in Harold Nicholson, *King George the Fifth, His Life and Reign*, p 529.
[2] A L Rowse, *All Souls and Appeasement*, p 117.

war Britain. It explains a great deal about popular reactions –
the refusal of a majority to listen to Churchill's pleas for
rearmament, the widespread complacency about German occupation of the Rhineland ('Jerry going into his own back-
garden'), the hysterical relief and gratitude that greeted
Neville Chamberlain on his return from Munich. It explains
Labour policy on foreign affairs, the fact that from 1918 all
factions of that badly-divided party agreed on friendship for
the German people and on a policy aimed at reaccepting
Germany as a member in good standing of Europe and the
League of Nations.[1] In their brief moments of power in the
1920s the Labour Party was formally pro-peace, pro-League
and pro-German, their foreign policy officially designed to
demonstrate British regret for the harshness of Versailles, and
British intentions to honour the postwar pledges of universal
disarmament and unequivocal reliance on the League of
Nations; by the 1930s, as Josiah Wedgwood said, Labour
people 'had preached the iniquity of war and armaments so
long' that, to the threat from Nazi Germany, 'many wilfully
shut their eyes and brains'.

But if the plainest facts of this account of broad support of
appeasement are undeniable, what have we gained from it in
historical insight? We know that Stanley Baldwin and the
man in the street shared a profound longing for peace, and
that both a Tory Cabinet minister and, say, a member of the
Socialist League talked with feeling of the injustices done to
'poor Germany' – true, of course, but hardly enlightening. Or
we have an unlikely image of the identity of Christian pacifist
George Lansbury and Neville Chamberlain (a Prime Minister
remembered as 'uncommonly insensitive to political atmosphere') as spokesmen for the deepest desires of the masses of a
peace-loving nation. With such uninformative generalities this

[1] In 1919 Beatrice Webb recorded her 'impatience' with France and with
French hatred of Germany; 'My thought and feeling,' she continued, 'goes out
to Germany in her heroic struggle to reconstruct her political and social machinery'
– the struggle that was, perhaps, the German 'transition to socialism'. *Beatrice
Webb's Diaries, 1912–1924*, ed Margaret Cole, p 144.

explanation of appeasement as a *national* response to the Fascist
challenge smooths over the different paths along which different
people retreated before the threat of Nazi aggression and, as
well, ignores the disparate levels of participation in and
responsibility for the details of that policy.

For it was the Conservative politicians, in impressive control
of a powerful government, who directed foreign policy in the
1930s – who were, as A L Rowse said, 'in charge of our destinies'.
An examination of the sources, of the records by and about
the Conservatives of the appeasement era, suggests a rather
more complex picture than one of simple harmony of leaders
and people on a policy that somehow turned out badly for both.
Surely it is clear from the records that the leaders both shared
and reflected the views of the mass of their countrymen. As
much as any informed Briton they were fair-minded in their
willingness to accept Germany as an equal partner in the
European community of nations. And they were men of peace,
not in a doctrinaire sense – like Lansbury Socialists – but as
practical men, businessmen, who knew the human and material
destruction and had suffered the losses of total war. But what
is also clear from the records is that Conservatives followed a
policy fashioned by themselves, not by the mass of their
countrymen.

To make an interpretive leap: the study of appeasement
properly begins here, with the recognition that it was a Conservative policy, a product of the particular content of the
Conservative insistence on peace and on friendship with Germany, of the particular way in which Conservatives filtered
these typical British opinions through their own attitudes and
ideas, their own necessities and designs. There was much besides
in their policy that bore the stamp of traditional British statesmanship – the dislike of 'European entanglements', the reluctance to be committed in any way to the 'faraway nations' (as
Chamberlain called them) of Eastern Europe; there was much
in their policy that was reminiscent (pathetically so in 1938–39)
of nineteenth-century Liberalism – the reliance on the nego-

tiations of the conference table, the firm, even moralistic, faith
in the right of 'self-determination' of peoples – that is to say, of
Germans outside the Third Reich. But there was more in the
policy of appeasement that reflected a new Conservative
uncertainty in the conditions of the postwar world, in a world
that seemed suddenly jarred by war into new and disturbing
shapes.

Perhaps we might illustrate with a story which is of 'appeasement' of a sort (it was so labelled); the main point is that it
demonstrates something essential about Conservative attitudes
in foreign affairs after World War I. It is a story that has been
painstakingly recreated[1] from the records of 1918, about Lord
Milner, the Imperial statesman whose achievements as High
Commissioner of South Africa during the prolonged crisis with
the Boers had made him a man almost revered by the extreme
Right of the Conservatives in Britain. Milner became part of
the War Cabinet in 1916 – a coup of a Lloyd Georgian appointment, delighting as it did a wide range of Tory diehard opinion
– and Secretary of State for War in 1918; it is an episode from
the latter tenure that deserves attention.

Taking over as War Secretary in early 1918, Milner could
see only the bleakest prospects for the Western Powers. On the
front in France, German armies smashed again at the Allied
forces, threatening in a massed offensive to end the stalemate
of the war of position; in the East, Bolshevik revolution had
removed the Russian ally from the war, and the treaty of
Brest-Litovsk – the Carthaginian peace by which the German
Government had permitted the Bolsheviks to quit – had opened
to the German war machine a vast wealth of material resources.
In this dark situation, Milner grew more and more pessimistic
about defeating Germany, more and more inclined to seek from
the Germans a negotiated peace. He was, apparently, persuasive with some of his colleagues on both points. According to
The History of The Times (the 'authoritative work on "appease-

[1] A M Gollin, *Proconsul in Politics*. The following summary is based on Mr
Gollin's chapter on Milner as 'The Appeaser', pp 522–577.

ment" in Britain'),[1] 'Milner certainly, and Lloyd George
probably, had been forced to the conviction that, with Russia
not merely out of the war but in the hands of Germany, the
Allies must abandon the hope of winning in the West. Germany,
by possessing Russia, had, in a sense, already won the war. . . .
Their new estimate of the possibility of the immediate future
led Lloyd George and Milner to think of settling the war on
what the latter had called "moderate" terms in the spring of
1917.' And what moderate terms seemed a basis for settling the
war in 1918? An answer comes in pieces of second-hand testimony. In the diary of Beatrice Webb is a note which she jotted
after a visit with the Prime Minister: 'What is clear from our
talk is that the PM and Milner are thinking of a peace at the
expense of Russia. . . . I am not at all sure whether his desire
to meet us and his desire that we should meet Milner is not
connected with this possible sacrifice of Russia and her Revolution.' A letter of Clifford Sharp, editor of the *New Statesman*,
pinpoints Milner's role: 'It appears that the chief exponent of
the idea of a negotiated peace with Germany at Russia's
expense is *Milner* who has gradually converted two or three of
his colleagues to the idea.' The writers of *The History of The
Times* summarised what is known of this 'very discreet' yet 'concrete' peace plan: by the spring of 1918 'the Prime Minister,
Ministers and ex-Ministers, including members of the War
Cabinet and some members of the Labour Party,[2] had privately
discussed the possibility of ending the struggle in the West by
giving the Germans a free hand in the East. It seemed an
admirably complete and well-timed scheme, backed as it had
been by the great Western German offensive of March and
April. The Brest-Litovsk treaty offered, in the view of some, a
a perfect pretext for the Western Powers to appease Germany
by sacrificing Russia.'

---

[1] The phrase is Gollin's, *Proconsul in Politics*.
[2] Mrs Webb's reaction was the tart remark that the idea revealed Milner's
lack of 'moral fastidiousness' and Lloyd George's 'cynical opportunity'. *Diaries,
1912–1924*, p 116. Editor Sharp was appalled by the idea, found it 'very disturbing
. . . sinister'. *History of The Times*, IV, 1, 360–361.

These 'secret appeasement plans' – the words are in *The History of The Times* – were not, of course, brought to the light of action, largely because of the stiffening of the Western Front by American armies, and the swift German decision for surrender. Interestingly, even as Allied prospects improved to positive brightness in the summer and early autumn of 1918, Milner continued with his idea of a negotiated moderate peace with Germany. He felt so strongly on the matter that he tested it in the Press, in an interview published in the *Evening Standard* that was briefly a *cause célèbre* in the political upperworld of London (with Milner's critics asserting that he, German-born, was something of a Junker himself). With his interviewer,[1] Milner's main theme was that negotiated peace was the quickest way to 'complete victory' for the Allies for several reasons: if, instead, the Allies insisted on the hard terms of unconditional surrender, the necessary invasion of Germany would result, first, in terrible losses of Western manpower and, second, in the stiffening of the resistance of the German people, further, invasion and heavy fighting in Germany could set up an unmanageable long-range situation – could 'create in Central Europe a state of chaos, confusion and desperation congenial to the spread of Bolshevism'; finally, and relatedly, political reforms in Germany (in September and October of 1918) had destroyed 'Prussian militarism' and had produced the kind of 'stable government' with which it was in the interest of the Allies – unless they wished to see 'Bolshevism and chaos rampant there' – to deal.

Lord Milner – to summarise – had put his impressive administrative talents into war against a Germany which had threatened the British Empire; when that threat was eliminated the British task, as he saw it, was done (for 'we did not go to war for Czechoslovakia, Yugoslavia, Rumanians or Poles'). As an Imperialist he was dedicated to the organic unity of the

---

[1] The interviewer was Arthur Mann, whose article on Milner's ideas appeared in the *Evening Standard*, 17th October 1918. See also Mann's informal account of the meeting in *History of The Times*, IV, 2, 1091–1092.

British Empire, and firmly opposed to 'entangling alliances' on the Continent, especially in Central and Eastern Europe. On the other hand, Milner did not consider a total withdrawal from the affairs of Europe. He was gravely concerned about the victory of Bolshevism in Russia and apprehensive of the spread of 'revolutionary fever' among the masses of Western Europe – most particularly, among the working classes of the British Isles.[1] Precisely these fears led him to the conclusion that the British must support and deal with a stable German government – shorn of the 'Prussian militarism' that had challenged the nation – as the chief European bulwark against the Communist disease. Thus, 'when the Germans were beaten in the West and no longer threatened the Empire in an immediate sense, Milner had no objection to the conditions established at Brest-Litovsk',[2] conditions which did indeed give to Germany a 'free hand' in the East.

Milner was an extraordinary man, of great influence and power within 'exclusive regiments of the Tory Party'. Not only was he venerated by 'the right wing of the Tories . . . the supporters of the generals, the bulk of the Conservative Press, Imperialists generally, the King and his friends',[3] but as High Commissioner in South Africa he had gathered around him a group of disciples in the Imperial cause, able young men from Oxford and the Colonial Office, who, thereafter, as alumni of 'Milner's Kindergarten', remained true to his ideas and ideals, his dedicated followers and defenders. By the 1930s, most of Milner's young men had become persons of stature and influence at the peak of important public, academic, or business careers – and some involved in the absorbing work of dealing with the Germany of Adolf Hitler. The biographer of Lord Milner had no doubt that they carried with them the 'legacy' of the

[1] Gollin, *Proconsul*, pp 538–540 and *passim*. Milner 'gave his blessing' to, and even 'played a part of some significance' in, General Kornilov's plot to overthrow the March Revolution and the Kerensky Government in Russia in the summer and autumn of 1917. *Ibid*, pp 550–551. He also was influential in the early Allied intervention in Russia after the Bolshevik Revolution. *Ibid*, p 557, fn.

[2] *Ibid*, p 577.

[3] *Ibid*, pp 370, 374–375.

master's teaching on the problems of Germany and Russia, of revolution and stabilisation, into the era of appeasement.

This much, in any case, we can here extract from the story of Lord Milner's 'appeasement': the apprehensions and anxieties that Milner felt in surveying the European scene pressed, too, upon many other Conservative minds; and the method by which he tried to allay his fears, his 'discreet' plan for dealing with a stable Germany as a bulwark of strength against Eastern and Central European revolutionary explosions, appeared and reappeared as a kind of subterranean policy hope in the 1930s.

Thus, in the study of appeasement, we concentrate on the leaders rather than the led, on the policy-makers and opinion-moulders rather than the 'people' or the public mind. Indeed, a key to appeasement is to be found in the Conservative mind, in the thinking, the attitudes, the fears and illusions of the inter-war political élites of Great Britain. Ministers of Cabinets, members of the Commons, peers of the Lords, respected journalists, leaders of society – among these we will find witnesses to the 'why' of appeasement.

PART ONE

BACKDROP TO APPEASEMENT
The Paralysing Postwar World

I
Conservative Crises

THE SEED TIME of appeasement was in 1918, in the deep-furrowed soil of the postwar world. It was then that the appeasing spirit was born, in the upper-class reaction to the chaotic conditions of that world, the torn and troubled state of society. Perhaps the reality of the reckoning of four years of total war was ominous enough to unsettle the judgment and shake the perceptions. In Europe the Old World tottered, its very foundations almost visibly deteriorating under the 'ground swell of international unrest'. Worse, there was no immunity, no apparent strength, on the English side of the Channel: expensive promises demanded fulfilment, the Lloyd Georgian programme of social reform; demobilisation riots, continuing conflict in the coal fields, the overhanging threat of a general strike – here was indicated the mood of the working classes; civil war loomed in Ireland – bloody product of the prewar opportunism of Tory diehards – while overseas in the colonies native groups were awakening to national awareness in the kind of crises that would provoke the slaughter at Amritsar. British capitalists were faced with unprecedented crises of their own: in four years of war the economy as a whole had suffered the loss of markets and credits and gained a burden of massive indebtedness; worn and outmoded, British industry was at an increasing disadvantage before the American producing colossus across the sea; and perhaps most serious was the final loss of nineteenth-century confidence and faith, the open disillusionment among quite respectable groups with the prewar system of social economy and the clear sense that somehow men had to find better methods to produce and distribute national – in fact, world – resources.

Spokesmen of the British upper classes stressed certain

causes, sources of both domestic and continental problems. 'When the war ended,' Stanley Baldwin remembered, 'we were in a new world . . . class conscious and revolutionary it was.' Class conscious and revolutionary – but had it not long been so? The final, depression-dogged decades of the nineteenth century, Liberalism with its Labour tail in the election of 1906, workers' syndicalism from 1911 – were these not class-conscious years? Not, apparently, like this; in the narrowing Conservative view, postwar society had taken a dreadful new twist which led unmistakably toward – what? Social democracy, socialism, Bolshevism – all, to the Tory, were part of the same heretical caste; from the frightening mask of Bolshevism in Russia – or Hungary or Germany – to the insolent face of political democracy in Britain, Conservatives saw the image of the enemy, the class forces gathering for what would surely be the 'historic conflict' with the old order.

In this age of disappearing certainties and indistinct guidelines the known and familiar took on sudden luminous value; the Tory creed, especially, became a cherished legacy, a precious bequest to be handled with reverence and care. In the 1920s there appeared a crop of speeches, books, and pamphlets presenting the 'principles of Conservatism'. 'Toryism in the 20th century', the 'Conservative point of view', all of them explaining in nostalgic detail the Tory concern for continuity and tradition – and all of them revealing with desperate frankness the Tory fear of the concrete present. The composite message of these tracts concentrated on the peril of the times, on the transformation of the national political scene. In golden nineteenth-century days – so the explanation ran – the stability of constitutional government had been possible because the major political parties, Tory or Whig, Conservative or Liberal, had agreed upon fundamentals, because both groups had accepted Christianity and the established Church, the structure of King, Lords, and Commons, the participation of legalised electorates, the capitalist system and the glory of the Empire. But this pleasant unanimity, this political gamesmanship between like-minded opponents, was gone; the 'grim reality' of the postwar world was the struggle of Conservatism – alone with its value-sense of tradition – with the Labour Party, with Labour-socialists acting in the name of ideas which denied the bases of the Establishment and which were 'obsessed with the desire to destroy'.[1] And how had this perilous reality come about? The initial error, according to the Conservative spokesmen, had been the grant of the democratic franchise, the 'reckless prodigality' of electoral reforms that had transferred 'so much political power to ignorance and irresponsibility'.[2] Britain was 'demoralised' by the democracy that, in ironic fact, no one had wanted: 'The rich have never liked it or believed in it. The middle class . . . would have preferred almost any other form of government. The labouring class used it as a weapon to destroy privilege, but is now thoroughly out of patience with it.'[3] Strong with the gift of democracy the working classes had poured their power into a Labour Party 'consciously antagonistic to the rest of the community' and led by members of parliament 'avowedly retained to promote the interests of one class only'.[4] Here, then, was the genesis of the national problem, of the emergence in Britain of a 'state of chronic civil war' in which the forces of law and order were helpless before the 'anti-social organisations' which were determined to 'wreck the State and destroy our existing civilisation'.[5]

We are talking, still, of the 1920s, as the British Conservative Party was settling into a stretch of political supremacy which would last, with negligible exceptions, until the 1940s. Yet – even as their victory solidified – the upper classes entered the age of Baldwin and Chamberlain with uncertain steps, half-crippled by their aversion to and fear of the society over which they were to preside. Was this a traditional British

[1] Duff Cooper, 'The Conservative Point of View', *Conservative Pamphlets*, p 12; Arthur Bryant, *The Spirit of Conservatism*, p 87.
[2] F J C Hearnshaw, *Conservatism in England*, p 268.
[3] William Ralph Inge, *Labels and Libels*, p 155.
[4] William Ralph Inge, *England*, p 262.
[5] Inge, *England*, p 261.

ruling class, a worthy addition to what had been unquestionably one of the most successful governing groups in the modern record? Or were essential qualities all too glaringly absent as postwar representatives moved into their moment of history? Certainly, despite their stress on the sanctity of links with the past, the new group seemed incapable of sustaining the proudest note of that past. Consider the immediate comparison: in the majestic self-confidence of the nineteenth century the British ruling classes had conceded the principle of electoral reform, the reform that would, in Macaulay's word, 'preserve' the freedom of propertied classes and the structure of the Establishment; with Disraeli they had gambled on 'Tory Democracy' as a sure way to deepen the loyalties of the lower orders; with Lord Randolph Churchill they had even weighed the possibilities of 'trusting the people' as junior partners within the national whole. It was the sure sense of this self-interest that had disappeared, gone with the optimum conditions of the age of Victoria; the new generation manœuvred uneasily, displaying kinship less with Disraeli reformers than with the intractable anti-democrats of the near past, men of 1867 like Robert Lowe who had warned against democracy, the 'parasite' growing on the British constitution that would 'eventually kill the parent tree'. 'Once give the working men the votes,' Lowe had predicted, 'and the machinery is ready to launch those votes in one compact mass upon the institutions and property of this country'; then the working classes would become 'masters of the situation, all other classes being of necessity powerless in their hands.' Terrible words these were, and terribly pertinent to twentieth-century Conservatives convinced as they had become that Disraeli democracy was in truth a 'moral disaster' inflicted on Toryism, that universal suffrage was leading remorselessly to the class crisis in which they – and this was the secret knowledge of their despair – would surely lose.

As the 1920s took shape the leaders of British Conservatism grimly accepted their sacred obligation to protect the rights of property and traditional privilege, the Britain of caste and class. At the same time they were assuming the larger responsibility for the essential values, the 'moral order' of civilisation. It was black and white, a matter of survival; Winston Churchill had put it neatly when he held up the capitalist-democracy of the West against the inexpressible horrors of socialism, Bolshevik-style: 'It may be a very imperfect organisation of society, but it is all we have got between us and barbarism.'

If, in the revolutionary disturbances of the postwar world, the Tory purpose was the maintenance of the *status quo ante bellum*, the first strategic necessity was the retooling of that venerable vehicle, the Conservative Party. Herein lay a problem of considerable dimension: in opposition to the front-line group of Conservative leaders a growing faction of party members considered independence the first step in reconstruction, insisted, that is, on wrenching the Party from the wartime coalition with Liberalism and the personal grip of David Lloyd George. Stanley Baldwin emerged from obscurity to take a central part in this political drama: 'I felt that our Party was being destroyed,' he explained, 'and I determined to do what I could to rescue it.' Rescue it Baldwin did – he and Andrew Bonar Law – with simple and direct tactics; in the postwar jungle of political machinations a Tory Party majority dumped the Lloyd Georgian coalition government – and the strong personalities who dominated it – and planted the Conservative reign that prevailed, through two brief periods of ostensible Labour leadership, until 1940.

The power play that established unadulterated Toryism in 1922 was a key and crucial move. The ending of the coalition provided, for one thing, the final push in the collapse of Liberal England, marked the burial of Liberalism as philosophy, creed, custom and value. For another, it proved for Tory purposes a highly successful gamble: while all over the world nations were to experiment with radical innovations from both the Left and the Right, the Conservative hand first steadied and then held firm the British social and political structure. It might be suggested, parenthetically, that the same accomplishment was possible in alliance with the remnants of the Liberal Party; this was, in fact, the contention of all the wartime leaders of the Conservatives, ministers like Austen Chamberlain and F E Smith (Lord Birkenhead), who feared that the split of the traditional parties would hand an easy victory to socialism and the Labour Party.[1] But most important, the rebellion against the coalition, as the work of new voices and elements within the Conservative Party – minor leaders, junior ministers, back-bench MPs, and behind them insistent pressure groups of stubborn Toryism – decided the personnel and nature of governmental leadership for the interwar period.

Perhaps it is misleading to refer to the rebel groups that formed behind Bonar Law and Stanley Baldwin as 'new' elements of the Party – especially when many of them represented an encrusted, shellbacked Conservatism. Yet the Party, as it took power in the early 1920s, did present a new, or at least different, face. The change was related to a continuing trend, to a process that had been accelerating since the late nineteenth century. By the opening years of the twentieth the drift of the plutocracy, the great industrial capitalists, into the Conservative camp had become a steady stream, so much so that by 1911, with the choice of Bonar Law – member of a firm of iron merchants, director of merchant banks – as Tory chief, the Party was well on the way to being ruled by its business wing. What was different in the postwar world was the completion of the process and, as the Liberal Party slid into oblivion, the polarisation of British politics – the direct clash of Capital – that is, Conservatism – with the organised body of the labour movement.

The manifest result of the change in the postwar decades

---

[1] Or even to 'anarchy and Bolshevism' – as *The Spectator* (28th October 1922) put it. See *The Times*, 14th October 1922, for Chamberlain's argument that the coalition was the best 'defence of the social and economic order'. Diehard Conservatives replied that an independent party was the 'stoutest bulwark we have against revolutionary courses'. *Ibid*, 17th and 18th October 1922.

was the increased number of Conservative businessmen in Parliament and in ministerial office. The 1918 'coupon' election provided Britain with what has been called 'the wealthiest, the least intelligent, and the least representative House of Commons since Waterloo'[1]; three hundred and eighty-four Tories sat in this House, a homogeneous mass that prompted Lloyd George to refer to the assembled group as the 'associated Chambers of Commerce'. Stanley Baldwin, after contact with the new MPs, referred to the 'hard-faced men who looked as if they had done very well out of the war'. Here was no passing phenomenon: Duff Cooper, coming into Parliament in 1924 and initially elated at the prospect of working with the heirs of Pitt and Disraeli, was sadly disillusioned by the Tory regulars. They were, he said, 'mostly businessmen who had recently made fortunes, often by methods that did not invite close scrutiny. Some of their more ribald critics within the party would refer to them as the "forty thieves".'

The bulk of those Conservative MPs, 'self-made self-seekers', according to the blunt estimate of Randolph Churchill, representing 'the most squalid and acquisitive segment of the [business] community', entered the House with concrete purposes; they were irreconcilables, there in the first instance on behalf of private and personal interests, and in the second, to maintain unchanged the class structure of Britain. Their methods were time-tested: financial orthodoxy and the admonition against interference – except through protective tariffs – with the affairs of business; strict governmental economy and no nonsense about social welfare measures; low taxes on industry, the reduction of consumption and imports – the traditional squeeze on the labouring classes; and parliamentary manœuvring to avoid the demands of a newly-broadened electorate, to deflect widespread hopes for reform through legislation.

The solid mass of representative Toryism is a constant part

[1] D C Somervell, *The Reign of King George the Fifth*, p 206.

T.H.M.—B

of our story, an ever-present moving force behind the ministerial élite upon which we will concentrate. For this was an era of uncommon party regularity, not so much in the rigidity of discipline and control, but in an iron resistance to the erratic, the different, the dynamic. By 1922 a party hard core, trusted representatives of the British ruling classes, had imposed control, had cut off the tenure of the 'great ones, the giants of the Edwardian era and of the war',[1] and handed the party to little-known names of the second line. And why did Tory regulars oust Lloyd George – even then a leader without significant political support – and his stable of Conservative ministers? This was no casual political murder, but a calculated decision for survival in the ominous reality of the times: the coalition became suspect in the postwar world of national political strikes, of rumblings of revolt in the colonial areas, of the nightmare come true in bloody workers' rebellion in Europe and total social revolution in Russia. Why the 'dim leadership' of Bonar Law?[2] Why Neville Chamberlain, competent but colourless, rather than his half-brother Austen, who had been chosen and trained for statesmanship by their famous father? Why Stanley Baldwin, whom Churchill called a 'mild socialist', rather than Churchill himself, or Lord Birkenhead, those happy warriors who welcomed an opportunity to settle the issue once and for all with the working classes? An obvious answer is that Bonar Law or Stanley Baldwin or Neville Chamberlain were safe, reliable, *understandable* – and untainted by the initiative, the 'recklessness', of the Lloyd Georgian association. Stanley Baldwin had been talking of Lloyd George, but his words at the Carlton Club in 1922 applied to the wartime Conservative ministers as well: they were, he said, 'a dynamic force, and it is from that very fact that our troubles, in our opinion, arise. A dynamic force is a very terrible thing; it may crush you.'

In the relative lull of the later 1920s, Conservatives admitted

---

[1] Charles L Mowat, *Britain Between the Wars, 1918–1940*, p 142.
[2] Philip Guedalla, *Mr Churchill*, p 228.

the exiles; the party split was publicly healed as Baldwin 'recaptured' the old coalitionists: Birkenhead became Secretary of State for India – not without a stiff fight, with Baldwin being told that 'the feeling against FE in the Party was so strong that it was hopeless to take him in'[1]: Austen Chamberlain was named Foreign Secretary, the post from which he proceeded to such varied accomplishments as the negotiation of the Treaty of Locarno, and a quiet arrangement with Mussolini, permitting the latter's widening influence in Northern Africa; even the renegade Winston Churchill was reaccepted by the Party, and handed the plum of the Chancellory of the Exchequer. But with the deepening of tension after the depression in 1929, with social and economic disintegration that seemed to threaten the very roots of Conservative supremacy, the government was purged again of its unpredictable few. Austen Chamberlain was perhaps ready to leave the Foreign Office; at any rate, the party was 'tired' of him, this Secretary who had been 'far too friendly to France'.[2] Churchill withdrew to a posture of individual opposition, reiterating in his most exasperated moments his early judgment that a government of his ex-colleagues was 'brainless, spineless, and dangerous'. The minister with strong ideas, with commitment, was more than ever out of place in the 1930s: Leopold Amery, dedicated to Imperial – and the new Commonwealth – cooperation and integration, had been one of the original junior ministers who brought down the coalition in 1922, hoping thereby to be part of a Conservative government that would make 'Tariff Reform and Imperial Preference' (the twin themes of imperialists since Joseph Chamberlain) the policy of Britain[3]; frustrated by his colleagues during the 1920s, Amery was increasingly isolated in the Baldwin Cabinets

[1] Keith Feiling, *The Life of Neville Chamberlain*, p 110.
[2] G M Young, *Stanley Baldwin*, p 139.
[2] Amery's principled Imperialism went back to the days of Joseph Chamberlain and the Tariff Reform League. From the years of the Boer War, too, Amery was close to Lord Milner – although he had not been a member of Milner's 'Kindergarten'; throughout his political life he remained a crusader for the basic elements of Milner's ideas of Imperial unity.

until, with the 'National' Government of 1931, he was left out altogether. Back then to a decade of unquestioned leadership came Baldwin, Neville Chamberlain, and the ministerial host whose names and activities mark the dreary processional of the 1930s. The intellectual deficiency of British leadership in that decade was no chance occurrence, nor simply a stroke of bad national luck; instead, it reflected the wishes of a Party and of ruling classes conducting a last-ditch defence of property and privilege and, consequently, willing to risk nothing, dare nothing, and deviate only with painful caution from a preferred policy of absolute inaction.

This is, to be sure, an oversimplification. Clearly, the Conservative Party was a great deal more than a monolithic machine, powered by the simple one-two relationship of business groups and their chosen leaders. Here was a complex interplay of political forces, of contending factions and clashing personalities. Within the Party and among its closest supporters there was rather less than unanimous acclaim for the Baldwin-Chamberlain Governments. Steady criticism came not only from Churchill and imperialists like Leopold Amery or Lord Lloyd, but from younger progressives, advocates of a 'New Conservatism', led by ministers-of-the-future Harold Macmillan and Robert Boothby. Lord Derby, head of the powerful Stanley clan and political 'King of Lancashire', brusquely ordered Baldwin to resign in 1930 in a letter which, after sound scoring of the sins of the government, wound up with a contemptuous dismissal of 'the old gang and the old policy'.[1] Press Lords Beaverbrook and Rothermere, in their attack on the Tory no-tariff policy before 1931, conducted what often seemed a personal vendetta against Baldwin himself. Of the coalition government that was put together in the wake of the depression panic, Boothby, a bitter Conservative critic, judged it no 'National' Government but 'simply a get-together on the part of the Boys of the Old Brigade, who climbed on the bandwagon and sat there, rain or shine'.

[1] Randolph S Churchill, *Lord Derby, King of Lancashire*, p 584.

But this is precisely the point – that neither criticism nor party in-fighting dislodged the governments of the interwar decades. Within a year after his letter Lord Derby was warmly congratulating Baldwin on the Conservative sweep in the election of the national government; the kind of revolt hoped for by Churchill against Baldwin's do-nothing leadership dwindled in 1936 into a polite deputation of 'Privy Councillors and a few others' to the Prime Minister, merely warning him of the dangerous lag in Britain's defence preparations. Weathering every crisis, the 'old gang' survived: the lethargic Baldwin, exasperating even his closest colleagues; Neville Chamberlain, whom Leo Amery thought 'humdrum, commonplace, and unenterprising' ('but I know that charge is groundless', noted Chamberlain); Sir William Joynson-Hicks, Cabinet diehard, 'a London solicitor of limited intelligence', in the words of Philip Guedalla; Sir Thomas Inskip, whose appointment to the newly-created post of Minister for the Co-ordination of Defence was 'received with astonishment by Press and public' – there had been nothing like it, said the political wags, since Caligula named his horse a consul; Sir John Simon, leader of the National Liberals, an 'unexpected and unfortunate' choice as Foreign Secretary in 1931[1]; and others of the national government that 'shambled its unimaginative way' to 1940[2] – Edward Wood (Lord Halifax), Sir Philip Cunliffe-Lister, Sir Samuel Hoare, Douglas Hogg (Lord Hailsham), Sir Kingsley Wood, Lord Londonderry, Walter Runciman. It is often pointed out that the uninspired and uninspiring Conservative leaders of the 1920s and 1930s reflected a national ostrich-like reaction to war and revolution, to social and economic insecurity; more precisely, they were indicative of the mood and temper of a fearful Conservatism, of Tory groups clinging to the familiar and the safe as a shield against the threatened changes of a dangerous age.

[1] Mowat, *Britain*, p 414.
[2] *Ibid.*

2
Conservative Cliques

THE MINISTERS of the Baldwin-Chamberlain Governments held, then, a mandate from the ruling classes of Britain, had been entrusted with office by groups that were in the dangerous postwar world 'less interested in the policy than in the biology of Government' – or, to be more precise, select Conservative circles were 'intuitively' convinced that correct policy would be pursued by these particular members of the 'hereditary English governing class'. In spite of the criticism of Tories who were certain they knew better how to rule, the chosen leaders remained, their assignment limited to guiding the nation – unchanged – through the trying times of the postwar world. The recognition of the caretaking nature of the task was fairly explicit: to Baldwin, office was often a dreadful burden, he himself an 'asylum attendant'; Neville Chamberlain noted that his chief objective was 'to keep the ship steady on the course'.[1]

What kind of men were the Conservative ministers? What were the ideas and attitudes they carried as part of their on-the-job equipment? What were the common bonds that united them, a hard ministerial core, for more than a decade and a half? Individual differences clearly existed among them: a temperamental gulf, for example, separated Baldwin from Neville Chamberlain, precluding a close personal relationship between the two. On such bases, as Keith Feiling remarks, groups form within cabinets – 'less on the identity of public conviction than on seeing life in the same way'; thus Baldwin's good friend was the easy-going William Bridgeman, First Lord of the Admiralty in the 1920s, 'a true patriot but hardly

[1] Keith Feiling, *The Life of Neville Chamberlain*, p 221.

THE
UNIVERSITY OF WINNIPEG
PORTAGE & BALMORAL
WINNIPEG 2, MAN.
CANADA
CONSERVATIVE CLUBS
39

a leader',[1] while Chamberlain, hard-working and conscientious, chose as intimates Halifax and Hailsham, Hoare and Cunliffe-Lister. Yet the group was knit together by overall ties. The most obvious tie was their participation in the revolt against the Lloyd George wartime government. As the 'first-class brains' of the coalition never let them forget, the Conservatives of the Baldwin-Chamberlain Governments had been back-bench MPs and minor ministers before 1922; there was the further implication that under the forceful leadership of a Lloyd George they would never have risen above the under-secretarial level. Leo Amery, who found his element in the Colonial Office in the 1920s, was stung by the taunt of the 'intellectual mediocrity' of the Cabinet in 1922 into this (rather equivocal) retort: 'Its defenders could point out that it contained three Fellows of All Souls, viz Curzon, Edward Wood [Halifax] and myself. It also included, as Attorney General, at any rate one newcomer of first-rate ability in Douglas Hogg [Lord Hailsham]. Most of its members had ministerial experience as under-secretaries, if not in the Cabinet'. On the other hand, frustrated after years of dealing with his colleagues, Amery had this to say about the Cabinet of 1929: 'I often thought of a comment of Lord Milner's, in reference to an earlier Government, on the difficulty of persuading a lot of empty sacks to stand upright.'[2] In any case, one notes that Amery perhaps tactfully refrained from specific assessment of such associates as Cunliffe-Lister, Joynson-Hicks, Sir Thomas Inskip, and Sir Samuel Hoare. That these politicians – and, indeed, the majority of the Conservative ministers – were defensively united in a kind of league of the mediocre, cannot be discounted.

But deeper bonds cemented the Conservatives of the inter-

[1] Mowatt, *Britain*, p 346.
[2] L S Amery, *My Political Life*, II, p 493. Amery was engaged here in a drawn-out battle with Chancellor of the Exchequer Winston Churchill – stubbornly a Free Trader and, as Amery felt, disastrously wrong in financial policy in the crisis of unemployment and decreasing trade that faced the nation. Thus, Amery was trying to push those of his colleagues who favoured protection – supposedly a majority – into a stand against Churchill and Free Trade. See *ibid*, II, 478 and *passim*.

war governments, gave them both 'identity of public conviction' and ability to 'see life in the same way'. As Baldwin
formed his first Cabinet in 1923, Neville Chamberlain, the
Minister of Health, wondered how he would get on with the
new Premier; after assessment of Baldwin, Chamberlain concluded it would be right, for 'after all, he is a business man
himself'. On such a criterion Chamberlain was assured of
moving comfortably among most of his colleagues of the suc-
ceeding years: solid men they were, men of practical affairs,
who would share with Birmingham industrialist Chamberlain
a common outlook on the essential matters of public life.
Chamberlain himself, sent by his father into the family metal
works, had bought into and become a director of multiple
associated industries. Stanley Baldwin, son of a Worcestershire
ironmaster, had inherited the family firm and had had a
career in its management when he entered politics and the
House at the age of forty-one. Sir Samuel Hoare was son of the
'oldest banking family in the City of London'; even Lord
Londonderry, descendant of the Castlereagh of the Napoleonic
era, was no idle aristocrat but a mine-owner, chairman of
Londonderry Collieries, Ltd.

One might catalogue the fact of the business character of the
interwar governments. With a few exceptions – like Halifax
or Londonderry – cabinet ministers were non-aristocrats, their
backgrounds different from those of Conservative leaders of
the days of Salisbury or Balfour. Most of them had emerged
from middle-class, Nonconformist, industrial, and commercial
families; their appearance in politics is clear evidence of the
shift of big business to Conservatism toward the end of the
nineteenth century. Stanley Baldwin's 1908 maiden speech to
the House of Commons, announcing his opposition to the
Liberal Government, has direct bearing on this shift: he was,
said Baldwin, a representative of 'a class which today was
thought little of, though it had played some part in the State –
the class once called masters, then employers of labour, and
now capitalists'. His kind of people, capitalists like himself,

continued Baldwin, were now critical of Liberalism because it accepted the principle of state interference with commerce and industry; Liberal ministers, he concluded, were 'rapidly alienating the support of the middle and lower-middle classes who helped to put them in power'. Capitalists, then, had turned to the Conservative Party for specific purposes and concrete needs; their capture of the leadership of that party, with Bonar Law and Baldwin, inevitably stamped it with their imprint and remade it in their image. (It is perhaps not irrelevant to note an observation of Joseph Schumpeter: 'The bourgeois outside his office and the professional man of capitalism outside his profession cut a very sorry figure.')

Almost uniformly, Conservative leaders were products of the prewar generation, men whose careers had been set before 1914, their education, training and ideas immutably set within a nineteenth-century framework. Young men were scarce in Tory circles of the interwar period, Anthony Eden and Duff Cooper being the most notable exceptions (and both ultimately demonstrated the differences of outlook that separated them from their elders). Yet there was more involved here than a closed company of the Old Guard hanging on to political office in deliberate exclusion of younger men pushing up from the party ranks: Duff Cooper, in his twenties at the start of World War I, tallies in his memoirs the incredible number of friends and former schoolmates killed in France, in battle especially punishing to young line officers; four years of such warfare had decimated the sons of the upper class, the suitable candidates for political places. That a new generation, even one well trained as hereditary defenders of the verities of the Establishment, might have opened a corner of the sealed package of élitist attitudes is at least a possibility. The kind of religious intensity, for example, that prodded Conservative ministers Joynson-Hicks and Inskip in their stubborn resistance to the proposed 'popish' revision of the *Prayer Book* was an inconceivable anachronism to the secular mind of the younger generation: Duff Cooper, in offhand reference to religious views, airily remarked that 'for the majority of English people there are only two religions, Roman Catholic, which is wrong, and the rest, which don't matter'. But to the Conservative power group, from Inskip and Joynson-Hicks with their evangelical background, to a Lord Halifax raised in the cloistered air of English Catholicism, religion and the Church were neither wrong nor inconsequential but massive cornerstones of the structure of tradition and stability.

As chosen caretakers of the Establishment, chief trustees of law and order, Conservative leaders pointedly displayed their sense of responsibility for the lower orders in their charge. Chamberlain, product of 'generations linked by the habit of public service',[1] both as Lord Mayor of Birmingham and national Minister of Health, was proud of programmes that included such benefits as modest housing projects and old-age pensions for the poor. Stanley Baldwin fondly remembered the easy familiarity of the family business and the ruling of his iron-works with a benign paternal hand: 'It seemed to me,' he wrote of the great coal strike of 1912, 'a monstrous injustice to these men, because I looked upon them as my own family, and it hit me very hard.' Lord Halifax, who recalled with almost palpable nostalgia an ancestral way of life, preserved at least the gentry image, a picture of 'the landowner living on his estate, among farm and cottage tenants, with something of a feudal atmosphere surviving'. These men made a careful distinction between themselves and rightwing diehards who in their blindly reactionary ways would push the nation to revolution. In the House of Commons in 1924, with the Labour Party preparing to form a government, Baldwin bravely repeated the principles of Tory paternalism: we are not afraid of social reforms, he said. Indeed, 'improvement of the welfare of the people' was a Tory policy, a cornerstone of Tory faith. (And in any case, Baldwin added, 'we will hold our fire', for 'we do not know whether the Jacobins or the Girondins are coming in'.)

[1] Feiling, *Neville Chamberlain*, p 52.

But the posture of the Tory Democrat was hard to maintain in these difficult, swiftly-changing years. Conservative leaders remembered vividly the period of labour's 'great unrest' before the war, that terrible age of epidemic strikes, when the British working man – that long-suffering figure, soul of conservatism and self-restraint – seemed seized with an unfathomable passion and inflamed with wild syndicalist doctrines. And fresh in the Conservative mind was the new strike fury of 1919 – when even the London police joined the strike lists – which briefly seemed to be carrying the 1911-12 outbreak to a certain revolutionary end. This was fact, this rebelliousness of once-docile masses, and its import was obvious to the most sanguine Conservative. The Tory was aware of the declining hold of his class: he recognised, like Baldwin, that the 'Two Nations of Disraeli were arming against each other'; he admitted, with Halifax, that he 'looked back wistfully to the conditions that [were] long past'; or he was forced to acknowledge hard truth, like Chamberlain, when the latter left his old family constituency of Ladywood – which, 'full of class feeling', was no longer safe for a Chamberlain – for the Conservative 'fortress' of Edgbaston. If he repressed that awareness, or if he spoke soothingly of social harmony and peace, his reaction to social change anywhere, at any time, belied his confident pose. Thus, Neville Chamberlain greeted with shock and disapproval the *first* Russian upheaval in March 1917 with the acid comment that the liberal-led 'Russian revolution is fermenting in all the unsteady brains of the world'. Chamberlain was unable even to adjust to the existence of the British Labour Party, his outrage at its presence running as a constant theme through his private notes: 'Although I never shout at Labour members or insult them', he wrote, 'I cannot understand the psychology of some of our men who . . . endeavour . . . to reason with them'; or again, he recorded that 'Stanley [Baldwin] begged me to remember that I was addressing a meeting of gentlemen. I always give him the impression, he said, when I spoke in the House of Commons, that I looked on the Labour

Party as dirt.' This distaste for the representatives of the working classes covered at once the Tory view of society, rigid and unchanging in its hierarchical certainties, and the fearful knowledge that society was being eroded by massive irrepressible forces.

In the retrospect of 1920s and 1930s, Chamberlain would, no doubt, have reiterated his judgment of the revolutionary activities of the Kerensky government in Russia; after all, look what these moderate revolutionists had loosened! As a key factor in the Tory fear psychology, the explosive appearance of the Soviet Union is almost impossible to overrate. From the period of the Allied intervention in the Russian civil war, Britain was saturated with accounts of the Bolshevik 'nightmare of unbridled anarchy',[1] and Bolshevik leaders were pictured as 'assassins and thieves', the scum of European conspirators, perpetrators of unspeakable crimes against man and society. Personal contact with the Bolshevik rabble was to British leaders inconceivable; few at any rate could muster the aristocratic style of Winston Churchill who, in referring to a meeting of Lloyd George with a Soviet representative, inquired, 'I suppose you have shaken the baboon's hairy hand?' Yet to the Conservative mind the Russian Revolution was no isolated event, no savage product peculiar to a semi-civilised land. Heritage of 1848, the spectre of proletarian revolution had haunted the Western bourgeois for generations; Bolshevism in Russia was the materialisation of a ghostly figure that now cast a long shadow over Europe and the British Isles.

The Conservative Red-obsession was translated in the interwar period into obstinate governmental rejection of Soviet attempts to settle primary issues between the two nations and a steady Communist-baiting in domestic affairs. The latter

---

[1] Colonel John Ward, *With the 'Die-hards' in Siberia*, p 267; see also *The Times*, 6th, 14th, 18th November 1919, for descriptions of the 'odious and bloody tyranny' in Russia, or *The Spectator*, 7th September, 28th December 1918, 2nd August 1919, for editorial certainty that 'torrents of blood' ran in Russia, in what was 'probably the worst Terror in the history of revolutions'.

was a curious blend of real and imaginary fears, of crusading zeal and blatant opportunism. Conservatives were in dead earnest in their fear of Comintern 'plots and intrigues', of Communist attempts 'to incite mutinies in the fighting services and strikes in the ranks of labour'[1]; militant international Communism added new dimensions to industrial conflict and deepened the Conservative suspicion of threatening moves from the working classes. Yet on another level, real apprehensions could be quite cynically used: the opportunity to blacken the Labour opposition with charges of its pro-Bolshevism, or to play upon propaganda-fostered fears of the middle-class electorate, was too good a thing to pass up. The 'Zinoviev Letter',[2] whatever its origins, was a scare-factor made to order for the national elections – which brought a resounding Conservative victory – in 1924. And citizens could be kept alert to the Communist menace – and to the vigilance of their Conservative protectors – through such stunts as the Arcos raid of 1927, when the Home Secretary, anti-Bolshevik zealot Joynson-Hicks, ordered a massed police force to search for subversive material in both the offices of a British company trading with the Russians and of the Soviet Trade Delegation. If the stated objectives of the raid were non-existent it could be justification, nevertheless, for a satisfying end – the breaking of trade and diplomatic relations with the Soviet Union that had begun during the brief life of the Labour Government.[3]

But that the deeper element of Tory anti-Communism was an almost obsessive fear of its ultimate effects was well illustrated in the reactions to social problems in the post-Bolshevik

[1] Sir Samuel Hoare, *Nine Troubled Years*, p 350.
[2] This 'extraordinary concoction', the probably-forged Zinoviev Letter, concerned alleged subversive activities begun in Britain as a result of the Anglo-Russian trade treaty signed by the Labour Government. It was published just before the elections in 1924; although the election in any case would probably have brought a Conservative victory, the Letter created a highly charged atmosphere at the polls. See Mowat, *Britain*, pp 187–194.
[3] See the editorial in *The Spectator*, 28th May 1927: 'It was never doubted that the meeting of the Arcos raid was that the Government would end diplomatic relations with the Soviet.'

world, the revolutionary jitters of the ruling classes in such crises, say, as the General Strike of 1926. If anything, the Conservatives were overprepared for class warfare: negotiators of Baldwin's Cabinet had managed to postpone the threatened strike for nine months, a purported investigative period that was used by the Government for the mobilisation of administrative forces, courts, army, and police, and for the enlistment besides of a force of citizen strikebreakers, called the Organisation for the Maintenance of Supplies. Thoroughly familiar to the Government, the private plans of the latter divided Britain into districts and topped the lines of command with respected public figures like Fleet Admiral Sir John Jellicoe and Lord Hardinge of Penshurst. The OMS – the Labour opposition called it the beginning of 'legal fascism' – had a dual purpose: it was both an additional arm of governmental power, providing a determined middle-class citizenry that would keep moving the essential services of the nation, and a lever that would insure governmental firmness against the workers.

Despite the massive weight of constitutional and extra-constitutional preparation – against workers' organisations ill-equipped except in their solidarity – the Conservative mind in 1926 was a study of apprehension and fear. By a decision of the courts the strike was declared illegal and the strike leaders outlawed; obediently, then, the strikers – the leaders and the bulk of the led – retreated from an 'unconstitutional' action and called off the general strike. Yet Prime Minister Baldwin, in a broadcast to the nation, sombrely pronounced the strike 'a challenge to Parliament, and . . . the road to anarchy and ruin'. 'Constitutional government', wrote Neville Chamberlain, 'is fighting for its life; if we failed, it would be the revolution, for the nominal leaders would be whirled away in an instant.' Prominent members of official society panicked under the tension of the nine days of the strike: the wife of Duff Cooper (Lady Diana Manners) 'could hear the tumbrils rolling and heads sneezing into the baskets'. And Duff Cooper – generally calm and judicious in comparison with his senior colleagues about relations with the democracy – is the source for this amazing exchange: 'Diana asked me this morning how soon we could with honour leave the country. I said not till the massacres begin.'

The verdict of history declares the old-guard politicians of the Baldwin-Chamberlain era a lacklustre, undistinguished lot. Had they governed in a more placid age, this group, so 'very representative of the nineteenth century',[1] might have left at least a respectable record. They were skilful enough in the use of governing techniques which had carried the British upper classes so successfully through the nineteenth century; they were, moreover, soberly committed to the properly paced extension, the adaptation, of the progressive Toryism of the Victorian and Edwardian periods. Thus, Neville Chamberlain – who often seemed more the nineteenth-century man than his maverick father – earnestly tinkered with revision of the Poor Laws and with National Health Insurance and talked of completing 'the circle of security for the workers', or at least of helping those 'who have the will and desire to raise themselves to higher and better things'. And Baldwin possessed a remarkable talent for the language of democracy, and a unique ability to appeal for popular support – invaluable qualities, both for his personal career and for the fortunes of the Party.

But it was not a placid age, and the pace of change, rather than slow and measured, was accelerating to a dizzying speed. The world familiar to Baldwin and Chamberlain was fast disappearing; behind them lay the far-flung hegemony of imperial Great Britain, and with it, the ruling class sense – essentially an aristocratic sense – of confidence and solidity. What had gone, actually, was the complex of conditions that had supported Disraeli's kind of Tory Democracy – in which a Tory-aristocracy had fed out piecemeal social and political reforms as a restraint on the Victorian capitalist plutocracy.

[1] Feiling, *Neville Chamberlain*, pp 120–121.

Ironically enough, Baldwin and Chamberlain were sons of
that capitalist plutocracy, destined to rule as the Disraeli
pigeons were coming home to roost, tapped for leadership in
the new democratic age, when the democracy of Britain coin-
cided, furthermore, with Labour politics, socialist programming
and international Bolshevism. The power of the people was a
new and dangerous affair; and if Baldwin could still pretend
to communicate in his homely way with the man in the street,
Chamberlain had no patience with such a sentimental approach. Chamberlain perhaps had Baldwin in mind when he
talked in these terms of the 'weakness of modern democracy':
'The system has produced men who have not the courage to
handle the animal firmly, though if they did, it is at least
possible that it would prove far more responsive than it does to
weakness.'

These were strong words, stronger, in fact, than any overt
action interwar governments were prepared to take. The
ineffectual nature of the Baldwin-Chamberlain Governments
stems in great part from this, from the inability of top ministers
to find solutions to their most pressing fears. They had, remember, exiled their more forceful colleagues. Birkenhead, for one,
knew how to handle the threatening democracy: 'Put up your
barricades . . . you wolves of Moscow,' he once shouted at a
heckling audience, 'we've beaten you with brains and if it
comes to fighting, two can play at that game. . . . We'll slit
your soft white throats for you.' And Churchill was attracted
for rather a long time by the Fascist siren song from the
Mediterranean: in Rome in 1927 he congratulated the Italians
on their 'triumphant struggle against the bestial appetites and
passions of Leninism', which had 'rendered a service to the
whole world'; 'Italy,' he added, 'has shown that there is a way
of fighting the subversive forces which can rally the masses
of the people, properly led, to value and wish to defend the
honour and stability of civilised society. She has provided the
necessary antidote to the Russian poison. Hereafter no great
nation will go unprovided with an ultimate means of protection

against the cancerous growth of Bolshevism.'[1] But if, in common with strong-minded Tories, the Baldwin-Chamberlain group was appalled by the insolence and rebelliousness of modern democracy, it had no stomach for the brutal approach. Following the inclination of Baldwin, Conservatives tried another method: the entry into the electoral competition minus the fire-eating right wing; bland, unchallenging leadership (except in back-to-the-wall situations like that of the strike of 1926) and the judicious use of the popular emotional issue; the reliance upon built-in legal and constitutional bulwarks against change – plus the hoary practice of attempting to fool the people most of the time.

Quoted in Frederick L Schuman's *Soviet Politics at Home and Abroad*, p 283. It was strange, thought Conservative Stanley Salvidge, that Churchill should be ostracised, this talented warrior, whose 'flashing blade could be effectively used in the fight against the rising forces of Socialism'; the 'Anti-Socialist Campaign', said Salvidge, was Churchill's 'political aim'. Stanley Salvidge, *Salvidge of Liverpool: Behind the Political Scene, 1890–1928*, pp 270, 272.

3
Conservative
Fantasies

CONSERVATIVES MOVED CAUTIOUSLY enough in their domestic dilemma of coexistence with a possibly socialist-oriented democratic electorate; when they turned to matters of foreign affairs they fairly floundered in the quicksand of the ominous unknown. Neither by inclination nor aptitude was the attention of the new set of Conservative leaders drawn to the international – especially continental – field; when events forced that attention the response was directed not by pondered policy, but by a haphazard combination of feelings, attitudes, and prejudices. Typically, after the war, the Conservatives favoured a withdrawal – almost as total as that of the United States – into isolationism, 'insular-prejudice', Keith Feiling called it, the safe immersion into the affairs of island and empire. By the mid-1920s the Conservative projected upon the Western world his own national experience. Barring Russia, Europe had weathered its terrible crisis and had emerged relatively intact; the job of each country was to retire within itself, plug up the holes—with whatever available material—in its national edifice and see to the return of peace, stability, and business.

In a general way, of course, such attitudes were British as well as Conservative. 'Public opinion' reflected isolationism, pacifism, longing for normality; commonly, Britons reacted against the passions of the wartime – the jingoism that had sustained the war effort, the hatred of the Hun that had spilled over to the immediate postwar vow to make Germany pay 'till the pips squeaked'. And commonly, Britons wanted a cessation of European crisis, which meant primarily a relaxation of French pressure against Germany, a yielding of French determination to keep the Germans a defeated and prostrate enemy. It was from the starting point of such attitudes that the Labour Party shaped its foreign policy – the initial implementation of which, incidentally, was the most creditable aspect of Labour-in-power in 1924 and during 1929–31. Labour supporters were profoundly pacifist and pro-German in their reaction to the horrors of the war and to the 'revisionism' that had undermined the charge of German war guilt; they, too, resented French resistance to German recovery and French efforts to find security against the inevitable revival of Germany in a network of alliances (encirclement of the German menace) in Eastern Europe. The Labour policy-answer to the Franco-German problem lay in reliance on the League of Nations – in the 1920s not yet a hopelessly impracticable position. The promise of the League Covenant, to France or to Germany or to any victim-nation, of collective resistance to acts of aggression, the use of League machinery for arbitration of international disputes, the effective implementation of postwar agreement on universal disarmament – these were the concrete blocks of Labour foreign policy, upon which Prime Minister Ramsay MacDonald and Foreign Secretary Arthur Henderson briefly, in their short tenure of power, began to build.

Again typically, Conservative attitudes on foreign affairs did not translate into such clear and positive policy. The imperialists, of course, knew what they wanted to do to buttress Britain's place in the international sun. Crusaders like Leopold Amery argued for the tight imperial and commonwealth organisation, for the economic and political unity of British and associated peoples, that would give Britain a position of strength from which to deal with any foreign contingency, in Europe or elsewhere.[1] Outside the Commonwealth it was still a Darwinian world – if a tired one – that Amery saw, in which the competition of nations was the dominant fact; to him, consequently, schemes of international co-opera-

---

[1] We might remember the 'conviction' of Amery's instructor in imperialism, Lord Milner, that 'Britain was no part of Europe'. See Gollin, *Proconsul*, p 535.

tion, of disarmament and arbitration, were to be dismissed not just as visionary but as simply irrelevant. With much of this Amery's less positive colleagues (his 'empty sacks') would agree – the 'insular-prejudice', the dislike of the League of Nations, with its pointless plans for disarmament, and its covenant pledges which could commit Britain to economic and military action that had no relation to her own national interest; they would share, too, a distaste for involvement in continental affairs, particularly for the old Entente tie with France that could conceivably drag Britain into some sort of guarantee of the French system of security alliances in far-off Eastern Europe, Czechoslovakia, or Rumania. The 1925 Treaty of Locarno – the chief positive Conservative accomplishment in foreign affairs in the 1920s, presented to the public as the final settlement of the Franco-German problem – appealed broadly to Conservatives on precisely these points: if Foreign Secretary Austen Chamberlain hoped that Locarno would stand as the British pledge to France of assistance against German aggression, the majority of his associates saw the treaty as an excellent circumvention of the indefinite commitments of the League of Nations, and as a clarifying statement of the British refusal to become involved in the east of Europe.[1]

Yet the Conservative majority produced no explicit, definable policy to carry its views on European matters – other than the insistent hope for order and recovery. It was, wrote Harold Nicolson, an old refrain, 'egoistic, traditional and limited': 'Let England have peace upon the continent and therefore an expanding market. Let England have the balance of power on the continent, and thereby security at other people's expense.' In practice, Conservative leaders followed what Hugh Dalton called the 'Montagu Norman'[2] line – 'pro-German and anti-French'. They were pro-German because Germany was the key to the problem of European stability, because a revived and prosperous Germany meant the revival

[1] See Amery's discussion of official views on Locarno, Amery, *Political Life*, II, 300–302.
[2] Norman was Governor of the Bank of England.

of the sagging structure of European capitalism and an end to the threat of 'Communism on the Rhine', and because a prosperous Germany was an expanding market, especially an investment market, with desperately important opportunities for British capital. They were anti-French because of the chronic instability and electoral restlessness of that alien Gallic land, because of French paranoiac notions of dictating to the rest of Europe, and because it was the French, in their perverse suspicions of Germany, who refused to allow the West to get back to the business of business.

For guidance on the point of Conservative pro-Germanism we might follow the highly literate testimony of Sir Robert Vansittart, from 1930 to 1938 Permanent Under-Secretary of the Foreign Office. By his own admission, Sir Robert was anything but a neutral observer; his detestation of things German was strong enough to constitute a school of thought known in Tory parlance as 'Vansittartism'. Yet as a career official Vansittart had a unique opportunity to contemplate the intricacies of Anglo-German relations during the Baldwin-Chamberlain era, that period, in Vansittart's words, in which 'our best brains' [sic!] made such an 'unholy mess'. 'Human nature fell low in the inter-war period', Vansittart wrote, 'and the chord of self-interest was rarely twanged in vain. Germany played many a tune upon it, and all the dupes fell a-dancing. They ended by even taking German thuggery for "the bulwark against Bolshevism", but by then they were completely dizzy ... and ready to condemn anything and anybody that Germany told them to condemn. The brain reels at the performance.' Vansittart's reference is to the 'Great German Swindle', in which British financiers – and Americans too, for Wall Street was the supreme goat – became willing victims of the trap laid by Chancellor Stresemann and sprung by Dr Schacht.[1] The first step was the granting of enormous loans to the German Government with which to pay reparation debts. Did the Germans pay? A very little, and all the time they

[1] Hjalmar Schacht was president of the Reichsbank from 1923.

complained of the drain; while the German national income rose by 1929 to a level 77 per cent higher than in 1913, Germans appealed to their creditors on the grounds of poverty for a reconsideration of 'political' debts – the plea that led first to a year's moratorium and finally to the cancellation of the whole reparations scheme. It was an incredible episode, wrote Vansittart, this example of the legerdemain of Dr Schacht: 'It was as though a mere conjurer had suddenly performed a genuine but shady miracle.' And this was but half of it. From 1924 both private investors and the great banking houses of Wall Street and London, attracted by high interest rates and the fabled honesty of the German businessman, poured money into Germany recovery, underwriting the revival of great industries – including that of the armament firms of Krupp and Thyssen – with the extension of apparently unlimited credit.[1] Who, from Montagu Norman, lord of the Bank of England, to the smallest private creditor, could afford to let Germany go down in financial collapse and social chaos, to lose such stakes? In part, cancellation of reparations during the depression was the result of the hope of the British and American Governments that Germany would subsequently repay her 'commercial' debts. The most powerful institutions and individuals of the British financial world were deep in German economic affairs – and the interests and wishes of the City were of primary significance to the ministers of Conservative Governments.

Such practical issues, then, were important elements in Conservative pro-German attitudes, in governmental concern for the well-being of the German nation. Clearly, Germany could not be cold-shouldered or isolated – or driven to flirtation with the Russians (as in the 1922 Treaty of Rapallo) for want of friends and allies in the West. The official idea was, as *The Times* put it, 'to show sympathy with Germany's grievances and to emphasise her qualities of neighbourliness'. The French, of course, refused to do either. French intractability on the

---

[1] See Paul Einzig, *Appeasement Before, During and After the War*, pp 47–48.

German question, French inability to love the Germans, was a trial to the Tories[1] and indeed reawakened the lingering Francophobia that they – like most Britons – had only shelved during the exigencies of the Allied war effort.

Anti-French prejudice is a hallowed tradition, with deep roots in the British mind; what concerns us is its manifestation in the attitudes of the Edwardians who guided the Conservative Party in the 1920s and 1930s. On this point Sir Robert Vansittart is, again, a relevant witness. The Victorian England in which Vansittart grew up (contemporary to Baldwin, Chamberlain, et al) was 'almost entirely anti-French', accepted, indeed, as a general axiom Carlyle's comparison of 'vapouring, gesticulating, quarrelsome, restless and oversensitive France' with 'noble, patient, deep, pious and solid Germany'. Victorians, said Vansittart, 'were vaguely convinced that nineteenth-century France had too good a time; that France laughed too much and cooked too well for this vale of tears'. The solid British bourgeois regularly visited Paris, it is true – although largely at the pleading of his womenfolk – where he had a miserable time; hardly anyone, on the other hand, travelled to Berlin, or even entertained 'so insane a desire'. Therefore, 'nearly everyone was pro-German'. He was reminded of this, Sir Robert added, by the instinctive disapproval of the Baldwin-Chamberlain Governments toward his pro-French diplomatic policies, the Conservative certainty that from his French contacts he had emerged with 'no morals and a Latin mind'.

However one weighs Vansittart's evidence, it is demonstrably true that animus against the French was one of the most common of Conservative expressions and that that hostility was increasingly accompanied by warm gestures of friendship for the Germans. *The Times* in its apologia for its appeasement delusion, presented precisely this fact: 'Years of difficulties with France had increased sympathy for Germany, and the romantic appeal of almost anything German, to so

[1] And, to be sure, to Labour men as well. Irritated as they were with the French, the Labour Party maintained a fairly consistent record of trying to understand and soothe the latter's fears of Germany.

many English minds . . . made *The Times* so pro-German
after 1922 that the paper could not, in 1936, even consider
the necessity to modify its policy'. French occupation of the
Ruhr in 1923, on Germany's default of reparation payments,
was an irritant that upset Anglo-French relations for the rest
of the decade. France, Neville Chamberlain commented coldly,
was the stumbling block to European recovery, for 'although
France wants the money which can only be got out of a strong
Germany, she always shrinks from any course which would
help Germany to pay'. And Conservatives become obsessed
with the unwisdom of the French creation of a security system,
a ring of allies around Germany – the 'Little Entente' with
Czechoslovakia, Yugoslavia and Rumania that was consummated precisely because the British had been unwilling to
guarantee their help against a revived German power. The
Entente was, to the Conservative mind, simply a sign of irrational French suspicion and ill-will, direct evidence of French
paranoid viciousness. By the early 1930s, when it was clear
that something had spoiled the picture of a pacific prosperous
Germany, Conservatives were unable to see the complexity of
the situation; the whole thing was the fault of the French, and
of beguiled Francophiles in the British Foreign Office like
Austen Chamberlain and Vansittart. One of Stanley Baldwin's
correspondents complained in 1932: 'France's postwar policy,
with our connivance, has brought about the present German
outburst of nationalism and demand for equality of arms.
Why are we afraid of France? With the knowledge that Italy
and ourselves are with the Germans she would pause.'[1] Even
in 1936, in the crisis of the Nazi occupation of the Rhineland,
Baldwin himself was annoyed with the French rather than the
offending Germans. About French pressure for joint action to
preserve a demilitarised Rhineland, Baldwin grumbled that it
'was no friendly act of France to force us into a decision for
which we were not ready' (and surely, he added, could France
not 'be brought to see that a Germany crushed by France and

[1] Jones, *Diary*, p 57.

Russia [the new French ally] would be a Communist Germany?').

In the end, perhaps, one's main impression in rounding up Conservative views on foreign affairs in the 1920s is the necessary narrowness of the project. Inexperienced in European matters, Conservative ministers were too absorbed with their domestic troubles to look much to the outer world – and, when they did, it was perforce to continuing thorny problems like the status and future of India. G M Young recorded this pertinent passage:

> I once asked [Stanley Baldwin]: 'You remember your interview with Poincaré?' ('I do indeed,' he answered, with a wry mouth.) 'Did you ever talk to any other leading men in Europe?' 'No,' he said simply, 'I didn't like them.' Ribbentrop once lunched, and recited *Mein Kampf*. Brüning also lunched and they were heard discussing whether Brüning and Browning were the same name. There were others, but he preferred to forget them.[1]

It was Baldwin, too, master politician and three times supreme spokesman of His Majesty's Government, who expressed most poignantly a characteristic feeling – a baffled sense of incompetence and impotence within the turbulent period of the post-war decade. Vacationing at Aix-les-Bains in 1933, Baldwin shared with a correspondent his reflections on the contemporary scene: 'Walking alone among these hills', he wrote, 'I have come to the conclusion the world is stark mad. I have no idea what is the matter with it but it's all wrong . . . at times I am sick to death of being an asylum attendant.'[2]

Probing for the ideas of Conservative leaders one gets, in short, a persistent sense of their isolation from important phenomena of their times. Nothing in the experience of these businessmen-politicians, these old-school-tie groups of solid

---

[1] Young, *Baldwin*, p 62. In the interview with Poincaré in 1923, Baldwin had been 'defeated, and indeed humiliated', by the French Premier, who got from the meeting Baldwin's apparent agreement on French occupation of the Ruhr—this not at all Baldwin's, or his Cabinet's, previous policy and intention.

[2] Jones, *Diary*, p xxxii.

Edwardians, had prepared them for a European encounter; nothing had prepared them for the ideological battle that raged on the Continent in the backlash of the Russian Revolution, for the strong-arm methods of rule that were establishing *Fascisti* gangs in Italy, for the violence of the racism and fanatic nationalism exploding in Germany. Their personal records reveal shock, distaste, dismay, despair – that is, an awareness, but no understanding; it is as though a late-Victorian veil separated them from the swirling currents of the modern reality. And surely this was significant in the story of appeasement in the next decade: the chief decisions of the 1930s were to be made by men who seemed out of touch with the symptoms, let alone the causes, of the profound disturbances of the twentieth century.

PART TWO

THE BALDWIN YEARS
'Muddle, Bungle and Blunder'

4
Appeasement,
Empirically
Evolved

'WHAT A PITY IT IS,' Hilaire Belloc observed, 'that the English governing classes are taught no history, and for that matter, little about contemporary affairs. The diplomats know a good deal, and are always well acquainted with the French tradition, which is full of history, but the average gentleman, let alone lady, knows nothing.'[1] Mr Belloc's point is a good one and entirely relevant to the subject. One thing is certain: uncommon types were few in Conservative councils in the 1930s and 'average gentlemen' stood tall in affairs of state. And a pity it was, this void of leadership in a decade in desperate need of men of acumen, unusual sensitivity and perception.

In the Conservative inner circle, in the 'cosy ring of Tory politicians' that formed around Stanley Baldwin, the concern was for politics as usual, the recapture of power in form as well as fact from the disintegrating forces of Ramsay MacDonald's second Labour Government. The 'National Government' of 1931 was a gratifying accomplishment: with depression heavy over the country a fearful electorate rejected the Labour Party to return an overwhelming Conservative majority, its leaders the old ministers, the 'humdrum figures' of the 1920s. Nor was that all; in 1935 Conservatives demonstrated again the tactical skill of their political professionalism, securing what bitter Socialists called 'another immense trick-victory'.[2] It was a Tory triumph, this mandate for the keepers of the *status quo*, a victory which made unnecessary any thought of change in the Party, of new faces and fresh ideas; politically speaking, 'the government had nothing to fear behind it or in front'. The benign countenance of Stanley Baldwin seemed at

[1] *Letters from Hilaire Belloc*, ed Robert Speiaght, p 256.
[2] A L Rowse, *All Souls*, p 21.

this point the perfect expression of Tory self-satisfaction, and his the Tory voice that seemed to say, 'so even in this terrible situation we have handled the threat of the democratic electorate; was this not our one pressing problem?'

There was, of course, a gathering storm of problems, a thunderhead hanging low over Europe; its force, when it broke, was sufficient to shatter even the complacency of the master British politician. Stanley Baldwin was, as his old opponent Winston Churchill put it, the 'ruling force' in British politics from 1922 to May of 1937; at that latter date – to follow the rolling Churchillian prose – 'loaded with honours and enshrined in public esteem, he laid down his heavy task and retired in dignity and silence to his Worcestershire home'. Sir Winston's final phrase is significantly to the mark: true it is that the retired Baldwin wrote no memoirs, indulged in little public retrospection on a political career notable at least for its longevity. Why Baldwin's 'silence'? A possible answer might be found in foreign events during the last years of his rule, so disastrous that in the quiet of his Worcestershire home he hoped only to forget them. By the end of Baldwin's term of office the best hopes of postwar foreign policy had vanished. The League of Nations with its ideals of international co-operation and collective action against aggression – this was smashed, buried under the debris of Mussolini's Ethiopian adventure. The Versailles Treaty and the Locarno pacts had been tossed aside by unilateral British approval of German naval expansion, by Allied acceptance of German rearmament and finally and officially stamped as obsolete by Hitler's unchallenged reoccupation of the Rhineland. In Spain the peace of Europe had been broken by bloody civil war in which Fascist nations interfered with insolent disregard of Anglo-French pleading for non-intervention. In such a dangerous world Mr Baldwin's England stood, in 1937, in self-imposed Imperial isolation, separated by its own suspicions even from its French ally. Baldwin was, one would say, rightly reluctant to discuss the details of such a record.

Baldwin's reticence notwithstanding, it is quite possible to trace out the affairs of his ministry, to reconstruct the activities that reduced the British nation to the sorry state of 1937. One starts with Baldwin himself, this clever resourceful man whose political skill and insight deserted him entirely in dealing with the perplexing continental world. It was not just that Baldwin was both untrained and disinterested in international matters[1]; he was simply not made to the measure of the statesman, and especially to the kind of statesmanship needed in the raw violence of the postwar world. Here was a man who – as A L Rowse noted – had never had to fight for anything; born to the firm security of the upper-middle-class home, Baldwin followed life paths neatly and tidily marked out for the progress of the only son – from Harrow and Cambridge to inherited position in business and parliament. A combination of sheer luck and a canny party sense brought him to the political limelight, and a combination of sheer luck and an uncanny feeling for the British political pulse sustained him as Conservative leader for fourteen years. Actually, in the political crisis, the tight spot – and there were many of them – Baldwin more often than not retreated into a defence of absolute inactivity, apparently waiting for the saving solution to present itself; often the solution did appear – the Zinoviev Letter in 1924, the collapse of the Labour Government before depression pressures in 1931, the Simpson affair, and Edward VIII's abdication in 1936, the last the event that permitted Baldwin to depart his career with a halo of national acclaim. In all of this it is Baldwin's passivity – Rowse called it an 'incurable vice of indolence' – that is the striking thing. It was as though the lessons of Baldwin's life had convinced him that one did not *do* anything; direction, even ideas, came from the outside, from some mysterious source. In a much-quoted answer to a query about the preparation of his speeches Baldwin explained, 'there is a cloud round

[1] See the pointed assessment of Baldwin as statesman in Young, *Baldwin*, pp 62–63.

my mind, it takes shape, and then I know what to say'. This peculiar intuitive approach carried him safely through many a domestic emergency, but in the baffling morass of European affairs his intuition failed him, the cloud refused to take shape. It was under the pressure of foreign crises that Baldwin was brought to despair: in 1936, after the fiasco of British policy in Ethiopia, after the Rhineland occupation, after the outbreak of war in Spain, Baldwin took a kind of vacation from leadership and buried himself almost incommunicado in Wales. Privately, his friend, Thomas Jones, dismissed reports of the Prime Minister's illness: 'There is nothing organically wrong with him. He lost his nerve and every burden became a nightmare.'

Perhaps it could be said with truth that the Baldwin record was in part the consequence of more impersonal forces, due, that is, to the immense difficulties of his position as leader in this transitional age; his was the responsibility of steering the nineteenth-century men of his Party through the uncharted course of political democracy, or of hanging on until modern successors, acclimatised to the twentieth century and armed with a 'New Conservatism', arrived to take over direction of a mass democratic society. And in this, Baldwin did his job faithfully, seeing in his intuitive way the necessary outlines of his role. Read Keith Feiling's assessment of the Baldwin leadership at the time of the King's silver jubilee in 1935:

In Britain's silver age he [Baldwin] had come to the height of his influence, in his personality old civic unkindness seemed to be buried, and in the rejoicing over a good King he might find just proof that he had accomplished what he had set out to do, to root democracy in parliamentary institutions by adjusting Labour to 'the good old humour' of England.

Yet it was clear, too, that like his colleague, Chamberlain, Baldwin was afraid of the 'animal', although he preferred to soothe rather than coerce it. The power of the electorate, its ability to dispossess its leaders, was a fearsome, unforgettable thing: Baldwin was haunted, for example, by the memory of the by-election at East Fulham in 1933, in which the Conservative position had been invaded and a traditionally-safe seat won by the Labour opponent on the charge of Tory 'warmongering'; the Conservative candidate, who had advocated, rather than international disarmament, the strengthening of the British armed forces, was lost, Baldwin noted, 'in a wild flood of pacifism'. The content of popular pacifism will concern us later: Here, the point is that Baldwin interpreted the defeat at East Fulham quite rightly as a judgment of Conservative rule, and that, further, it profoundly affected his confidence that he 'could sway opinion this way or that'; hereafter, he would avoid coming to grips with that opinion, would avoid the risks one took in standing, in public exposure, for any positive policy.

Perhaps, then, it is the two together – the unforseeable difficulties in controlling democratic opinion and the personality of Stanley Baldwin – that lie behind the story of his calamitous term. How very different he was from Churchill, the scion of the class of 'natural rulers' of the past! 'Tell the truth,' Churchill said, 'tell the truth to the British people. They are a tough people and a robust people. They may be a bit offended at the moment, but if you have told them exactly what is going on, you have insured yourself against complaints and reproaches which are very unpleasant when they come home on the morrow of some disillusionment.' Churchill would tell the truth to make the people accept his desired policy; Baldwin would use deception to achieve the same end. Deceit, for Baldwin, was a natural and unavoidable practice in the game of political leadership, a most valued part of his political repertoire; he could even use candour as a deceit, as political capital, as he did in his famous 'frankness' address of 12th November 1936, in which he informed the House of Commons that the low state of British defences was due to the calculated decision against rearmament as the programme which might have lost an election for the Conservative Party. It was an amazing Baldwin performance – carrying, as Churchill said, 'naked truth about his motives into indecency' – and amazingly effective in charming his listeners into forgetting for the moment that he had not, after all, authorised a go-ahead on rearmament. An even more revealing – because unconsciously ironic – incident occurred in the Commons in the same year, when Baldwin told the Members that he had not had time to prepare a speech, and thus would talk to them 'truthfully, sincerely, and plainly'. Baldwin was totally absorbed in manipulation of the democracy; it was an exhausting struggle, which sapped his strength and left him without mental energy to deal with foreign, unreal problems. Yet, even in the domestic matters to which he devoted his attention, ambivalence, indecisiveness, a critical failure of nerve – qualities so maddening to critics of his foreign policy – marked Baldwin's behaviour: this popular politician, so often warm and moving in his public expression of faith in the virtues of 'the people', could remark in private conversation, 'I doubt if we can go on like this: we shall have to limit the franchise.'

Baldwin's domestic preoccupations made him indifferent to discussion or consideration of foreign affairs: 'Wake me up,' he was reported as saying in the Cabinet, 'when you are finished with that.' Because of his disinterest – and incompetence – there was no guiding hand in foreign policy, no one to check the kind of *ad hoc* decisions made by ministers like Sir Samuel Hoare, in the unfortunate negotiations that ended in the Hoare-Laval pact, that sorry response to Italian aggression against Ethiopia. There was no one to gather up the frayed edges of British defences, no one to supervise a chronically lagging air rearmament – or the Air Minister until 1935, for that matter, Lord Londonderry, whose open admiration of the Nazi chiefs so compromised his position that his kinsman, Winston Churchill, felt it necessary to write a special affirmation of his 'unquestionable loyalty and patriotism'. Then, too, Baldwin's weaknesses, his mental vacuum on foreign questions, left him wide open, vulnerable to the ideas and pressures of more sure-thinking friends, the prime example the peripatetic Thomas Jones, self-appointed contact man from Nancy Astor's Cliveden group, Baldwin's boon companion and confidant.

Ignorance, apathy, and apprehension – it was a melancholy combination of attitudes in the first British Prime Minister to face the terrible threat of the 1930s, the rise of Hitler's Germany. Baldwin's intuitive approach to leadership set the tone of the British response in the first years of the Fascist challenge; the nation was reduced to a policy of no policy or, more precisely, to a policy hastily devised and empirically arrived at as each foreign problem arose – the empiricism, however (and most importantly), well within the framework of the fixed ideas and attitudes of Mr Baldwin and his associates.

In January of 1933 Adolf Hitler became Chancellor of a Germany already militarily stronger than the limits imposed by the Treaty of Versailles.[1] The Disarmament Conference, the hope of the pacifists, had been dragging on since 1932, from the beginning paralysed by French reluctance to grant equality of arms to the Germans, and by the refusal of all powers to give up favourite weapons. When, in October 1933, Hitler announced withdrawal of Germany from the Conference and from the League of Nations, the spirit of peace in Europe and of Locarno co-operation was clearly a precarious thing.

With Stanley Baldwin as a sometimes guide, British Conservative leaders (most of them) as well as the British people (most of them) sauntered through the period of the early 1930s, only casually glancing outward, and largely unaffected by the alien affairs of Central Europe. True, a few observers took a hard look at what would be identified as the Nazification of Germany – Winston Churchill, for example, who was com-

---

[1] Churchill, *Gathering Storm*, pp 44–50, for a discussion of the secret and evasive ways that the Germans sought, throughout the 1920s, to rebuild army, navy, and air force – as well as their industrial war machine. An excellent summary of German militarism and rearmament is in John W Wheeler-Bennett, *Munich: Prologue to Tragedy*, pp 208–210.

pelled by what he saw there to attempt to inform his country-men. Driven by his sense of danger Churchill became a mine of information on the regeneration of German power and the self-appointed educator of the English governing group. To the Tory illusion of well-being in Europe, Churchill posed the facts of increasing friction in international relations. When Conservatives talked of 'poor Germany' he inquired blandly for evidence of the 'Carthaginian peace' that had supposedly devastated that vanquished land; what he saw, said Churchill, was a Germany that had 'received an infusion of blood from the nations with whom she went to war', a Germany 'absolved from all the burdens of reparations, with a moratorium upon all commercial debts, with her factories equipped to the very latest point of science by British and American money', a Germany which only awaited 'trade revival to gain an immense mercantile ascendancy throughout the world'.[1] And Churchill grasped some of the significant characteristics of emerging Nazism: in 1933 he spoke of the 'fierce passions' raging in Germany, and sombrely noted 'the tumultuous insurgence of ferocity and war spirit, the pitiless ill-treatment of minorities, the denial of the normal protections of civilised society to large numbers of individuals solely on the ground of race'. It was his insight into Nazi Germany, said Churchill, that lay behind his steady opposition to disarmament and his repetitive prayer of 'Thank God for the French army'.

The Churchillian lessons were pounded home in many a Commons address. Month after month – that became year after year – Churchill hammered at what were to him the most obvious matters of concern for British statesmanship. What, he asked in 1934, was the dominant fact of the European situation? It was, he answered, that Germany was rearming, particularly in air power. And what did this mean to Britain?

It is no use disguising the fact that there must be and there ought to be deep anxiety in this country about Germany . . . at present

[1] Winston Churchill, *While England Slept*, p 18.

two or three men, in what may well be a desperate position, have
their grip on the whole of that mighty country. . . . . Men in that
position might very easily be tempted to do what even a military
dictatorship would not do . . . because you have men who, to
relieve themselves from the peril which confronts them at home,
might easily plunge into a foreign adventure of catastrophic
character to the whole world. . . . People may say that we have
no quarrel with Germany and that Germany has no quarrel
with us, but do not doubt that there is very sharp resentment
against England in Germany.[1]

Behind Churchill's apprehension lay a tradition-bred instinct
for the supremacy of Imperial Britain:

Germany is already well on her way to become, and must become,
incomparably the most heavily armed nation in the world and
the nation most completely ready for war. . . . We cannot afford
to see Nazidom in its present phase of cruelty and intolerance,
with all its hatreds and all its gleaming weapons, paramount
in Europe.[2]

Churchill reacted to Nazi Germany, then, both with unusual
insight and with the spontaneous roar of the tough Tory
imperialist. But what about the business-politicians who –
rather than he – had the responsibility of dealing with the new
rulers of Germany? In the early years of Nazi power, in 1934
and 1935, Conservative ministers were not inclined to grant
immediate trust and approval to Hitler and the Third Reich.
One must dig for evidence of Baldwin's involvement in the
subject, and what emerges is characteristically ambivalent. At
the same time that his Government signed an Anglo-German
naval agreement permitting Germany 35 per cent of parity with
Britain – this the British way of admitting that the Versailles
prohibitions against German rearmament were dead[3] –

---

[1] Churchill, *While England Slept*.
[2] *Ibid*, pp 227–228.
[3] The Naval Treaty was especially surprising – and a straw in the wind –
because in this formal Western flouting of the strictures of Versailles, the British
bypassed their French allies. See D L Fleming, *The Cold War and Its Origins,
1917–1960*, I, 54–55.

Baldwin was saying to his friend, Thomas Jones: 'We don't know what Germany really intends. We do know . . . that France is pacific, and is not a potential enemy. We cannot say that about Germany.' Neville Chamberlain was privately indignant about the murder, in 1934, of Austrian Chancellor Dollfuss by Nazi thugs, the signal for a planned Nazi uprising in Austria.[1] The murder was, Chamberlain said, an 'ominous tragedy', in which Germany was 'once more behind, instigating, suggesting, encouraging bloodshed and assassination, for her own selfish aggrandisement and pride'; note in the words of the aging Chamberlain his apparent association of Hitler's Germany with that of Wilhelm II, his memory that Germany was the 'bully' of Europe and the *'fons et origo'* of European troubles and anxieties. And on the fringes of officialdom there was, as yet, little warmth for the Nazis. A L Rowse reported the disgust with which Lord Lothian[2] – who would be, by 1936, hot after the friendship of Hitler, Goering, and company – heard the news of the Nazi purges of 30th June 1934: 'We can't have any dealings with these people,' said Lothian, 'they are nothing but a lot of gunmen.'[3] Even Lady Astor, from politically involved social circles that would soon become the soft underbelly for the invasions of Hitler's propaganda legions, reportedly displayed general distaste for the vulgar masters of the New Germany.

Furthermore, this was but the opening stage in European gangster diplomacy, the period of swift developments that brought an initial shocked awareness of the changing power structure of international politics. It was the period in which France, nervously watching German conscription proceeding in blunt defiance of the Versailles treaty, tightened her alliances with the Soviet Union. It was the period when Mussolini, after his first interview with Hitler, described the German Fuehrer

[1] Hitler's eager grab for Austria here in 1934 was stopped by Mussolini, who was furious at this move by his junior-in-dictatorship. Italian troops were mobilised to maintain the independence of Austria. See Gaetano Salvemini, *Prelude to World War II*, p 162.
[2] Ambassador to the United States, 1939–40.
[3] Rowse, *All Souls*, p 31.

as a 'barbarian' who talked 'only of *Anschluss* and war', a man with whom Mussolini could 'never have a meeting of minds'. In this moment of flux, this period of fumbling for strategy against a barely-rolling German aggressiveness, Britain was drawn into the Franco-Italian circle of resistance. Lending strength to one another, the three governments formed in early 1935 the 'Stresa Front', which amounted to a loose understanding that they would work together in dealing with Germany.

Did this anti-German activity and sentiment mean that British Conservatives took an initially hard line against Nazism? Hardly. Not even apologists for the Government would advance such a point. In the midst of a passage explaining Neville Chamberlain's hardheaded assessment of the Nazi challenge, Keith Feiling summarised British action in these words:

> Neither Italy nor France were pleased with the British in the first half of 1935. Our separate protest against German conscription seemed unduly mild, we condoned Hitler's breach of faith by the visit to Berlin, [Foreign Secretary] Simon's zeal for an Eastern pact was reckoned cool. At Stresa itself we refused to hear of immediate sanctions against further treaty violations, or to make bilateral air pacts in advance of a general agreement. Finally, three weeks before Stresa, Simon had invited Germany or enter on naval conversations, and within six weeks of condemning the German repudiation of the Versailles military clauses we were negotiating a separate naval treaty, which carried that repudiation further still.

The British Government was not, in short, intending a stiff stand against German aggressiveness, against a Nazi regime that, in openly rearming and in building a conscript army, had already knocked over some of the most hallowed straw men of international agreement made since 1918. The British refused to get tough – indeed, they were discovering, even as they echoed the alarmists on the 'German menace', good and compelling reasons for doing nothing about it.

The fateful moment was here in the early 1930s, in the

response of Conservative leaders to danger signals from foreign fields, in the cautious, narrow steps with which they picked their way. The businessman out of his office – of whom the shock of the Great Depression had already taken its toll – faltered before the special imperatives of statesmanship in the 1930s, although in his arrogant manner he thought himself the very model of the good manager, the sensible architect of national policy. Observe, as an excellent focus, the indecision of Neville Chamberlain, Chancellor of the Exchequer, and responsible, as his biographer put it, for 'husbanding our resources'. Chamberlain was ever quick to point out the deficiencies in his colleagues, for example, in the Foreign Secretary: 'Simon's weakness', he noted in his diary, 'has given rise to much criticism. . . . He can always make an admirable speech in the House . . . but the fact is that his manner inspires no confidence, and that he seems temperamentally unable to make up his mind to action when a difficult situation arises.' It was on the basis of such judgment of the head of the Foreign Office that Chamberlain decided to take a hand in foreign affairs, to lend his capability to his ineffectual associates; once there, however, he was no more willing than anyone else for strong action, for policies that might 'earmark our forces for unknown commitments'. Thus, Chamberlain talked resolutely in 1934 of checking the German bully, and even the Japanese, who had been running amuck in Manchuria for three years; this was the opportunity, he said, 'to put ourselves right with the world, take the lead, and incidentally stage an example of an international police force'. Yet as he gave it second thought the resolution faded, for 'we cannot provide simultaneously for hostilities with Japan and Germany, and . . . the latter is the problem to which we must address ourselves'. And so Chamberlain concentrated on the single problem of Germany – although, it turned out, there were still areas of equivocation: on the one hand, he could see the necessity of a programme of air rearmament, for 'we shall be more likely to deter Germany from mad-dogging if we have an air force which, in case of need, could bomb the Ruhr from Belgium'; but, on the other hand, such rearmament had to be carefully considered since 'if we were now to follow Winston's advice and sacrifice our commerce to the manufacture of arms, we should inflict a certain injury on our trade from which it would take generations to recover'. By 1935 Chamberlain was so successfully husbanding British resources – that is, eliminating unnecessary expenditures – that he grasped at any straw of reason and moderation from the bully abroad: 'You asked me what I thought of Hitler's speech,' he answered a query, 'well, frankly, I was intensely relieved . . . while I recognised, and indeed insisted on the necessity for . . . a recasting of our air programme. . . . I have been greatly alarmed at some of the proposals, which appeared to me panicky and wasteful.' And this was the businessman-politican who had taken over, announced himself the most capable of Tory officials, the man 'practically' in charge 'of the defence requirements of the country'.

Government leaders, then, were carefully avoiding any risks to foreign policy, and risks there might be in blocking Nazi determination to break the bands of Versailles. War, especially, was unthinkable, the nightmare possibility that triggered Conservative anxieties. Stanley Baldwin's public statements on modern warfare were expression, not so much of the pacifism that went deep into British society, but of a governing group that had lost its nerve, a collapsing leadership. He wanted the man in the street to know, said Baldwin, that 'there is no power on earth that can protect him from being bombed. Whatever people may tell him, the bomber will always get through.' Playing upon his own fears, Baldwin pictured for his listeners – in the House of Commons – the horrors of attack from the air, cities in smoking ruins, millions of people dead or fleeing in panic of terror. And what was the point of this public prediction of destruction? Apparently there was none – except a kind of catharsis of Baldwin's fatalistic despair. He had been advised, 'If London is bombed three nights running, nothing can avert a revolution' – words that had seared the Conservative mind; 'when the next war comes,' Baldwin would conclude his scare speeches, 'and European civilisation is wiped out, as it will be' – how certain he was that his world, 'civilisation', could not withstand another blow!

There was another distinguishable element in the Conservative retreat before the first thrust of foreign aggression. Since the 1920s, Tory interest in the League of Nations, Tory faith in the principle of collective security, had been feeble at best. Into the Covenant of the League had been written the understanding that all member-nations were pledged to maintain international peace, that they would join in military action or in economic sanctions against any aggressor, in any part of the world. The typical Conservative attitude was explicit in this paraphrase of the League promise: 'If the Covenant meant what it said, we were pledged to keep by force the frontier of every existing State, and to protect an indivisible peace by making every war universal; as if the defence of a vast vulnerable empire were not enough for forty million Britons. Now it was, and always had been, certain that no British Government would fulfil such commitments.'[1] That was as plain as words could make it; in action, Conservative regard for the Covenant pledge was clear as early as 1931, when Japanese troops overran Manchuria, a blatant aggression against China. At this initial test the Covenant pledge had been conveniently shelved. War against Japan and on the basis of an abstraction? The very thought, to British leaders, was an absurdity. At any rate, Japan had assured the British of an 'open door' trading policy in Manchuria; and perhaps it was a neat solution to the chaotic social conditions of the Far East to have the Japanese at once bring order into revolutionary China and patrol the Asian borders of the pariah Soviet Union.[2]

---

[1] Feiling, *Neville Chamberlain*, p 261.
[2] See R Bassett, *Democracy and Foreign Policy: A Case History, the Sino-Japanese Dispute, 1931–1933*, pp 31–32 and *passim*. Also Henry L Stimson and McGeorge Bundy, *On Active Service in Peace and War*, p 248, for Secretary of State Stimson's note that the British 'held back' from joint action against the Japanese aggression, that Sir John Simon, British Foreign Secretary, was unable 'to take Chinese territorial and administrative integrity very seriously'.

Japanese aggression helped the British set a pattern for the future; hereafter it was easier to bypass the League, to judge each foreign problem on its individual merits, to define with narrow care the vital areas of concern for Britain and the Commonwealth.

Nevertheless, in the early 1930s, the Covenant stood, to Conservative leaders an irritating relic of diplomatic nonsense – or worse, the dangerous device by which Britain might be pulled into an impossible European trap. Suppose, for example, there were an issue of aggression in Eastern Europe in which the aggrieved nation were a member of the French 'Little Entente', or even – getting to the heart of the matter – the Soviet Union; under her League duties, and prompted by her French neighbour, Britain could be drawn into the defence of the victim, into even the protection of the Soviet Union. It was the inconceivable nature of the dilemma posed by League responsibilities that lay behind the new precision about areas of British concern, the talk of the 'narrow sphere where our interests are direct and obvious'[1]; British interests, it seemed, were restricted to *Western* Europe, and British security related only to the borders of France and Belgium.

From Conservative sources, then, there came an undercurrent of insistence that the Covenant of the League be changed, 'revised' in the euphoristic word of the day, which meant that the anti-aggression clauses be eliminated, that the organisation be reduced to a properly unobtrusive role. Tory negativism on the League struck a variety of notes. There was the Baldwin-type disregard of the whole thing—although he habitually vacationed only a few miles from Geneva, at Aix-les-Bains, Baldwin had never visited the League headquarters nor observed assembly sessions. Or, the bulk of 'responsible' opinion agreed with Neville Chamberlain that the League should be kept as 'a moral force and focus',[2] a high platform, that is, for sounding the absurdities of collective security. And

[1] Austen Chamberlain, quoted in Salvemini, *World War II*, p 499.
[2] Feiling, *Neville Chamberlain*, p 295.

there was blunt rejection and open contempt, mostly from Tory lords, in remarks about 'foolish faith in an impotent League', the League existing as a 'mutual admiration society manned by well-meaning busy-bodies'.[1]

Still, except in the sanctity and remoteness of the House of Lords, criticism that struck at the heart of the League of Nations was a thing to be quietly done. The League was a symbol to millions of Britons, the promise of enduring peace that would be preserved by statesman of nations that had learned at last the senselessness of war. Popular idolisation of the League and faith in its principles were powerful political forces: Baldwin, for one, spoke in public 'beautifully' about the activities at Geneva – 'Only there do you get the argument, the friendly pressure that can be brought by men constantly meeting, men deep and true in conviction'; well did the master-politician know that to reveal his scepticism and disbelief was to 'invite political extinction'.[2] The gulf between Conservative cynicism and popular hope led necessarily to the Baldwin solution of deceit. Clearly, the only possible official line was to profess adherence to the League – a public profession that would cover the search for some way to avoid the logic of its principles.

Indeed, in the early 1930s the important factors were on the negative side of the ledger—that is, operating against the Churchillian demand for an adamant stand by Britain and her allies to forestall the real or potential aggressor. The narrow concerns of a Chamberlain fused with the apathy and disinterest of a Baldwin in the shaping of Conservative policy in foreign affairs. Mark the disastrous drift of the product: Britain was led by men weak in the crisis of the capitalist world, haunted by the possible social effects of depression and decline, and chiefly involved in the exigencies of political survival; why, they asked, should a nation 'on the edge of financial catastrophe' be responsible for, or even concerned with, the actions

[1] Lord Londonderry, *Ourselves and Germany*, p 134; *House of Lords Debates*, Vol 104, Fifth Series, p 315.
[2] Young, *Baldwin*, p 173.

of far-off aggressors? Why, above all, should the nation run the risk of war with foreign adventurers?

In summary, Conservative leaders were – to put it mildly – badly prepared for the explosion of Fascism, weighted down by their caution and ignorance, hamstrung by their fears. They saw the potential danger of the new movement in Germany – this is an interesting point; they even made a few half-hearted stabs toward preparation for that danger. But from there the retreat began, the second thoughts and the rationalisations. Conservative leaders moved with relief to the easier occupation – of stripping themselves of the few weapons, particularly those of collective security, that might have given them strength. Sham-leaders they were by 1935 and 1936 – when the dictators started to move – capable only of pretending, for public consumption, that they would not yield, step by step, before the dynamic of Fascist aggression.

5
'The Accursed Matter
of Abyssinia'

FROM THE SUMMER of 1935 to the end of the political term of
Stanley Baldwin, crises in foreign affairs shattered the British
sense of isolation, of insular-preoccupation – those attitudes so
prominent in the Prime Minister himself. There was no relief
from foreign pressures: the 'accursed matter' of Abyssinia[1]
shaded into the lost opportunity of the Rhineland, while the
brief flurry of that excitement was lost in the European crucible
of the Spanish Civil War. It was impossible now for the
knowledgeable to ignore the outside world; as Thomas Jones
reported from a weekend at Cliveden: 'The talk is never of
home but always of foreign problems.'

First, then, consider the matter of the Italian conquest of
Ethiopia, an episode in which a great many things were clarified, not least among them the attitudes of British Conservative
leaders toward war, rearmament, and the League of Nations.
Clarified, too, was the wholesale incompetence of the Baldwin-
led Government, although illumination on this point occurred
only after the Tory victory in the election of 1935. Nevertheless,
important discoveries were made: 'It might have been
expected', wrote A L Rowse, 'that Baldwin and his friends
would make a mess, but not such a very shocking mess.'

Mussolini's move against Ethiopia, the Italian aggression
against the feeble forces of Emperor Haile Selassie, presented
a dilemma for the Tories from the start. As the issue developed
in mid-summer of 1935, Conservative reaction was a broad
sympathy for Italian interests and designs in North Africa.
There was long precedent for this ready understanding, dating
from the turn of the century, when the British had shared
with Italy and France spheres of influence in and encircling

[1] Feiling, *Neville Chamberlain*, p 278.

Ethiopia; the last British word had been given in 1925 by Austen Chamberlain, then Foreign Secretary, who had pledged British support to Mussolini's attempts to acquire economic rights in Ethiopia – a gentlemen's agreement that was surely made with the awareness that the Italians might be forced to military methods to get their way with the Ethiopian Government.[1] To the Conservatives, this was a colonial area, to be so treated; they stoutly protested the French-drafted invitation that made Ethiopia a member of the League of Nations – as Churchill put it, it was ridiculous to pretend that that backward desert land was a 'fit, worthy, and equal member of a league of civilised nations'.[2] Why hedge this country with the protections of proper communities; why deny European nations – have-not nations – the opportunity to satisfy their territorial ambitions in such places (dreary wastes) as Ethiopia? Thus, Conservatives understood, even shared, Mussolini's annoyance with the Ethiopian resistance to his demands for economic privileges; as Duff Cooper said, 'Italy had good ground for complaint against Abyssinia.'

On the other hand, if Conservative leaders felt a bond with

[1] Salvemini, *World War II*, pp 73–75. Salvemini points out the difficulties in citing evidence for the agreement between Sir Austen Chamberlain and Mussolini: 'There is not a single word on the agreements of 1925 in Sir Charles Petrie's book, *Life and Letters of Sir Austen Chamberlain*. We are merely told [II, 306] that on his way home from the Mediterranean, Sir Austen 'saw M Briand in Paris so as to kill the rumours that his meeting with Signor Mussolini had some sinister significance'. *Ibid*, p 76, fn 3. There is this item (which Salvemini uses) in a biography of Anthony Eden, written by a man who had been Private Parliamentary Secretary to Austen Chamberlain: 'Great Britain had Italy's backing in her claims against Turkey. A price for this support was demanded by the restless and apparently irresponsible Benito Mussolini, and was quietly paid by Sir Austen.' A G C Johnson, *Anthony Eden*, p 128. Keith Feiling refers casually to the agreement of 1925, 'whereby, in return for Italian support for a barrage on Lake Tsana, so vital for the water of Egypt, Britain would assist Italy to obtain a railway concession connecting her two colonies, and admit her exclusive economic influence in western Ethiopia'.

[2] Feiling quotes Churchill to this effect without giving his source. Feiling, *Neville Chamberlain*, p 264. For his part, Churchill touches only fleetingly on the British view that 'the character of the Ethiopian Government and the conditions prevailing in that wild land of tyranny, slavery, and tribal war were not consonant with membership of the League'. Churchill, *Gathering Storm*, p 149. One gets none of this, however, in Anthony Eden, *Memoirs: Facing the Dictators*, p 213 ff. Eden proceeded from the fact that Ethiopia *was* a League member, and that failure to act in its protection would endanger the League – and the existing political system of Europe.

Italian expansion in Africa – and hoped to remain Mussolini's friends – it was quickly apparent that the affair in Ethiopia was not a traditional, reasonable case of imperialism. Mussolini was seized with a most unreasonable kind of truculence: he seemed to have forgotten the reciprocal nature of the agreement of 1925 with Austen Chamberlain, the understanding that the price of British support for his African ambitions was his scrupulous regard for British prerogatives, 'special interests', in the area[1]; moreover, his invasion of Ethiopia was unnecessarily brutal, the irresponsible act of a deliberate troublemaker. And the whole affair truly became an accursed matter when Haile Selassie, ruler of the Ethiopians, dumped it into the lap of the League of Nations – according to his legal right – charging the Italians with wilful aggression against a sovereign member-nation and demanding the application of the anti-aggression clauses of the Covenant.

The Conservative dilemma took shape in the background of the developing crisis of Italian aggression in North Africa. On the face of it, the problem seemed about to be settled by other participants. The League of Nations swung into action, and economic sanctions against the Italians were initiated by a League committee with the apparent co-operation of member nations – and of the United States. In Britain, a major breakthrough occurred in the angry reaction of the Labour Opposition – as of public opinion in general[2] – to Mussolini's bluster and brutality; spreading was a new ability of millions of

[1] Salvemini, *World War II*, p 75. See also Eden, *Facing the Dictators*, pp 222–223. In a memorandum, Eden wrote in 1935: 'Personally, I have for some time past been anxious at the drift of events in Ethiopia. It is hard to believe that Italian ambitions are limited to a few wells. It would seem now that Italy aims at no less than the absorption of Ethiopia morsel by morsel. In this connection it is perhaps not without interest to note that Sir Miles Lampson fears that, were our ships absent during trouble in Egypt, Italian ships would arrive on the scene. . . . I venture to think that it must be a matter of serious concern to us that Italy should seek to secure such a dominating position in this part of Africa.'

[2] The Conservative Press, too, was calling for 'effective action' from the League, for 'swift and firm' punishment of the Italian aggressor. *The Spectator*, 4th, 11th October 1935. See *The Times*, 6th September 1935, for the editorial comment that Great Britain 'with others, has taken her stand by the methods of the League and means to abide by them'; also, *ibid*, 27th, 30th September 1935, the editor's view that League action against Mussolini was an 'endeavour of civilisation to ban war as an institution incompatible with itself'.

Britons to see that extraordinary measures were necessary to counter the threat of Fascism. The latter was of quintessential importance: here was a sign of the end of blind pacifism, as well as of Labour's refusal to approve rearmament; to stamp the change the Trades Union Congress, by a large majority, resolved to support the League of Nations in its defence of peace – recognising clearly that 'defence of peace' meant the possibility of war.[1] The language of the resolution was, of course, significant. Labour pacifism, the popular opposition to rearmament that had terrified Baldwin in the East Fulham election, had been a manifestation of a basic lack of trust in Conservative governing classes: 'Would you support another imperialist war?' the Labour Party had asked. The thundering answer was 'Never!'[2] The new mandate for rearmament given by millions of Britons in 1935 specified that the effort be linked to the purposes of the League of Nations, that if war against the Fascist aggressor were necessary it would be the united action of League member-nations. Still, there was consensus in Britain on the need for an expanding defence programme, and this was a great stride forward, an essential condition to British fulfilment of League obligations.

To the casual observer the way seemed clear, with the League moving to punish or censure the Italians, with British public opinion aroused to the issue, prepared to support any action to stop the aggressor.[3] To Conservatives, one way was clear – to a political calculation; the Baldwin Government made the decision to hold a national election in the autumn of 1935, the chief campaign issue to be Conservative handling of the international crisis, the policy of resistance to aggression through the collective action of the League.[4]

[1] See *The Times*, 6th September 1935, for the report of the TUC meeting which approved sanctions against Mussolini—at the risk of war. Also Clement R Attlee, *As It Happened*, pp 139–142.
[2] See *New Statesman and Nation*, 25th July 1936, for the article on Labour pacifism.
[3] As *The Spectator* saw it, Britain had undertaken, through the League, a 'momentous action in an uncharted field' (11th October 1935).
[4] Anthony Eden's reaction to the proposal of an election was interesting. Asked by Foreign Secretary Sir Samuel Hoare for an opinion, he replied that in his view

This was the first step in the Conservative creation of a shocking mess in the Ethiopian affair. In the electoral campaign Conservative candidates went to the nation proclaiming their faith in the League, exploiting the popular approval of rearmament under League auspices and of the collective stand against Mussolini. In campaign oratory Stanley Baldwin rose to eloquent heights of pride in the League:

> Judgment may lead to action, cautionary action, restraining action, at the extreme to coercive action. We mean nothing by the League if we are not prepared, after trial, to take action to enforce its judgment. Look at the alternative. When I spoke, so inadequately, of the horrors of war, was it not clear that we must be prepared to take risks to prevent that evil thing stalking again across the world?
>
> The judgment of the world, given, as it must be, unanimously in open Assembly, after long discussion, is no light and hasty thing. The last few weeks have taught us what it means. *Securus judicat orbis terrarum.* That is the power of the League of Nations.

British voters believed such public pledges – and why not? The deep-toned sincerity of a Baldwin gave a kind of glow to the campaign, enhancing the Tory image as the party of tradition and experience. The results of the election brought a comfortable majority for the Conservative Party, a victory won on the strength of official professions – that 'the keystone of British foreign policy' was the League of Nations, and that 'there would be no wavering in the policy pursued over Abyssinia'.[1]

Yet the private views of Conservative ministers about using the League as a force against Italian aggression were rather different from their campaign rhetoric. The Prime Minister,

it was the 'right moment' for the Government to secure a sufficient majority, which would be for the 'national good' for the next five years. But he added 'that the country might have the impression that we were playing a "dirty trick" by calling for an election at a time when a virtually united nation was supporting us'; he wrote, 'rather our majority was less striking than that the country should feel any resentment at the way in which we gained it'. Eden, *Facing the Dictators*, pp 313–314.

[1] Amery, *Political Life*, III, 180. Mr Baldwin's Government, thought *The Spectator* (22nd November 1935), had been given and had accepted a 'mandate' for sanctions against Italy.

for example, was not sanguine in the situation: even as Baldwin spoke so firmly of adherence to the principles of collective security, 'gnawing' at the back of his mind was the 'innermost conviction that the League could not stop the career of Mussolini'.[1] And if the Prime Minister was not sure that Mussolini could be stopped by the action of the League nations, the Chancellor of the Exchequer apparently doubted the wisdom of even attempting such a check. Leopold Amery – Tory MP and Churchillian in his contempt of the Baldwin group – reported a conversation with Neville Chamberlain: 'His [Chamberlain's] whole view . . . was that we were bound to try out the League of Nations (in which he does not himself believe very much) for political reasons at home, and that there was no question of our going beyond the mildest of economic sanctions such as an embargo on the purchase of Italian goods or the sale of munitions to Italy.' A few days later, Chamberlain delivered a campaign speech on the subject of the 'solemn pledges' that the nation had made to the League, concluding that 'the choice before us is whether we shall make one last effort at Geneva for peace and security or whether by a cowardly surrender we shall break our promise and hold ourselves up to the shame of our children and their childrens' children'. Quoting those words, Amery commented: 'After the frank cynicism of his talk to me only a few days before I thought the unctuous rectitude of this effort a bit thick.' Privately pulled in one direction, publicly pushed in another, Conservative ministers pursued a 'double policy', according to Chamberlain's apologist, Keith Feiling, 'to intimidate the aggressor, but to attempt conciliation', a policy, in G M Young's phrase, 'of sanctions in principle, so to speak, and a simultaneous search for ground of accommodation'.

It is not altogether clear that, in the late autumn of 1935, Press and public were aware of the working of the 'double policy', this situation in which some members of the Cabinet were committed, for political reasons, to a programme for

[1] Young, *Baldwin*, p 216.

Italy and the League in which they did not very much believe. In the midst of the widespread enthusiasm for the Government's part in collective action – the League-imposed sanctions against Italy – one finds only an occasional sceptic word: the *Manchester Guardian*, for example, although in general certain the Government intended to support an economic boycott of the Italians, reported that 'hints of possible lines of compromise are floating about'; and the editors of *The Spectator* commented, the day after the Conservative electoral victory, that 'there is some excuse for the suspicion that we are concerned primarily to maintain normal relations with Italy, subject to the regrettable necessity of a little interference with her trade' – an acid remark that was immediately sweetened by the note that it was nevertheless 'not at present justified' to doubt the Baldwin group.[1] But if the outside world assumed the British Government united on the principle of League action, confusion prevailed within – confusion that was the product of the split in Conservative thinking, the contrary content of Conservative goals.

Chief witness on the difficulties inherent in the double policy is Anthony Eden, in whose *Memoirs* has appeared a most detailed account of the Conservative contribution to the Ethiopian muddle. Eden was Minister for League of Nation Affairs, and as a member of the Cabinet, almost co-equal with Foreign Secretary Sir Samuel Hoare; it was his job to represent Britain at Geneva, and to advise his government on its responsibilities in the League effort against aggression. Poor Eden: try though he did to fill out his public image as the British knight at the Geneva roundtable, he was steadily frustrated by unsympathetic associates. There were, he wrote, 'many counsels' opposing his plans of employing the League machinery against Italy: in Rome, British Ambassador Sir Eric Drum-

---

[1] *The Spectator*, 15th November 1935. Nor were proponents of the League alone in believing the Government loyal to Geneva. See especially *The Observer*, 9th, 23rd February 1936, for editor J L Garvin's résumé indictment of the governmental commitment to the League (that 'inadequate ark') and of governmental responsibility for the 'muddle, mischief, and danger' of imposing sanctions against M ssolini.

mond (later Lord Perth) 'was advocating some form of protectorate over Abyssinia, lest worse befall'; or, Foreign Office, Sir Robert Vansittart, obsessed with 'principal danger' which Nazi Germany presented to European security, persuasively argued that Britain should 'pay almost any price' to Mussolini to hold him in the defensive alliance of the Stresa Front.[1] But Eden's continuing problem was the vacillation of his Cabinet colleagues, who constituted the ministerial source from which his authority and orders came. His assignment had seemed plain enough to Eden in the beginning: as the Geneva representative of a great power he was to assume, with his French counterparts, the leadership of League measures – in the first instance, economic sanctions, which amounted to an international boycott of Italian exports and a denial of key products to Italy; this policy which Eden thought 'had been ours from the first' had the 'unequivocal' support of 'almost all Europe and the Dominions'. A corollary tack, the difficulties of which Eden did not underestimate, was to keep the French – particularly Prime Minister Pierre Laval – in close collaboration; despite French uneasiness about antagonising Mussolini, and thus losing his strength in the war of nerves with Germany, Laval would, Eden was sure, fulfil his obligations to the League if British pressure upon him were 'firm and persistent'. Yet as Eden worked with his policy assignment he found it slipping away from him. In London, he would be given 'comparatively firm language at a ministerial meeting with the Prime Minister', instructions that would later, in dispatches, be negated by 'limiting clauses'; he was 'too often given [his] head and then curbed', plagued by the Cabinet's 'indefinite attitude', dismayed by a leadership that was 'troubled and uncertain'. Perhaps, wrote Eden in a significant passage, the confusion in the Cabinet was the result of a kind of myopia, 'an insufficiently clear view of whose side we were on'.

Eden, *Facing the Dictators*, pp 271, 270. Eden does *not* say that the determination to hold the Stresa Front against Hitler was a primary concern of the Cabinet.

The issue between Eden and London was a fundamental difference of opinion about Britain's role in this international affair. The Cabinet had no enthusiasm for collective action, for a co-operative effort that might mean trouble in the Mediterranean and naval expenditure for the British economy. His superiors were convinced that Eden was far too dynamic at Geneva and were fearful that his drive for sanctions was incurring the risk of war with Mussolini; in spite of Eden's arguments – that a great power that did not lead would lose its greatness, that Mussolini was bluffing and would back down when he realised the resolution and unity of the League, that France would stand by Britain in the League, provided Laval and his Government were assured of British intransigence – the conviction and the fear remained. And so Eden was time and again pulled up short, informed of the 'great perturbation' in the Cabinet at his pace in Geneva, told that the Cabinet trusted he would 'not allow any haste on the Council [of the League] in regard to the discussion of sanctions', or ordered 'to go as slowly as possible and take the initiative as little as possible'. After frequent and extended communications with London on the subject of Laval – in which Eden had stressed his view that Laval would follow a strong lead – he received an 'extraordinary' directive suggesting that he align British policy with that of the French: 'I was now told that in no circumstances should we take any action on our own account; to that extent it would be more correct to say that we should be adjusting our position to that of France.' Eden's strong protest prevented further instructions to subordinate his actions to Laval, but he was never able to stiffen his colleagues to resolution. At a late stage in the League arrangements for sanctions he was informed from London 'that the Board of Trade and the Admiralty were very nervous of refusing to allow Italian shipping to use the ports of the members of the League. They thought this policy provocative and impossible to realise, except by force. Any such proposals should be referred to London. It also seemed that uneasiness was now felt about refusing supplies to Italy. The Government wanted to get assurances that all members of the League would stand together if one of them were attacked when applying sanctions. They also hoped that, as a starting-point, we could discuss any League proposals which might be available, rather than work on the basis of a British initiative.'

Eden's testimony – providing almost unique access to Cabinet proceedings in the Ethiopian crisis[1] – becomes a vantage point from which to observe the denouement of the British side of the story. 'Troubled and uncertain', or wrapped in a dilemma of their own making, the Conservatives had to find a way out – to avoid both a clash with Mussolini and placate the public opinion which demanded that the aggressor be stopped. Perhaps a remark of Neville Chamberlain's illuminates their thinking: the perfect solution, Chamberlain was reported as saying, was to 'act so that no charge could lie against the Government of deserting the League of Nations. France, however, would not apply sanctions, and this would be Great Britain's chance to refuse to act alone, and embark on a big naval reconstruction effort.'[2] The French, that is, were to be the key to the working of the dual policy, the French who, as Eden steadily insisted, required special British nursing to bring them to the break with Mussolini. Truly, Pierre Laval was a frustrating ally, twisting and searching in negotiation for ways to soften the action against Italy, even to settle the whole matter in the time-tested tradition of secret diplomacy. Yet Eden was sure that Laval would have responded to a strong British lead. While he certainly blamed the French in the ultimate disaster of League policy, Eden's explanation is that Laval, rather than destroying British will to act through the League, was used by those in Britain who had not wanted League action from the start: 'The effect of Laval's sophistry, as he may have intended, was to strengthen the hands of those

[1] The Press, apparently, avoided hints of dissension in the Cabinet—although *The Times* knew of it, enough to deny top-level trouble with Eden. *The Times*, 21st October 1935.
[2] Quoted in C F Adam, *Life of Lord Lloyd*, p 268.

in England who thought that we had been pressing too hard for sanctions.'

Thus, it would be all the fault of the French if the League were paralysed and Mussolini rewarded, rather than censured, for aggression. To be sure, if the League failed, the Conservatives had a second line of face-saving devices: the British public, with its deep aversion to war, was warned of the risks involved in thwarting Mussolini ('sanctions mean war!') and even told that the British navy was inferior to the Italian fleet.[1] But the French were the chief scapegoats, the French Government reluctant to lose Mussolini as a bulwark against Hitler; for public consumption, Conservatives could point to the record of the strong-minded British Government, instantly accepting its League obligations and fully ready to support the oil embargo, even if it brought war with Italy – with only the proviso that the other League members, and particularly the recalcitrant French, would display equal integrity and strength.[2] It was a fine story, designed to appeal to the current high enthusiasm for the League, to the popular faith that its members really intended that the League save the peace and the honour of Europe. It was a fine story – except that in its direct contradiction to the private thoughts of some British leaders, it was a dangerous story, one to be used only by the skilful and experienced political manipulator. And it was a disastrous story for Sir Samuel Hoare, Baldwin's new Foreign Minister and, as it turned out, sacrificial victim for the Conservative Cabinet.

Sir Samuel Hoare had become part of the Baldwin Cabinet in June of 1935; he had been a member of Parliament since

[1] Most insistent on these points were Lord Rothermere's *Daily Mail* and *The Observer*. See especially the interview of the *Daily Mail* correspondent with Mussolini, 26th August 1935; also, *The Observer*, 15th December 1935, 19th January, 9th February, 2nd April 1936, for J L Garvin's editorials. Anthony Eden scoffed at the excuses of those afraid to face the Italian Navy: 'We were powerful in those days,' he wrote, 'both in resources and influence. Though our military equipment was in poor shape, it was adequate for the immediate task.' Eden, *Facing the Dictators*, p 274.

[2] See *The Spectator*, 18th October, 29th November 1935, and *The Times*, 19th October 1935, for examples of Press acceptance of primary French responsibility for delaying tactics in Geneva.

1910 and had held a succession of ministerial posts since 1922. It was not, then, that he lacked experience, but rather the kind of native ease with which a Baldwin played at duplicity. And he had the difficult task of handling in public the dual policy of the Government, of dealing with the shady Laval, of explaining – as Anthony Eden's superior – British action to the representatives of the nations at Geneva. Hoare tried valiantly to follow both lines of government policy. On 11th September 1935 he delivered before the assembly of the League a speech that was a brilliantly encouraging expression of the public version of official policy.[1] As spokesman for His Majesty's Government he pledged, said Sir Samuel, 'unwavering fidelity to the League and all that it stands for', to the 'ideas enshrined in the Covenant', and to 'steady and collective resistance to all acts of unprovoked aggression'; these ideas, principles, 'precise and explicit obligations', Hoare said, had become part of the British national conscience, rules for conduct to which the British people and their government would hold with 'firm, enduring and universal persistence'.[2] It was a speech full of clichés, of sonorous phrases that would be remembered – to Hoare's misfortune, for in three months he was party to the deal that exposed both the hollowness of his words and the double mind of the Baldwin Government.

The Hoare-Laval Pact, the quiet arrangement made in Paris in December of 1935 between the two ministers, proposed, in brief, to end the international crisis over Italian aggression by ceding to Mussolini two-thirds of Ethiopian territory, much more land than the Fascist troops had conquered as yet; out of this division of their country the Ethiopians would be allowed to keep a narrow strip that stretched to the sea.[3]

---

[1] The speech was so strong an endorsement of League action that Eden was 'puzzled', particularly 'in the light of their [the Cabinet's] refusal to allow me to give warning to Laval earlier of our intention to fulfil the Covenant.' Eden, *Facing the Dictators*, p 293.

[2] The full text of Hoare's speech is in *The Times*, 12th September 1935. Hoare immediately became the hero of the pro-League journals: see *The Times*, 30th September 1935, and Sir Evelyn Wrench in *The Spectator*, 25th October 1935.

[3] See Salvemini, *World War II*, pp 385–394, for an excellent account of the pact.

This was, in truth, political realism: providing the Italians accepted this gift-solution, the issue would be neatly concluded; European war would be avoided and the whole embarrassing matter of obligations to the League simply ignored. Laval's signature on this hardheaded pact meant that the French could return to their primary preoccupation with the menace of Germany on the Rhine, secure in the knowledge that the Italian neighbour to the south would be grateful for services rendered. For his part, Hoare played at Paris a caricature role of the slow-witted English diplomat outmatched by the wily Latin. Hoare agreed with Laval on this day as he had agreed before to the practical ideas of a realistic fellow, to ideas that truly expressed the general sense of his own government; he did not focus, apparently, on the fact that this was different from other private consultations with the French Foreign Office, that Laval had proposed a final solution to the Ethiopian crisis, a 'compromise' that would present to Mussolini most of what he was fighting for.[1] The next day, when the details of the agreement were published in the French Press, Hoare was exposed in this astonishing piece of stupidity.

The publication of the Hoare-Laval Pact brought, in Britain, a public explosion, a storm of shocked, shamed, angry protest that was virtually nationwide; even the solidly Conservative *Times* condemned the immorality of betrayal of the League and of awarding Mussolini the bulk of Ethiopia, leaving to its people only a 'corridor for canals',[2] In its first reaction to the pact, the Cabinet approved its terms (this 'commonsense arrangement . . . the best day's work any Foreign Secretary had done for years . . .'),[3] but the courage of the Baldwin

---

[1] Hoare, *Nine Troubled Years*, pp 184–188, gives a short (still embarrassed) review of the incident. Much more satisfactory is Eden, *Facing the Dictators*, pp 335–348.

[2] *The Times*, 16th December 1935. For a further Press sampling see *The Spectator*, 13th December 1935, for the editorial shock at this 'disastrous betrayal of League principles'; or *Manchester Guardian Weekly*, 13th December 1935, and the editorial query, 'Who will now trust the British Government in this affair?' See, too, *ibid*, 'Comment and Criticism': the great mistake, said the writer, was to entrust the work of the League to ministers of England and France, for 'once away from Geneva those Governments find it easier to remember past imperialist bargains'.

[3] Amery, *Political Life*, III, p 183.

clique evaporated before the national outrage. T
Minister, 'feeble, toneless and unhappy', it was
the Government was discredited, that defeat w
defeat in the House first, and then, after dissoluti
the country'. Conservative ministers were, suddenly, terribly
sorry – sorry that the nation was in an uproar, that there was
revolt in the Party, that the government was tottering,
and that to save the political situation it would be necessary
to cashier the unfortunate Hoare; they were sorry, that is,
not that the thing had been done, but that it had been done
so clumsily and had been found out, leaked to the Press.

Note the responses of individuals within this government
under attack. Stanley Baldwin – wearing 'the air of a man
crushed by some appalling disaster' – fell back on the well-
practised tricks of his political trade. He tried to pretend at
first that a grave national emergency prevented his discussion
of the pact: 'My lips are not yet unsealed,' he told the House
of Commons, 'were these troubles over I would make a case. . . .'
When that failed to quiet the clamour of criticism, Baldwin
decided to be 'perfectly frank' with the Commons, to confess
his error and bad judgment:

> Never throughout the week had I or any one of my colleagues
> any idea in our own minds that we were not being true to every
> pledge that we had given in the Election. . . . I was not expecting
> that deeper feeling which was manifested . . . in many parts of
> the country. . . . The moment I am confronted with that, I
> know that something has happened that has appealed to the
> deepest feelings of our countrymen.

He had not understood these deep feelings of faith in the
League, said Baldwin (although he had recently had insight
enough to make political capital out of them), but now that he
did understand, the Hoare-Laval proposals were 'absolutely and
completely dead', and there would be no attempt to revive them.[1]

[1] It was not Baldwin's most effective performance. Press observers felt that he
had 'disappointed woefully', that in the end he was still 'bereft of any rational
defence of his conduct'. See *Manchester Guardian Weekly*, 27th December 1935.

Spectacular as was his public humiliation, Baldwin's confession revealed nothing but the desperation of the pinned politician; the private postmortem thoughts of some of his colleagues cast the greater light on the Conservative view of the affair. A week after the exposure of the pact Neville Chamberlain commented in a letter to a friend:

> When Sam left for Paris on Saturday the 7th, we had no idea that he would be invited to consider detailed peace proposals. I believed, and so far as I know, my colleagues believed also, that he was going to stop off at Paris for a few hours on his way to Switzerland, to get the discussions with the French into such a condition that we could say to the League, 'don't prejudice the chances of a favourable issue by thrusting in a particularly provocative extra sanction at this moment'. Instead of that, a set of proposals was agreed to.

This is, one would say, a revealing statement: according to Chamberlain, Hoare was instructed to find, with Pierre Laval, a way for their governments to persuade the League to table the oil embargo – the 'particularly provocative extra sanction' – against the Italian Fascists; Sir Samuel had done precisely this, although his execution of the order was somewhat crude. On the very day, incidentally, that Hoare concluded the pact with Laval, Chamberlain had been nervously considering Mussolini's bombastic threats that the addition of oil to the sanctions imposed by the League would bring European war. He jotted in his diary this bit of pure Chamberlainese: 'The object of sanctions being to stop the war, it would obviously be absurd to proceed with them if thereby one was to prejudice an opportunity of ending the war.' But to continue with Chamberlain's *ex post facto* letter: with the League dying or already dead, with the aggressor richly rewarded for his slight pains, Chamberlain was concerned with just one thing. 'Nothing', he wrote, 'could be worse than our position. Our whole prestige in foreign affairs at home and abroad has tumbled to pieces like a house of cards. If we had to fight the election over again, we should probably be beaten.'

Or, there was the contribution of Lord Halifax – at this moment Lord Privy Seal – who wrote to Chamberlain that 'the whole affair was a thoroughly bad business', the 'initial mistake' of which was Hoare's, in publishing the communiqué from Paris [the proposals were given by Laval to the French Press]; but 'I am still puzzled', Halifax wrote, 'by the condemnation meted out to proposals that were not, as you said all along, so frightfully different from those put forward by the [League] Committee of five. But the latter were of respectable parentage; and the Paris ones were too much like the off-the-stage arrangements of 19th century diplomacy.' Halifax's sincere bewilderment is the striking thing; uncomprehending, he wondered, distantly, about the moral and emotional issues that had stirred his countrymen. If such Conservatives, isolated in their tightly-closed world, were baffled by popular execration of the Pact, they might have listened to the explanations of the opposition. In House debate Clement Attlee – now leader of a Labour Party working to line all its members behind the League and collective punishment of the Italian aggressor – went to the heart of this 'extremely ugly' episode. 'If you turn and run from the aggressor,' said Attlee, 'you kill the League, and you do worse than that, or as bad as that: you kill all faith in the word of honour of this country.'

But the Baldwin Government hung on, relieved when the tension subsided and the nation sank back into a kind of stunned apathy. The men of the Conservative clique had achieved a part of their goals; there was no general European war, and although they had irritated Mussolini – tragically, as they saw it[1] – the Duce was still able to mop up in Ethiopia unhindered by censure or force from the European complex of nations. A semblance of sanctions – a mockery of sanctions – remained into the summer of 1936, the mummified memory of one-time resolution. Fittingly, Neville Chamberlain signalled their end, observing that the continuation of the form of

[1] Amery, *Political Life*, III, pp 184–185, for the old Tory contempt for a government that allowed the Italian ally to be alienated.

sanctions was the 'very midsummer of madness'. 'Is it not apparent,' Chamberlain asked, 'that the policy of sanctions involves, I do not say war, but a risk of war? . . . is it not also apparent from what has happened that, in the presence of such a risk, nations cannot be relied upon to proceed to the last extremity unless their vital interests are threatened?'[1] (No matter that in the House of Commons spokesmen like Lloyd George blistered a government that had admitted that 'Britain was beaten, Britain and her Empire beaten, and that we must abandon an enterprise we had taken in hand', a government that had never 'meant business over sanctions'.) The Government, indeed, had never meant business in this field trial for the principles of collective action, and the result – intended or not – was the death of the league.[2] From this point no one would worry much about the proceedings at Geneva, the 'arid pedantry', the empty romanticisms, the absurd notions that the actions of great powers should be subject to the review of a host of weak and insignificant nations. From this point it would be easier to do nothing about European crises provoked by the dictators.

---

[1] Feiling, *Neville Chamberlain*, p 296. *The Observer*, 14th June 1936, felt that Chamberlain had at last spoken 'like his father's son'.

[2] As editor J L Garvin announced with enormous satisfaction week after week. See *The Observer*, 23rd February, 26th April, 21st June 1936.

6

On to
the Rhineland

ONE WEEK AFTER his reference to sanctions against Italy as
the 'mid-summer of madness', Chamberlain recorded in his
diary his reasons for making the speech: 'I did it deliberately',
he wrote, 'because I felt that the Party and the country needed
a lead, and an indication that the Government was not wavering and drifting without a policy.' The policy in mind was
appeasement of the dictators, and Chamberlain, self-styled
strong man of the Cabinet and heir-apparent to Baldwin's chair,
was indicating his intention of guiding the fading Prime
Minister along its lines. Other people wanted to guide Baldwin
too: the new Foreign Secretary Anthony Eden for one, whose
appointment as Hoare's successor was judiciously based on his
unsullied reputation as a champion of the League.[1] The Old
Guard in the Cabinet, though, carefully circumscribed Eden:
Chamberlain had not even consulted him about the speech
against sanctions because the Foreign Secretary 'would have
been bound to beg me not to say what I proposed'. If the
Government was 'wavering and drifting' without a policy, it
was not Eden who was moving up to steady its course,[2] nor
the Germanophobe Sir Robert Vansittart, nor the tough
Tories with Churchill; the influential people, one feels, were
Chamberlain in the Cabinet, Baldwin's 'choice friends' like
Montagu Norman, Governor of the Bank of England, and
Geoffrey Dawson, editor of *The Times*, or the Prime Minister's
unofficial companion, the knowledgeable Thomas Jones.

To be sure, in 1936 an explicit British policy in regard to

---

[1] However, see Salvemini, *World War II*, p 361, for the author's view of Eden's
acquiescence in the death of the League and his continued co-operation with the
Cabinet Old Guard.
[2] Eden's repeated failure to counterbalance Baldwin's apathy and/or reserve in
foreign policy matters is clear in *Facing the Dictators*, pp 421, 432, 460–461.

the Fascist troublemakers on the Continent did not exist; a
government headed by Stanley Baldwin was not likely to be
stirred to such a clarification. But it is reasonable to suggest
that from certain Conservative circles a definable policy goal
was emerging, a feeling, perhaps among some a conviction,
that rather than court future Ethiopian fiascoes the British
Government should settle for an official line of appeasement of
the demands of the dictators. The point is illustrated by
Anthony Eden in his evaluation of the lessons of Ethiopia. As
Foreign Secretary, Eden became well aware that the failure
of collective action against aggression – essentially, as Eden
saw it, a failure of the French – had made a deep impression
in British officialdom: 'the effect of Laval's conduct of policy
over Abyssinia', wrote Eden, 'had been to weaken those who
wished to found British policy on an Anglo-French alliance and
to swell the number who were isolationist or considered that
we must come to terms with Hitler, even though the price
were high.'

On 7th March 1936, as the issue of Italian aggression dragged
miserably to no end, Hitler's troops occupied the Rhineland,
demilitarised by international treaty – by both Versailles and
Locarno – since 1919. Defiantly, the German Fuehrer asserted
his independence of prior European agreements and the right
to use German territory as Germans chose[1]; the occupation
was especially justified, Hitler claimed, because the Franco-
Soviet Pact, finally ratified in the French Chamber in February
1936, had been devised as an offensive weapon, deliberately
constructed to encircle and contain Nazi Germany.[2] Panicked
by this swift transformation of the West European *status quo*,
the French turned for stiffening and support to their British
allies, to a British Government bound by the Locarno Treaty
to maintain a demilitarised Rhineland. What was the result?
In answer first to the French, then to meetings of the Locarno
powers and the League Council, the British Government

[1] See the leader in *The Times*, 9th March 1936.
[2] For the testimony of the French officials, see *Les Événements Survenus en France*,
1933–45, III, 215–217.

flatly refused to engage in either military or economic sanctions against Germany. In a diary entry of 12th March, Neville Chamberlain noted a discussion with French Foreign Minister Etienne Flandin, in which he, Chamberlain, had stated that British public opinion 'would not support us in sanctions of any kind'.[1] Flandin's initial view was that if France and Britain held firm Germany would yield in the Rhineland without war but, Chamberlain added, the British Cabinet could not 'accept this as a reliable estimate of a mad dictator's reactions'. Instead, the British made their own estimate and decided it would be wiser to negotiate with the 'mad' dictator. That is, the Conservatives decided to accept Hitler's offer to talk – what amounted to a bribe for his *fait accompli* in the Rhineland – to discuss the possibility of a new demilitarised zone,[2] of an agreement on limitation of air rearmament, even of the return of Germany to the League of Nations. In the House of Commons, Anthony Eden explained the Government decision as part of its general aim of 'the appeasement of Europe', an objective that would, in the end, 'strengthen collective security, further Germany's return to the League, and, in a happier atmosphere, allow those larger negotiations on economic matters and on matter of armaments'. And thus Hitler was permitted the once-forbidden fruit, the fortification of Germany's borders on the Western Front.

The permissiveness with which the British accepted German violation of the Locarno prohibitions seems a crucial marker on the road to appeasement. What had Hitler done in occupying the Rhineland? He had shattered a treaty restriction that he had long and violently denounced as a humiliation upon German nationhood; but more, he had undermined the French security system, erected with his Western wall – the building of which proceeded rapidly, as the British Government knew, from March of 1936 – both a threat to France and a solid seal against interference in what he considered his private area

---

[1] Eden too was sure of this: see *Facing the Dictators*, p 389.
[2] It was known, however, that such a new zone was 'impracticable', and the offer made 'purely for propaganda purposes'. Eden, *Facing the Dictators*, p 387.

in Central and Eastern Europe. Faced with this achievement, the British asked only for a fresh guarantee of Western security, an assurance that British interests – as well as those of France and the Low countries – be undisturbed. But was this an unusual position for a British government to take? Certainly, the Conservatives were justified in assuming the mass of British people saw nothing amiss in 'Jerry going into his own back-garden'.[1] As for the governmental concern for the safety of Western Europe and the apparent disregard of the other side of the Continent, the British had no unilateral obligations in Central and Eastern Europe – except, and it was a large exception, under the anti-aggression clauses of the League of Nations – nor would a British government of any complexion have assumed such obligations. Still, it seems a perfectly proper thing to explore the matter further. Were the Conservatives here sidling toward the policy they would later make real at Munich – hopefully assuring Western security by abandoning Central and Eastern Europe to Hitler's ambitions, acquiescing to Germany's *Drang nach Osten?* Was it a vague idea of this kind that unnamed officials held, those who – so Anthony Eden claimed – hoped to 'come to terms' with Hitler? Even more intriguing, was it this sort of thinking that prompted Sir Robert Vansittart's scathing remark (made in 1935!) of the immorality of 'giving Germany a free hand to annex other people's property in Central or Eastern Europe'?[2]

[1] The first reactions in the Press were almost unanimous on doing nothing about the remilitarisation of the Rhineland. To *The Spectator*, the German *coup* was a 'small thing in itself', and the *Manchester Guardian* advised Britons to show that they had 'no longer the desire to limit or postpone Germany's legal equality'. (13th March 1936). *The Times* (9th March 1936) declared that this elimination of a Versailles injustice offered a chance to 'rebuild' an equitable European order. J L Garvin, in *The Observer*, explained that the occupation of the Rhineland might have been expected, not only because Germans had a perfect right to 'equity within their own land', but because of the Franco-Soviet Pact; Hitler was bound to strike out at the 'encirclement' of Germany by France and that 'colossal' power, the USSR (15th March 1936). For the Left, the *New Statesman and Nation* (14th March 1936) spoke soberly of the 'complacent' British acceptance of a move that could only have been designed to secure Germany on her Western frontiers – and thus free her for Eastern adventures.

[2] The free hand to Germany, Vansittart continued, was 'both absolutely immoral and completely contrary to all the principles of the League which form the backbone of the policy of this country. Any British government that attempted

By the witness of various commentators in 1936, kindred ideas of coming to terms with Hitler were being considered in circles of the political upper-world of London. In his *Memoirs*, Eden related the problems he had encountered in pursuing, after the *coup* of the Rhineland occupation, his insurance policy of formal discussions between the French and British military staffs: 'Before the debate on the ratification [of reaffirmation of assistance to France], I had a few words with the Prime Minister in his room in the House of Commons. Though he did his best to conceal it from me, I could see that he was anxious. He admitted that Kingsley Wood [Minister of Health] had been to see him to tell him, in characteristic phrase, that the Staff talks were unpopular on the Conservative back benches. "The boys won't have it" was his verdict.'[1] Apparently, it was not only backbench Tories who chafed at an anti-German policy in tandem with the French; when Eden drafted a questionnaire to submit to Hitler, an attempt to ascertain his future intentions in foreign relations,[2] unnamed 'members of the Government', Eden's colleagues, withheld approval of the draft until its 'provocative' sections had been cut or modified. Or Claud Cockburn, editing *The Week*, and operating on the tips circulating in the rumour mill of Whitehall and Westminster, repeated stories he had heard of thinking in the Cabinet, of hopes among the Old Guard around Baldwin that the 'German menace' would become preoccupied in an 'eastward drive'; in the month after the Rhineland march, Cockburn printed a story of a split in the Cabinet between an Eden-led group and the Old Guard, the latter countering Eden's French ties with a demand for an Anglo-German

to do a deal would almost certainly be brought down in ignominy – and deservedly. . . . Any suggestion that a British government, contemplates leaving, let alone inviting, Germany to satisfy her land-hunger at Russia's expense, would quite infallibly split this country from top to bottom.' Quoted in Nicolson, *King George the Fifth*, p 529.

[1] Eden, *Facing the Dictators*, p 407. Eden did not 'believe this judgment to be well-founded', although a message relayed through the Prime Minister would seem to be of the highest reliability. *Ibid*.

[2] The Foreign Secretary had had reports from Berlin, from the British Ambassador and his military attaché, that German officials considered it a 'matter of course' that Germany would expand eastward. *Ibid*, pp 414–415.

V

alliance.[1] And so respectable a source as Arnold Toynbee, evaluating the events of 1936 in *Survey of International Affairs*, discussed the importance of the German occupation of the Rhineland – the division of Europe into Eastern and Western halves, the closing off of the Eastern from (mostly French) meddling: after the march into the Rhineland, Toynbee wrote, 'a conclusion of a Western Pact, leaving Hitler tacitly free to do as he liked in the East commended itself in those British circles in which Anglo-German rapprochement was regarded as highly desirable (either from fear of Germany's growing strength or from dislike of Russia or from other motives)'.

Again – none of these was openly declared British policy.[2] If anything, people in those 'British circles' desiring rapprochement with Germany felt themselves out-weighed and out-manoeuvred by pro-French officials of the Foreign Office, by Eden and Vansittart, with their plans for closer cooperation with the French.[3] Yet it seems certain that a growing number of important persons was ready to argue for a new direction in foreign policy, for a British course that would 'get alongside of Germany'. Joachim Ribbentrop, working busily as Hitler's propaganda agent in London, reported home during the Rhineland crisis that 'in these critical hours Germany . . . discovered many a good friend in England'; Ribbentrop particularly relished a meeting with 'all our available friends', held at the Carlton Hotel, a meeting which was 'like a dovecote', a pro-German occasion attended by 'prominent leaders in politics and business', people who 'powerfully influenced public

---

[1] *The Week*, 1st April 1936. According to Cockburn, there was little difference in the ultimate strategy of the Cabinet groups; the Eden group thought only that Western unity would convince the Nazi expansionists that their moves lay necessarily in the East.

[2] They were not declared, according to Arnold Toynbee, because the Government considered it best to cloud its policy, to leave its European counterparts in doubt about British intentions. Thus Eden – or Baldwin or Chamberlain – would protest that the British Government had no idea of ignoring the fate of Central and Eastern Europe. *Ibid*, pp 280–281.

[3] See, for example, Jones, *Diary*, pp 183–184, for the opinion of one of Jones' correspondents that 'Flandin has triumphed all along the line in London' – that is, that the French Government had succeeded in persuading the British to join in its anti-German policies.

opinion'.[1] Ribbentrop did not identify his new friends, but he would perhaps have counted as an accomplishment of his campaign the journalistic efforts, in the summer of 1936, of Geoffrey Dawson. And no one would underestimate the opinion-moulding power of the editorial page of the great *Times* of London, or of such Dawson pieces as a July editorial which discussed the necessity of an understanding with Germany, argued weightily against British participation in an anti-German military alliance, and wound up with heavy criticism of the idea of British support for the French in any of their Eastern European undertakings.[2]

There is a singular source for the mobilisation of pro-German sentiment in 1936, one piece of evidence that stands, almost unique, as a kind of handbook for appeasement. Prime Minister Baldwin's friend Thomas Jones – Baldwin's companion, confidant, and unofficial adviser – kept a diary[3] which (published along with bits and pieces of Jones' correspondences) affords a considerable insight into the thinking of Jones and the circle of very important people with whom he was in contact. Jones possessed proper qualifications as a chronicler of the political upperworld: from 1916 he had been a civil servant, Deputy Secretary to the Cabinet, and thus in close working relations – and in the case of Baldwin, in close personal relations – with a succession of prime ministers and cabinet officials; in 1930 he retired to become, at Stanley Baldwin's suggestion, Secretary of the Pilgrim Trust, an endowed benevolent foundation. The

---

[1] *The Ribbentrop Memoirs*, introduction by Alan Bullock, p 56.

[2] *The Times*, 6th July 1936. Garvin's *Observer* made this even plainer. Much earlier, Garvin had angrily rejected French and British military cooperation: 'We must not be dragged into war at the whistle of Bolshevism or at the beck of the Little Entente.' *The Observer*, 15th, 22nd March 1936.

[3] The publication of Jones' *Diary* was a revelation to A L Rowse, who knew him slightly in the 1930s: 'And here is the place', Rowse wrote, 'to consider the case of Tom Jones – TJ as we all called him. . . . A former secretary to both Lloyd George and Baldwin, he wrote their speeches and remained on intimate terms with Baldwin. . . . He was a great busybody and contacts-man. . . . If I had known the dirty work he was doing for Ribbentrop I should have been less affable to TJ on his visits to All Souls. But he had the Celt's intuitive discretion, and never opened up on the subject of appeasement to me; he was the only one of them who didn't come into the open. I knew he was on that side, but I never knew to what a degree he lent himself to Ribbentrop's purposes until his *Diary with Letters* came out.' Rowse, *All Souls*, p 35.

exercise of these various responsibilities made him, Jones related with obvious pleasure, a 'person of some casual interest to London political hostesses', welcome in the homes and clubs of people of position, distinction, or nobility. He became, over the years, a man-in-the-know, the associate of ministers of the Crown and the companion of the social élite – the valued friend of Stanley Baldwin, as of Lord and Lady Astor. The latter names are deliberately selected: in the peak years of his influence with the great, Jones' social path zig-zagged between the residences of the Prime Minister – the weekend retreat at Chequers or Number 10 Downing Street – and the Astor homes, especially the Astor country estate of Cliveden in Berkshire. At Cliveden the talk, led by the hostess, who was MP for Plymouth, was always of politics, domestic and foreign; on a typical visit, Jones could review the current news with a select group of guests, people like Lord Lothian, Geoffrey Dawson of *The Times* or J L Garvin of *The Observer*, Lord Halifax or Arnold Toynbee, William Bullitt, then American Ambassador to the Soviet Union – or much-courted German visitors, like the charming Ribbentrop and his subordinates. Their discussion, a good sampling actually of the opinions of decision-making and high-level persons, Jones would carry back to the Prime Minister, to be used as ammunition in what became—the *Diary* reveals – a steady campaign to influence Baldwin's ideas on foreign policy.

Two things are interesting to note in Jones' records for 1936: first, the story they have to tell of the development of pro-Germanism in the circles in which Jones moved; and second, the impressions one gets there of Jones' relations with Stanley Baldwin, specifically of Jones' attempts to give shape to the formless attitudes of the Prime Minister on foreign affairs.

Jones' efforts toward appeasement of Germany began, in relatively low key, sometime in late February 1936. On 21st February, he noted that he had breakfasted with Baldwin to help the Prime Minister with the preparation of a scheduled speech. After gloomy discussion – he had found Baldwin, Jones wrote, 'rather sorry for himself' – of the eclipse of the prestige of the Government in the aftermath of the Ethiopian muddle, the conversation turned to the chief problem in Central Europe. In Jones' words:

> Defence . . . and our relations with Germany are the subjects which fill the PM's mind today. I keep on and on preaching against the policy of ostracising Germany, however incalculable Hitler and his crew may be, and the duty of resisting Vansittart's pro-French bias. It need not be 'either' or 'or' in an absolute sense if we are skilful. We have abundant evidence of the desire of all sorts of Germans to be on friendly terms with us . . . men and women in Germany who have not forgotten the War and its horrors, and who are in no hurry to precipitate another.

At this meeting – held before the Rhineland occupation – one would judge that Jones took a moderately pro-German tack, or a line that was mostly pro-peace; the strongest impression one gets from his words, beyond a mild surprise at the peremptory manner with which he advised the Prime Minister, is the sense of his latent distrust of the French, and his feeling that pro-French officials like Vansittart dominated the course of British actions.

The tone of Jones' reports was only a little less moderate on the decisive day of 7th March, the day of the Nazi invasion of the Rhineland. When the news of the occupation was broadcast he was weekending, as usual, with a glittering group, the party including Lord and Lady Astor, Lord Lothian, chairman of *The Economist* Sir Walter Layton, the historian Arnold Toynbee, the American financier Norman Davis, and Sir Thomas Inskip, new Minister for the Co-ordination of Defence (a most important Cabinet post). As Jones related it, the group resolved itself into a 'Shadow Cabinet' to deliberate the wireless report of the German move; in dead-serious political parlour game, the guests drew up a list of recommendations which Jones – and this, apparently, was the point of it all –

telephoned next morning to Baldwin, for the Prime Minister's 'enlightenment'. In brief, Baldwin was told to condemn German entry into the Rhineland, but as 'the last and least of the series of breaches' of the Versailles Treaty and 'not to to be taken tragically in view of the peace proposals which accompany it'; the German seizure of the forbidden zone should be treated 'as assertion, demonstration, of recovered status of equality and not as an act of aggression' – although, the recommendations stated, should there be an act of German aggression Britain would 'stand by France'.[1] Most of all, and here the group's advice was direct and pointed, the British Government should examine Hitler's peace programme, which struck 'a new "European" note', and as such should be welcomed 'wholeheartedly' and put to the test of negotiation. These proposals were no idle exercise, but rather intended as heavy pressure on Baldwin's official action: 'What I am trying to secure,' Jones concluded, 'is that SB should have his mind made up on the big major issue of accepting Hitler at his face value and trying him out fairly now that the last trace of humiliation has been removed. One wants SB's mind firmly made up *before* he enters the Cabinet where he will encounter all sorts of contradictory advice.'

This weekend policy guide was a sign of things to come, although still very different in tone from similar projects to follow. It was the product of people of tentative pro-Germanism, pursuing a rational hope of finding bases of understanding with the difficult quantity of Nazi Germany. But in the weeks after the Rhineland occupation something happened to intensify the favour for Germany and to transform an unimpassioned design to prod the indecisive Baldwin into a driving campaign to ensure the appeasement of Germany. A part of that 'something' was cryptically stated by Jones on 4th April:

These last weeks have been anxious ones for the Government. I saw SB for a half hour yesterday just before he started for

[1] Jones, *Diary*, p 180.

Chequers. He was tired but not rattled. Said he thought by
June we should be in calm weather again. . . . He thought Eden
was doing well and that is the general opinion. . . . The country
is pro-English, rather fed up with France than actively pro-
German, but more pro-German than the Cabinet[1]. . . . Part of
the opposition to France is influenced by the fear of our being
drawn in on the side of Russia. I found Ribbentrop just as
much obsessed with the fear of Bolshevism as Hitler is in his
public speeches. R[ibbentrop] is for peace and quoted his
previous attempts with [former French Foreign Minister]
Barthou and Simon's failure to respond. R urged that he was
now offering us another chance, 'perhaps the last'.[2]

And what was this message about? It might better be para-
phrased. As Jones and his friends assessed the situation after
7th March, France was teetering on a decision for war, insanely
creating the possibility that the British and French might
plunge into the self-destruction of conflict with Germany; thus,
in Jones' circles, the resentment against France rose sharply.
Further, with the Rhineland crisis the significance of the
French mutual security pact with the Soviet Union had fully
penetrated the mind of the London upper world of politics –
with, that is, a certain amount of assistance from the propagandists from Germany. There was nothing sudden about the
Franco-Soviet Pact; it had been hanging fire since it was first
negotiated in 1934 by Louis Barthou – before his work was
ended by an assassin – as the essential part of a French circle
of security against Germany. But its import became most
terribly clear in Britain in April and May of 1936 when it was
feared that the French might try to chase the Germans from
the Rhineland; should the British join their French ally in
upholding the dicta of Versailles and Locarno against Germany
they might, too, be joining with the ally of France, the Soviet
Union. An alternative to this inconceivable alignment, then,

[1] It is unclear from the text whether Jones is still quoting Baldwin at this point,
or adding his own observations. The reference to the Cabinet illustrates the feeling
– perhaps of both men – that the Eden group was dominant in national councils.
Eden, as we have seen, was not so certain of his strength.
[2] Jones, *Diary*, p 185.

was dangled by the German persuaders: in the atmosphere of a Cliveden, Ribbentrop assiduously spread his master's line – of the piling successes of the conspiracy of world Communism, to which the French, with their Soviet Pact and with their new Popular Front Government and its Socialist premier,[1] were heavily contributing; come with us, the Germans invited their new British friends, and you will have peace, as well as the protection of our unremitting anti-Communist crusade. This was 'perhaps the last' chance-offer that Ribbentrop used as bait in his conversations with Thomas Jones and his set at such places as Cliveden.

Jones' subsequent entries demonstrate his progress on these points. On 15th April, he recorded this item:

> Last Wednesday (8th) I had lunch alone at the Carlton with von Ribbentrop and went over the usual topics between us and Germany. He talks English very well and I'm sure does not want war in the West. He talks of Hitler as a being of quite superior attainments and fundamentally an artist, widely read, passionately devoted to music and pictures. They share the dread of Russia. Communism is the enemy which Germany cannot resist alone and successfully without the help of Great Britain. France is succumbing to the bribery of Moscow; so is Spain. The Paris Press and the French Deputies, a hundred of them, are in the pay of the Bolsheviks, so he assured me. Why were we so blind to all this?

At this date Jones reserved a sceptic corner of his mind as he listened to German scare stories, as he repeated casually, for the benefit of a correspondent,[2] Ribbentrop's tales of the victories of the Left in France and Bolshevism in Spain. We find him telling one friend – Dr Abraham Flexner, Director of the Institute for Advanced Study – of Ribbentrop's argument

[1] Leon Blum became Premier of the French Left-Centre Coalition Government in May 1936. See Feiling, *Neville Chamberlain*, pp 281, 284, for a sample of immediate Conservative hostility toward M Blum. On the other hand, Antony Eden spoke of his own pleasure at working with Blum, of a relationship 'which grew increasingly confident'. Eden, *Facing the Dictators*, p 418.

[2] Lady Grigg, wife of Sir James Grigg, Finance Member of the Government of India, 1934–39, a regular correspondent of Jones.

for an Anglo-German alliance to 'save civilisation' from Communist domination, and adding that he, Jones, had 'hinted' to the German in reply that 'some remedies might be worse than the disease!'[1] But this was in April; in the following weeks, Jones' further experiences wiped away his residue of sense. He entered this diary note on 25th May:

> Dined at the Astors. Bullitt, the USA Ambassador at Moscow, there, and made our flesh creep with his Bolshevik stories. . . . He corroborated all von Ribbentrop has told me of the amazing efficiency and widespread penetration of the Communist propaganda, and described the training through which the Spanish contingent had been put before they were sent back to Spain, loaded with money, to stir up strife. This was the real danger to the world, not the military preparations of Russia. Says Moscow foretells a Communist government in Spain in three months. The Japs were very clumsy colonisers and had made so many mistakes in Mongolia that Bolshevik influence had greatly increased there.

The next day, 26th May, Jones was wide open for more corroboration:

> Lunch with the Astors. Bullitt there and Geoffrey Dawson. Bullitt talked on the relations of France, Russia and Germany. Germany will do nothing menacing for twelve months – not before the fortifications on the West are well advanced. Is Russia safe from German aggression? France is the friend of Russia and Germany is the enemy of Russia. German fortification of the Rhineland is a threat to Russia which France has chosen to regard as a threat to herself. Blum depends on Russia and Delbos was Moscow's choice for Foreign Minister. No leader of the French Right in sight. Russia has issued orders to the French communists to go slow for two years. There is no honest journalist or unsubsidised paper in France. Germany cannot

[1] Jones, *Diary*, p 188. Of Jones' frequent correspondents, Flexner was the one consistently clear-sighted analyst of the nature of Nazi Germany, the one friend who had no patience with Jones' enthusiasm for the New Germany. It is worth noting that Jones moderated his views in writing to Flexner, after he felt the edge of Flexner's contempt for those who 'spoiled' Hitler. See *ibid*, pp 281–283, 311–314, 354.

now go through the Baltic countries, nor through Poland, nor through Czechoslovakia. The French can be relied on to cherish and nourish the military conversations with England. What should be unthinkable, on the British side, is a virtual alliance with France now that France has a virtual alliance with Russia, with Czechoslovakia and with other nations, so that automatically the area of engagements grows wider and wider.

By May 1936, then, Tom Jones had made these ideas his own – and had become, in the process, an easy mark for Ribbentrop's designs. It was Jones who was invited to visit Ribbentrop at his home outside Berlin, the object being a 'private and unofficial visit' to discuss leisurely the pressing matters of Anglo-German relations. (Jones protested, he wrote – surely disingenuously – that he 'was a person of no importance and entirely without official standing'. True, he added, 'I enjoyed the friendship of the Prime Minister and saw him occasionally', which meant that Ribbentrop 'must take the risk of my repeating anything he told me to the Prime Minister should any opportunity occur'!) Jones did indeed journey to Berlin, where he saw not only Ribbentrop but the Fuehrer himself; on his return, the message that he rushed to give Baldwin was that Herr Hitler very much desired to meet him, the Prime Minister, and to achieve at the highest level an understanding between Germany and Britain.

Parenthetically, Baldwin's laconic reaction to Jones' proposal was marvellously typical of the man. The Prime Minister was interested, certainly, and intrigued with the tale of Jones' trip – 'Go on,' he said at one point, 'this is like an Oppenheimer story' – and he invited Jones to Chequers to 'talk all this out'. But at Chequers Baldwin spent the greater part of the first evening in rambling talk of domestic political affairs, all the while playing, as Jones reported with understandable frustration, a game of patience. And when Jones finally related the exciting core of his message from Hitler, Baldwin was playing another game – of evading the issue: could the projected meeting between the two leaders be arranged even though SB 'did not fly and did not like the sea'? Or 'could the meeting wait until August when SB could go by car to some mountain rendezvous?' Jones ended the account on a note of some discouragement: 'Then some more Malvern water, and to bed.'

But, undaunted, Jones' crusade for understanding with Germany rolled on. Still at Chequers (23rd May), Jones wrote to his American friend, Dr Abraham Flexner, a summary of the foreign situation that revealed clearly his contacts with the German persuaders:

> The behaviour of the French over Abyssinia has thrown a lot of public opinion over toward Germany and there are signs of a more vigorous attempt to come to some sort of alliance with Germany which would not alienate France. The picture is complicated by the Franco-Russian agreement which is popular with the Left here and in France. We have to choose between Russia and Germany and choose soon, for if we do not do so, Germany and Italy will converge as, apart from Austria, they have no fundamental divergencies. *Hitler feels quite unequal to standing up alone to Russia and is disturbed by the way in which Russia and Czechoslovakia are concerting an air policy.* He is therefore asking for an *alliance with us to form a bulwark against the spread of Communism. Our PM is not indisposed to attempt this* as a final effort before he resigns after the Coronation next year, to make way for Neville Chamberlain.[1]

And, as he ended his visit at Chequers, Jones left Baldwin a set of directives – an amazing document – designed to smooth the course for the new understanding with Germany. In it, Baldwin was ordered (there is no other word) to consider a number of things. He was told to find a new ambassador to Germany, someone 'unhampered by professional diplomatic tradition, able of course to speak German, and to enter with sympathetic interest in Hitler's aspirations'. The Prime Minister was urged, further, to look with understanding upon German ambitions in Austria and Czechoslovakia. He was

---

[1] Italics are the author's.

told of Ribbentrop's 'passionate hostility' toward Czech President Eduard Benes and of the German anger about the position of their 'flesh and blood' in the Sudeten; 'can anything be done diplomatically,' demanded Jones, 'about this alleged persecution of Germans?' On the subject of Austria Jones concluded with this stern command: 'We should not be compromised into undertaking to protect Austria from falling into the lap of Germany. We do not mean to fight for Austria any more than for Abyssinia. We are not going to impose sanctions against Germany under any formula of collective security. Has this been made crystal clear to France?'

What effect had this pressure upon Stanley Baldwin – and through Baldwin, upon the policies of the British Government? Or had it any effect upon a Prime Minister, one of whose chief characteristics was a reluctance to commit himself to any action, or upon his Government that was still following, officially, the old policy of coordination with the French? The answers to these questions are, admittedly, much less clear than the fact of Jones' attempts to bring Baldwin to a German alliance. Let us try, however, to gather the evidence that exists.

There is no reason to condemn the testimony of Jones, to disregard it as a clue to the personality and mind of Stanley Baldwin. No better source is available as insight into this close-mouthed politician; the Baldwin whom Jones quotes and describes seems infinitely more real than the elusive subject of G M Young's biography or the stick figure of the apologia of his son, Alfred W Baldwin. Especially, there seems no reason to doubt Jones' importance to Baldwin, the evidence that Baldwin listened to Jones on subjects from art to foreign policy to political appointments.

The uncertain thing, however, is Baldwin's use of the advice that was asked for and freely given. Did he – who heard from many people, yet kept his own counsel – accept and implement Jones' ideas? The Prime Minister did not go through with Jones' pet plan of a meeting with Hitler. In June 1936, Jones admitted defeat on the project after it had been vetoed by Anthony Eden. He wrote to Ribbentrop: 'I have taken the matter as far as I can, without damage I hope to the cause we both have so much at heart, and my task is done. *You will, I hope, come over as soon as you can to see Eden yourself, and put to him what you have put to me with so much conviction.*'[1] Yet, better than Eden perhaps, Jones knew the Prime Minister. Months later he was still pushing Baldwin for a rendezvous with Hitler: in November 1936, he told Baldwin that he had been urged to 'beg' him to talk with the Fuehrer. And what was the Prime Minister's reply? According to Jones, Baldwin said, 'Well, it's not outside the bounds of possibility.' The story is consistent with the picture of Baldwin, the do-nothing leader: it was not, as A L Rowse put it, that Baldwin rejected Jones' arguments for a top-level conference; 'it was simply, as his entourage well understood, his inertia.' Rowse, in fact, was sure that Baldwin was wholly influenced by Jones, that to the Prime Minister 'TJ incarnated "the wisdom of the ages" '; 'Baldwin ceased to listen to Vansittart, whose warnings were so uncomfortable and preferred TJ, whose siren voice contributed the more soothing passages to his speeches.'

We can add to this Anthony Eden's discreet admission about his difficulties with the Prime Minister. Eden cited in his *Memoirs* 'two extracts' from his diary as 'revealing about the Prime Minister's attitude to foreign affairs'. The first entry was dated 20th May 1936 (in the initial period of Jones' enthusiastic propaganda for Germany): 'Talk with SB in evening,' ran the Eden entry. 'Did not get much out of it save that he wants better relations with Hitler than with Mussolini – we must get nearer to Germany. "How?" I asked. "I have no idea [said Baldwin], that is your job." ' The second item in Eden's diary was entered two weeks later:

Saw SB. Warned him that object of German foreign policy was to divide us from French. Hence Anglo-German Naval Agreement and Ribbentrop's repeated missions here. At the moment

[1] Italics used in Jones, *Diary*, p 224.

. . . we had asked Hitler a number of perfectly reasonable questions which in fact he could only fail to answer if his intentions were bad. It was therefore most important that he should be given no occasion to cloud the issue; above all that SB should not. I think SB saw the force and was rather alarmed.

The coincidence of Eden's remarks and what we know was going on – the pressure upon Baldwin from Jones – is too obvious to miss: Baldwin listened well enough to Jones to insist to his Foreign Secretary that Britain should 'get nearer to Germany', but with Eden's apprehension about German methods of achieving 'equality' in European affairs he backed down; and when Eden expressed his opposition to the projected Baldwin-Hitler meeting – unmistakeably the action that might 'cloud the issue' with Germany – Baldwin dropped that too. Under conflicting pressures in the unknown area of foreign affairs, Baldwin – one might speculate – followed his native inclination; he did nothing, or rather, he rode the fence, letting Eden know that he was 'rather alarmed' about German truculence, yet talking vaguely with Tom Jones of the 'possibility' of his meeting with Hitler.

Where, then, did British foreign policy stand after the Nazi occupation of the Rhineland? Perhaps the best answer is that like the Prime Minister it was indecisive and hesitating. And perhaps it was the indistinct form of Government policy that was in itself suspect, that alerted critics to listen carefully for slips from Government spokesmen. When Anthony Eden, for example, said in a major speech on the Rhineland, 'we made it plain at once that we were ready to negotiate with Germany, France and Belgium, new non-aggression and security arrangements for *Western* Europe',[1] his words were picked up as a significant admission; to some of his listeners Eden had given proof of their suspicions that the Government had, in fact, fixed its policy goals on safety in the West, eliminating Eastern Europe as an area of British interest.[2] Labour

[1] Italics are the author's.
[2] See *New Statesmen and Nation*, July 1936; Eleanor Rathbone in *Manchester Guardian*, 4th July 1936.

MP, Hugh Dalton, demanded bluntly, in House debate, a Government answer to these suspicions: 'There is a common belief, running wildly and dangerously in this country, that the Government is so frightened of Herr Hitler that it is prepared to give him a free hand in the East, and in the South-East and in the South of Europe. Is it true or not? Let the Prime Minister say.' Responding for the Government, Baldwin was typically ambivalent: he protested, on the one hand, that there 'was no foundation for a single word' of Dalton's charge; but, in concluding his retort, he explained that in future negotiations with Germany it was possible that the British Government would not be able to 'make provisions for the same security in the countries to the centre and the East of Europe as we hope to make for ourselves'. 'As we hope to make for ourselves' would seem to be clear enough – as clear as any statement Stanley Baldwin would make. The foreign policy of the Baldwin Government was, in Rowse's words, 'equivocal and confused', like everything about the Prime Minister. The surest thing one can say is this: the groundwork for the appeasement of Germany that would later carry through Tom Jones' urgent recommendations – when a more resolute leader would use them as his own – was under way before the retirement of Baldwin as first minister of the Crown.

7
And into the
Spanish Labyrinth

CONSERVATIVE LEADERS of the Baldwin Government were still climbing out of the Ethiopian fiasco, still grappling with the dilemma posed by the German occupation of the Rhineland, when they were given a third foreign problem, in many ways the most challenging: the explosive issue of the Spanish Civil War. Yet, as General Francisco Franco's Moorish troops and Foreign Legionnaires opened the rebellion against the Spanish Republic, there was a new flurry of energy in official Britain: briskly this time, the Baldwin Government grasped the reins of European leadership, intent on providing example and direction for international action in this delicate and difficult event – intent on a course that, whatever its initial objectives, assisted what was now a triumvirate of Fascist dictators.

Seething Spain, torn by political passions unresolved from the nineteenth century, the land where liberals and monarchists, socialist-anarchists and fascists faced one another in snarling debate and, after 19th July 1936, in naked conflict – Spain became the bloody field of instruction for the still-naive. The revolt of Franco and his generals, the Fascist *pronunciamiento*, had the enthusiastic backing of the army and a part of the navy, the Church, the landowning class, and the bourgeoisie – and had, too, the solicitous friendship and support of Mussolini and of the German Fuehrer. Against the insurrection stood the weak Popular Front Government, staffed by a coalition of liberal republicans, and working with the cooperation of Socialists, anarchist trade unions, and small groups of Communists and Trotskyists; the Government was shored up by (in fact, with Franco's attempted *coup* of mid-July, saved by) the anti-Fascist, anti-clerical working classes, the armed Spanish masses. There was never a possibility that the war

would be a private battle among Spaniards: by 1st August,
less than two weeks after Franco's landing the British Press
assumed public awareness that in Spain the European civil
war had begun. 'Across Europe,' ran a lead editorial in the
New Statesman and Nation, 'one sees the trench-lines drawn,
that had divided us unperceived. . . . The democracies face
the dictatorships – it is a war of ideas. The workers face the
owners – it is a war of classes.'[1] And openly now in this war
of ideas and classes, the sides had been taken, Rome and
Berlin on the Right, Paris and Moscow on the Left.[2] Newspapers printed weekly tallies of Italian and German assistance
to the Spanish Rebels, reports of Junker transport ships sent
to carry Moorish troops from North Africa to Spain, of German
and Italian pursuit planes and bombing planes of German
make, and the arrival in Rebel territory of Italian and German
'technical' personnel.[3] For the other side of the trench lines
the chief story was the appeal sent by the Spanish Government
to the French for arms and planes, and Premier Léon Blum's
immediate affirmative response.[4] Spain, in late July and in
August of 1936, was a swirling vortex, into which the main
actors of Europe were being irresistibly drawn.

What of the British participant in this developing battle
of giants? The British reaction was, apparently, swift and
sure: according to Keith Feiling, 'every decisive principle'

[1] *New Statesman and Nation*, 1st August 1936. Lord Rothermere's *Daily Mail* led
on the Right, by sheer volume of the printed word, in spreading the news of the
plot of World Communism to take over Spain. *The Observer* was not far behind:
on 26th July 1936, that journal warned that the Spanish war might spark the
(inevitable) Armageddon between the Red and the Black. See too *The Observer*,
9th August 1936, for this explanation from a correspondent with the Rebel
forces: 'As El Cid saved Spain from the Moors centuries ago, patriotic Spaniards
of today want to save their country from the new barbaric wave they feel is
threatening Europe.'
[2] *Daily Mail*, 17th August 1936, printed as a factual news story, reports that
Germany and Italy had pledged commitment to the Rebel cause, that both
governments were determined to prevent the victory of 'Red Spain'.
[3] See *New Statesman and Nation*, 1st, 8th, 15th August 1936; *Daily Mail*, 11th,
14th, 17th August 1936; *The Spectator*, 7th August 1936; *The Observer*, 2nd, 9th
August 1936. At this early stage in the war stories of Italian and German aid
reaching Franco's forces were daily fare, even in Rightwing papers that would
later qualify such reports.
[4] See Pierre Cot, *Triumph of Treason*, pp 340–341; also the testimony in *Les
Événements Survenus*, III, p 215.

in relation to the Spanish situation was set in 1936 'with unanimity in Cabinet and Party'. And what were the principles
so quickly decided at the outbreak of Franco's rebellion?
Chiefly, that the war be 'localised', 'circumscribed' by international action, prevented from causing the general European
conflict that could well be 'uncontrollable'.[1] Obviously, this
was a worthy and essential aim, one completely shared by the
French Government of Blum. There was a difference, though,
in French and British approaches to the Spanish crisis. Blum
and his Socialist colleagues were very much involved in what
was happening to the Spanish Government, and their concern
could not have been, and was not, concealed. The British
took a loftier stand. Their policy was to be pursued without
becoming entangled in the 'exceptional circumstances of the
conflict', the 'dangerous reactions' provoked in Spain; the
British course, made by men who had nothing to do with
'-isms' of any kind, would not be influenced by ideological
considerations, by the heated allegiances of volatile Spaniards
or of the 'unsteady brains' of Continental ideologues. Britain
would quite correctly stay out of the internal affairs of Spain,
concerning herself only with her own interests in the area –
the essential security of Gibraltar and of the sea lanes of the
Mediterranean and the protection of heavy private investments in Spanish industries and mineral resources.[2] In short,
the British Conservatives attempted to assume in the Spanish
Civil War a posture of old-fashioned neutrality.

But were they really neutral – or to put it properly, was
neutrality possible as a response to this clearly unprecedented
Spanish conflict? This much is sure: Spain was the final
clarification for a great many people. In journals like the *New
Statesman* contributors wrote with new awareness of the rolling
ambitions of 'international Fascism' and of the terrible

[1] Eden, *Foreign Affairs*, p 151 and *Facing the Dictators*, p 451.

[2] For example, the Rio Tinto Company (copper), the Armstrong Company
(cork), the Barcelona Traction, Light and Power Company, the Anglo-Spanish
Construction Company – all British owned; Britain took, too, almost fifty per cent
of Spanish exports, especially iron ore, before the Civil War. See *The Times*,
21st March 1938, 31st July 1936.

challenge to democracy and to the democracies posed by the Fascist powers, the 'group that acts as a unit'.[1] Or, in *The Observer*, the news and editorial pages were filled with explanations of another kind – of the 'historic crusade' that had opened in Spain against World Communism, against the 'one thick red thread' running through the web of international affairs. The 'true issue' in Spain, *The Observer* wrote editorially, was that Russian Bolshevism had 'produced all the dictatorships and challenged all liberty, in Europe. No stone had been left unturned by Moscow to ensure the present victory of the Reds in Spain. If the Reds do not conquer Spain – and it is now certain that they cannot (this in October and November, 1936, during the low point of Republican resistance) – then Communism is doomed in Western Europe. . . . It is General Franco's ultimate task, and it will take time, to safeguard liberty in Spain.' Indeed, Editor Garvin of *The Observer* produced, from his analysis of the meaning of the Spanish War, recommendations for the redirection of British policy: he wrote that if the Soviets continued to attempt the subversion of Europe, despite their rebuffs in Spain, the Soviet Union would likely be attacked by Germany, the 'great anti-communist dictatorship'; consequently, Britain's priority policy had to be a 'lasting settlement and friendship with Germany'.

There is no weekly record of the thoughts of Conservative leaders – no public record of Garvin-like interpretative leaps from the lessons of Spain; but there are indications that the politicians too were part of their times, that they could not abstain from alignment in the European schism that had opened in the Spanish War. Take, for example, Winston Churchill, who moved, on this issue, from his chronic dissidence to a position well within Conservative unanimity. 'In this quarrel I was neutral,' wrote Churchill, 'naturally, I was not in favour of the Communists. How could I be, when if I

<hr>

[1] *New Statesman and Nation*, 31st October, 28th November 1936. See also Kingsley Martin, in *The Political Quarterly*, VII, No 4 (1936), for a discussion of the transformation of many Socialists – who dropped their pacifism in 1936 and became (like traditional Tories) almost bellicose.

had been a Spaniard they would have murdered me and my
family and friends?' (One is reminded of Lloyd George's
remark about Churchill in 1919: Churchill the 'most formidable and irrepressible' anti-Bolshevik, whose 'ducal blood
revolted against the wholesale elimination of Grand Dukes in
Russia'.) Churchill was neutral – except that he was less
neutral toward the 'Communists' of the Government of Spain.
Or there was Tom Jones, tightening the screws of his pressure
on Stanley Baldwin: 'If the Government wins in Spain,' he
said, 'they will be superseded by the Communists to whom
they have issued arms'. (The Communists of Jones' reference
were, in the main, workers – most of them anarchist by leftist
affiliation – who were issued arms by the Government to
repel the July *coup* of the insurrectionists).[1] Or note the
contribution of Baldwin himself, a remark recorded on 27th
July: 'I told Eden yesterday that on no account, French or
other, must he bring us in to fight on the side of the Russians.'
The Times, that semi-official journal, attempted to be neutral –
and the paper did, in fact, cover both sides of the Civil War,
unlike, say, the *Daily Mail* or *The Observer* – but its headlines
were daily revelation of the way the Conservative eye saw
events in Spain: 'Burning of the Churches of Barcelona' by
'armed proletariat' ran the heading of the lead article on 23rd
July; the same theme appeared in the same spot almost daily
thereafter – 'Destruction of Barcelona', 'Red Rule in Barcelona', 'Extremists out of Hand', 'Murder Squad', 'Barcelona
under Reign of Terror'. 'It seems probable,' observed a lead
writer of *The Times*, 'that if the Government wins Spain will go
quickly Communist' – and he was expressing, no doubt, a
Conservative certainty. It seemed to matter not at all that
the Government in Madrid was, in the words of *The Spectator*,
'relatively liberal'[2] until September, when the reformed

---

[1] As even *The Times* recognised, 25th July 1936.
[2] *The Spectator*, 7th August 1936. *The Spectator's* stand was unequivocal: 'The
Government has never ceased to be the constitutional Government, and General
Franco and his supporters are rebels pure and simple.' This, said the editors, was
'incontestably the legal position.' 21st August 1936.

coalition, with Socialist Largo Caballero as Prime Minister, included two Communists in minor Cabinet posts. Conservatives insisted they would not take sides – even as they concentrated on one fact, that war had set off the revolutionary explosion, that under the banner of the Spanish Government the working classes were massing to overthrow 'Church, State, and property', and preparing the 'inauguration of a Communist regime'.[1]

With these private views circulating in the background, Conservatives proceeded to implement their neutrality – in fact, to organise international neutrality toward the Spanish Civil War. Foreign Secretary Antony Eden was author of the British contribution to the 'Non-Intervention Agreement', by his account in sole charge of policy in late 1936. Baldwin departed for Wales in July and remained there, almost out of touch with London, until October; further, the Cabinet did not meet from July to September, so that, Eden wrote, 'British policy was in fact decided in the Foreign Office'.

Eden's description of his own feelings about Spain is additional evidence of typical Conservative concerns. The Spanish Ambassador in London had implied to him that 'a Communist Government [was] the most likely outcome of the civil war', and this was certainly a disquieting thought; Eden was disturbed, too, by the news from Moscow, that Kremlin-inspired 'popular demonstrations' for the Spanish Government had been organised, and contributions to the amount of 'half a million pounds' sent to Spain. The Rebel side was little more attractive to Eden, for the generals were not, any more than the Communists, fighting a war 'of liberty and democracy against tyranny'; still, he felt the Spanish Ambassador 'near the mark' in observing that 'it was probably wrong to suppose that a Government of the Right would necessarily be close in foreign policy to Germany and Italy, since such a regime would not be stable and the traditional foreign policy of Spain

[1] Churchill, *Gathering Storm*, p 243.

would always make itself strongly felt'.[1] Eden was taking, he said, the 'pragmatic' view of a bad situation, as he made the diplomatic arrangements for the policy of Non-Intervention, 'the best which could have been devised in the circumstances'.

There is no reason to doubt the sincerity of Eden in his hopes for Non-Intervention, his fervent wish that all nations – and especially Italy, Germany, and Russia – would boycott both Loyalists and Rebels in Spain. Britain, of course, kept her part of the bargain with scrupulous care: the sending of war goods to Spain was cut off by 19th August, not that much of any kind of material had been available to Loyalist Spain – Government ships had been refused fuel and supplies at Gibraltar since July. The unilateral embargo was imposed, Eden wrote to Baldwin (in an effort to keep the Prime Minister informed), because he 'felt it necessary to do this even before we achieved international agreement in order that we might, by setting an example, do our best to induce others, more particularly Germany and Italy, to follow suit'. But, unfortunately for Eden's hopes, Germany and Italy did not follow suit, and the supply lines of the Spanish Rebels with the outside Fascist world were never disrupted: in July and early August both German and Italian Governments had been hurrying war goods to Franco's forces; and in late August, when the Non-Intervention Agreement was finally signed in Berlin and Rome, it was 'clearly understood that the flow of men and war materials should continue and increase', that it would be quite possible 'not to abide by the declaration anyway'.[2] The French were fully informed about the activities of the Fascist powers[3] – as was Eden himself. He recorded, for example, an interview with Alvarez del Vayo, Foreign

[1] Eden, *Facing the Dictators*, p 455. *The Spectator* (7th August 1936) was one source that refused such optimism. At the very start of the war that journal – generally Conservative in sympathy – warned that Fascism in Spain was a serious threat to Gibraltar and well might result in the Mediterranean becoming an 'Italian lake'.
[2] Hugh Thomas, *The Spanish Civil War*, pp 272, 260–261.
[3] See *Les Événements Survenus*, III, 215–217.

Minister of the Spanish Government, in which del Vayo
showed him 'documents and photographs to prove the extent
to which Hitler and Mussolini were violating the agreement'.
And he related a talk with French Foreign Secretary Yvon
Delbos, in which Delbos warned him of 'German activity in
connection with the Canaries' and 'Italian activities in the
Balearics' – evidence, it seemed to Delbos, of the close cooperation of Hitler, Mussolini, and Franco. But while the
French worried and Spanish Loyalists despaired about Fascist
intervention, Eden, for the British Cabinet, waved away their
apprehensions. He informed Delbos that he was 'watching
the situation in the Balearics'; as for del Vayo (a man of
'Communist sympathies'), Eden 'gave him no encouragement
to think that we would modify our policy'. Eden, speaking
for the British Cabinet, had but one policy – neutrality and
Non-Intervention – and he would stick to it with stubborn
devotion, even though it were exposed as hollow fiction and
in the end his position seemed one of utter hypocrisy.

In the closing months of 1936 evidence piled up on German
and especially Italian violation of Non-Intervention, evidence
that became public – common – knowledge. *The Observer*
approvingly tallied the Italian and German aircraft with the
Rebels, this 'open help from abroad', and applauded the
Portuguese who had 'never stopped helping the anti-Reds'.
The *Manchester Guardian Weekly* printed an eye-witness account
of a bombing of a Spanish town by Italian planes, and the
New Statesman described the 'revulsion' felt by delegates to a
Labour conference, as they listened to firsthand reports
of Fascist intervention from visiting Spanish Republicans. In
October, the Soviet Union made formal charges against Italy,
Germany and Portugal and announced to the Non-Interven-
tion Committee that unless the violations were stopped the
Russian Government would consider itself no longer bound
by the Agreement; with that, the public disillusion with Non-
Intervention was open. Non-Intervention, said *The Spectator*,
was not an instrument for isolating the Spanish War; rather,

'it isolates only the Spanish Government'. The *New Statesman* welcomed the Russian charges, which forced recognition of 'proven' Fascist intervention and predicted 'revolt against the farce' of the Agreement. And 'Our Diplomatic Correspondent' in *The Observer* referred to the 'bizarre pantomime' of the Non-Intervention Committee, to the unreality of a situation in which 'every delegate of twenty-seven countries knows that foreign arms of every kind are being increasingly imported into Spain'. British public opinion, which had generally, Right to Left, accepted Non-Intervention at face value, was now willing to admit that the policy was a failure, that it had proved totally ineffective in sealing off Spain from foreign interference.

The British Government, however, was not at all prepared to abandon the machinery of Non-Intervention. As far as the Government was concerned, the policy was operating with smooth precision: the only foreigners present in Spain were handfuls of 'volunteers' on one or the other side; of course, Portugal was not a 'conduit' for supplies to Franco's armies; there was 'no evidence' of the disembarkment of '15,000 Italians' in Spain and 'no information tending to confirm' reports of '1500 Germans at San Sebastian'.[1] In the winter of 1936–37 Anthony Eden was still chief spokesman for the Government – his break with his colleagues was a year away – and, if anything, he redoubled his efforts to keep the form of Non-Intervention alive. He was irritated with the Russians for pressing the issue of Italian, German, and Portuguese violations because, he said, it was done 'before even pretending to sift the evidence', and because – significant phrase – it 'had unnecessarily complicated matters'. That is, in making public what every diplomat already knew, the Russians had needlessly endangered the frail structure of the Non-Intervention Agreement.[2] By the early months of 1937, with

[1] *House of Commons Debates*, Vol 321, Fifth Series, p 1126; *ibid*, Vol 323, Fifth Series, p 1133.

[2] In his annoyance with the Russians, Eden made an observation that became a stock argument. After October 1936, he said, the 'Russians were openly sending

Spain

Russian supplies reaching pro-Government Spain, with Italian troops landing in division strength, with the German Condor Legion preparing to bolster Franco's sagging lines,[1] Eden was forced to a more candid position on the continuation of Non-Intervention. It was, he said, 'a device, admittedly a device, by means of which we hope to limit the risks of war. It is an improvised safety curtain.'[2] And in the House of Commons, under attack from an Opposition increasingly in favour of opening armaments markets to the Spanish Government, Eden tried another tack in defence of his policy. Non-Intervention was 'tattered and full of holes', he admitted, but since the policy was the only one the British had in the cause of preservation of European peace, they had better search their minds for good reasons to accept it. He himself had hit upon a useful idea; foreign intervention in Spain would defeat itself, would unite the whole Spanish people in common hatred of the outsiders; 'unless the whole past history of Spain is belied,' Eden told the House, 'the great mass of the proud Spanish people will feel the least illwill to those nations which have intervened the least'. As Eden described it, Non-Intervention was a plan designed by far-seeing statesmen to ensure the national interest in trade and future relations with Spain; 'in the long view,' he concluded, 'and in an issue of this kind it is the long view that counts – intervention in Spain is not only bad humanity, it is bad politics'.

Not only did Conservatives stand four-square for Non-Intervention in debate; the Government proceeded to legislative enactment of its neutrality – to a legal buttress to the 'facade'[3] of the Agreement. The Munitions to Spain Bill was an early example; the Bill was presented to the House in

supplies to Spain and the evidence we had at this time was more specific against them than against the dictators in Rome and Berlin'. *The Observer*, for one, gleefully used this, in unabashed reversal of its earlier open reporting of German and Italian aid to Franco, to assert that the Russians had intervened first in the Spanish war. *The Observer*, 25th October, 1st November 1936.
[1] See the estimate of foreign aid to both sides in Thomas, *Spanish Civil War*, pp 309, 337–343.
[2] Eden, *Facing the Dictators*, p 463.
[3] As Neville Chamberlain called it. Feiling, *Neville Chamberlain*, p 299.

November 1936 – after Franco had declared a Rebel blockade
of Loyalist ports – as an internal measure designed to demonstrate Britain's pledge of Non-Intervention. The Bill forbade
British ships to carry arms to Spain, from British or foreign
ports; it stated the right of the navy to search British merchantmen for war goods, and declared that if merchant ships
carrying arms illegally were stopped by Spanish Rebels they
would not be given protection by the British Navy. It was a
Bill, said Antony Eden, intended to close 'a small gap in our
arrangements in respect of the Non-Intervention Agreement'.
The measure touched off a howl of complaints (before it was
passed by an obedient Conservative majority on 1st December
1936) against a Government that had announced an incredible
thing, that had admitted that it could not – or would not –
protect British shipping. From the Left in the Commons came
a voice suggesting that the legislation was drawn up because
Franco threatened to stop all ships bringing Russian aid to
the Spanish Loyalists; the British Government, then, had
rushed to draw the teeth of Franco's threat – by offering to
do it for him. In defence of the Bill, Eden would say only that
it was a logical extension of Non-Intervention, and that – a
revealing enough explanation – the Government was determined that British nationals would not be in a position to
provoke trouble with the Fascist powers in Spain.

And the Conservatives had only begun their retreat from
possible friction with the dictators! Bent on prohibiting any
of its citizens from the environs of Spain, the Government
repeatedly discovered, to its dismay, other 'small gaps' in the
arrangements for Non-Intervention. In January of 1937, the
Foreign Enlistment Act was stretched to cover, and prevent,
the participation of British citizens as volunteers in Spain;
this was demanded, Eden said in the Commons, by the frantic
appeals of parents of impressionable boys lured away to be
cannon fodder for the Spanish Government.[1] But it was the

---

[1] In the discussion of the act, one hostile MP asked, 'Is it not the case that the
Foreign Secretary never became interested in volunteers until the volunteers
stopped Franco from entering Madrid?'

independent wanderings of Britons at sea that kept the Baldwin Government most on edge. The Munitions to Spain Bill did not, of course, prohibit the carrying of food and non-military goods to and from Spain, thus leaving open an area of profitable enterprise to British shipping. Not surprisingly, there were incidents at sea in which Rebel naval vessels stopped British merchantmen and even confiscated cargoes; the response of the British Government to this provocation was the filing of a routine complaint with the Rebel authorities. In the House of Commons an irate MP demanded from Eden a statement on 'ships loaded with Spanish iron ore for Britain', which had been stopped and stripped by the Rebels. Insisted the questioner: 'Do not these acts constitute, under international law, acts of piracy; and is this country merely to content itself with making protests?' And Eden's answer: 'I would not like the honourable Gentleman to think that,' he evaded. '[It is] a very complex question.'

It was a very complex question, too, at Bilbao, in April of 1937, where related events again set the Commons in an uproar.[1] The incident here developed during Franco's campaign in the North – subsequently successful – to eliminate the Basques as a pocket of Loyalist resistance. Under heavy attack, and backed up against the Bay of Biscay, the Basques badly needed foodstuffs – which were available on British ships waiting at the nearby French port of Saint-Jean-de-Luz. The British Board of Trade, however, acting on reports from Ambassador to Spain Sir Henry Chilton[2] and Admiralty officers in touch with the Rebels, sternly ordered British ships out of Basque waters, warning that the harbour at Bilbao was both mined and patrolled by Rebel vessels. Despite the warning, and on the strength of an all-clear from the Basques on shore, intrepid British captains sailed in with their

[1] For the debate on the Bilbao affair, see *Commons Debates*, Vol 322, Fifth Series, pp 1030–1142.
[2] See Claude G Bowers, *My Mission to Spain*, p 291 and *passim*. Bowers, United States Ambassador to Spain, was shocked by the attitudes of his diplomatic colleagues. Ambassador Chilton, he said, 'was violently against the loyalists from the first day, and he habitually called them "reds"' .

cargoes, safely and without challenge; they proved, that is, that the Government intelligence was incorrect, that Bilbao harbour was not mined and was not patrolled by Rebel ships. And the moral of the story is this, that the Baldwin Government had in effect put itself in the plainly non-neutral position of attempting to enforce Franco's declared blockade of Basque ports.

Clearly, British leaders were willing to concede a great deal in order to remain neutral in the Spanish Civil War, were ready even to jeopardise Britain's proud title of mistress of the seas. The latter willingness was evident not only in the waters patrolled by Franco's navy; it was demonstrated in the wider area of the Mediterranean – and in the whole morass of British relations with Italy.

The Italians were playing a complicated game in Spain. They were there, with their Fascist brethren, openly – exultantly – on an ideological crusade, participants in what Italian Foreign Minister Count Ciano identified as an 'ideological war'; the Black Shirt divisions, whose presence in Spain was publicly talked of by 1937, were to be tested in war, to prove themselves the vanguard of the Italy that was once again a nation of conquerors. Still, dazzled though he was with his illusions of Roman grandeur and his self-image as the greatest of the Caesars, Mussolini knew what the Spanish War was about: it had resulted, he told Ciano, from permitting national decisions to be made by 'the gelatinous mass, by definition irresponsible, which is the people'; the Black Shirts were sent, then, not only for the glory of Italian Fascism, but to halt the Spanish decline into rabble-democracy – that is, the Popular Front. Further, the Italians came to Spain for strategic gain, a kind of extension of their ideological assumptions. A Fascist Spain would bring enormous advantages – and enormous problems for the arch-enemy, the leader of the parliamentary nations of the West, Great Britain; with Franco sitting on top of Gibraltar, and with the Italians entrenched in the Balearic Islands and thus straddling the sea lanes, the Mediterranean would become an Italian, or at least a Fascist, rather than a British lake. This was no casual competition: the Italian Foreign Minister contemplated the inevitability of a German and Italian war against the West in 'the spring of 1939'; it would be a lightning war, Ciano thought, a war that would be won 'at Suez and in Paris'. With such enticing prospects, at any rate, the Italians were willing to invest heavily in a victory for Franco, to the extent of fifty thousand troops and planes and submarines. But it all worked out rather badly. Mussolini passionately wanted striking Italian victories in Spain, a sensational performance that would immortalise the valour of his Black Shirts; the battle of Guadalajara (part of the long unsuccessful Rebel campaign for Madrid in 1937) was, for example, an Italian action – four divisions, 'supported by 250 tanks and 180 varied pieces of mobile artillery, together with a chemical warfare company, a flame-thrower company, and 70 lorries per battalion.'[1] The result was that Guadalajara ended with massive counter-attack from Loyalist troops and the International Brigades and an Italian retreat that could only be 'named a rout'. The Italians found, in short, that they needed help in the Spanish crusade. Their failures pushed them to desperate acts – submarine attacks, for one, on merchant ships in the open Mediterranean, which registered hits on Russian and British shipping; this defiant assistance to Franco's blockade somewhat bolstered the Italians' sinking self-esteem. But, most important, the poor showing of the Italians in Spain drove them closer to their German associates: Mussolini's debt for the stiffening support of the Condor Legion was paid, in part, with the united Fascist front of the Anti-comintern Pact of November 1937, and wiped out entirely with his passive acceptance of Hitler's occupation of Austria in March of 1938.[2] Indeed, the Italian problem became, in the course of the Spanish Civil War, the overbearing German partner – who both fascinated and repelled (and frightened) the Duce and his cohorts.

What kind of policy did the Baldwin Government – and,

[1] Thomas, *Spanish Civil War*, p 383.
[2] See Chap 12, p 201 ff.

after May 1937, the Chamberlain Government – set up to deal with the Italian Fascists? In a nutshell – the Conservatives worked mightily to make an ally of Mussolini, to compensate for the irritation they had caused him in Ethiopia, to give him room in the Mediterranean – above all, to let him finish his war in Spain. The Italian diplomatic record in London showed an account of derelict promises, transparent lies, and open treachery – all of which the British took; they were discomfited, to be sure, embarrassed because of Italian violation of Non-Intervention, worried about Italian penetration of the Balearic Islands, and frantic with the attacks on British shipping, but to the end their patience with the Duce was inexhaustible.

The set of events that illuminate Conservative handling of the Italian problem began in January 1937 with the signing of a 'Gentlemen's Agreement' between the two governments. The words of this understanding about matters related to Spain were vague, but nevertheless comforting to the British: the Italians promised to 'maintain the integrity of Spanish territory' and both governments pledged friendly cooperation in the Mediterranean, explicitly; the Agreement did not deal with the issue of the presence of Italian 'volunteers' in Spain, because this, an international matter, was the responsibility of the Non-Intervention Committee.[1] The 'Gentlemen's Agreement' was such patent nonsense that it utterly convinced the Italian Fascists in their opinion of the British leaders as a flabby lot. Mussolini poured more Black Shirts into Spain and sent more submarines to plague neutral shipping in the Mediterranean, certain now that the British would confine any protest to an 'exchange of views'. But in September 1937 there was a surprise, a brief rerouting of British policy. Within the Non-Intervention Committee – of which Italy and Germany were, of course, members – Anthony Eden seemed to have achieved the acceptance of a plan of withdrawal of foreign 'volunteers' from Spain. And at the Swiss

[1] *House of Commons Debates*, Vol 319, Fifth Series, pp 104–105. 'The Gentlemen's Agreement', said *The Observer*, restoring 'an historic friendship', was concluded by Mussolini in 'his frank and open way' (15th November 1936).

town of Nyon a conference was held by Britain, France and Russia, together with the nations with Mediterranean frontiers, to discuss 'piracy' on the sea[1] – a conference from which Italy abstained; the conference concluded with the assignment of British and French patrols in the Mediterranean, with orders to attack any unidentified submarines. The Nyon Conference was an amazing demonstration of what firmness could accomplish; as Churchill pointed out approvingly, the Italians backed off from real resolution – 'the outrage stopped at once'. Such achievement, though, was only a deviation in Conservative policy, which made the main tale all the clearer. Neville Chamberlain, now Prime Minister, was not happy with the success at Nyon, which was had, he said, 'at the expense of Anglo-Italian relations'.[2] Chamberlain quickly set things back on a proper course. He sent personal letters to Mussolini – which he did not show to Anthony Eden – pleading for a reaffirmation of the 'Gentlemen's Agreement'. He eagerly accepted as sign of Mussolini's good faith the withdrawal of some three thousand Italian troops from Spain toward the end of 1937 – troops that would have been withdrawn in any case because they were unreliable or disabled. And Chamberlain had the last word, in fact rounded off Conservative policy with Italy with the conclusion of the Anglo-Italian Pact of April 1938; by its terms, Mussolini was induced to promise the withdrawal of his troops from Spain by the British offer to recognise his 'Empire' in Ethiopia – by the bribe, that is, that the British Government would obtain 'formal recognition' of his Ethiopian conquest; but the significance of the Pact was all in its qualifying clause, which stated that it would go into effect after the 'settlement of the Spanish question'[3] – in short, Mussolini had promised to withdraw his troops *after* the Spanish war was over!

[1] See Eden's discussion of the conference in *Facing the Dictators*, pp 518–538.
[2] Feiling, *Neville Chamberlain*, p 331. The full text of the Nyon Conference agreement is in *The Observer*, 19th September 1937. That journal judged the Conference 'ill-advised', saved from being worse only by Neville Chamberlain's 'coolness' to its conclusions. *Ibid*, 12th September 1937.
[3] See *The Times*, 20th May 1938, for a discussion that may have had direct

All this was done, remember, in the name of 'neutrality', in following a policy that was declared a deliberate and fair-minded refusal to take sides in the Spanish Civil War. It is hard to believe in such neutrality, hard to believe that the prejudices of the Conservatives against the Spanish Republic did not colour and, in the end, control their activities. Perhaps Eden was the most objective in his estimates of Spain – and he was a central actor in the course that permitted, as Pertinax said, 'an Italo-German monopoly of waging war in Spain'.[1] Eden resigned from the Chamberlain Government in February 1938, not because of the realities of the situation in Spain, but because he was humiliated by the spectacle of Chamberlain's attempts to placate Mussolini, shocked that the British Government would allow itself to be so flouted in international dealings.[2] (Churchill went similarly into opposition, growling about the blindness of the Government to the dangers of 'active Axis intervention in Spain'.) Eden's erstwhile colleagues were probably unfair, then, in implying that his new critical posture was based on an ideological preference in the Spanish War – Sir Samuel Hoare, for one, who observed that Eden saw the War as an issue of 'absolute right and absolute wrong in which the dictator should at all costs be totally defeated and democracy totally defended'. (Eden, alas, could tell us more than he does about sentiment within the Cabinet. He gives a brief glimpse with a quote of a remark of Hoare's – then First Lord of the Admiralty – about his (Eden's) policies as Foreign Minister: Hoare grumbled that, with Eden, 'we were getting to a point when, as a nation, we were trying to stop General Franco from winning'.) With Neville Chamberlain as Prime

bearing on the Anglo-Italian Agreement. The writer referred to the 'general depression of the last few weeks' because Franco's offensive seemed to be stalled, whereas 'easy estimates' of victory had been heard a month before: 'Depression is turned into anxiety at the reports that General Franco can hardly hope for victory unless his backing of foreign combatants and foreign munitions is greatly increased.' The inference seems to be that in April, when Chamberlain concluded the Agreement, he had thought the end of the war and a Franco victory certainties.

[1] Pertinax, *The Gravediggers of France*, p 433.
[2] See Chap 12, p 195 ff.

Minister, however, the British record leaves the declaration of neutrality in some classic category of diplomatic hypocrisy. Partisans of the Spanish Loyalists, of course, stated this bluntly and bitterly. The *New Statesman* had from the beginning pointed to the 'obvious sympathy of the British Government with the Fascist Powers'. The *Manchester Guardian* wrote sadly in 1938: 'We are still to connive at the death of a system which seemed to open out to the Spanish people an escape into a freer air of liberty, knowledge and independence.' Clement Attlee explained that Chamberlain, the businessman's businessman, set up his own hierarchy of values in Spain: what does Spanish freedom mean to the Prime Minister, asked Attlee, as long as 'Rio Tinto Mines pay a dividend?' Another well-known Labour Member, Eleanor Wilkinson, was convinced that Conservatives favoured General Franco because he was 'their sort of man'; the British Government, said Miss Wilkinson, regarded 'the Fascist powers as being run by people who somehow stand for their own class, who know how to keep their own working class in order'. And French comment, especially from members of Blum's Government, resentfully cited British duplicity – with an initial story that Premier Blum had been blackmailed into sponsoring Non-Intervention,[1] to the information that the French had stayed with neutrality because that seemed 'the only way to prevent England from aiding Franco'.[2]

Despite contrary hopes or predictions, General Franco did not get his victory in 1938; thus the war continued, and what

[1] See Cot, *Triumph of Treason*, pp 339–345, and the testimony in *Les Événements Survenus*, III, pp 216–217, for the story of British threats – to withdraw support of France against Germany, to take reprisals against the French economy – if Blum were to proceed with aid to the Spanish Republic; Alvarez del Vayo, *Freedom's Battle*, pp 66–70, repeats the story of Blum being forced to take responsibility for non-intervention, and tells of the French Premier's personal struggle in thus betraying – in the eyes of the socialist world – the Spanish Republic. On the other hand, Eden flatly denied that Blum had been brought to heel by the British – denied it in 1936, when he was charged with the story by a delegation of Labour Members. See Eden, *Facing the Dictators*, pp 455, 456. Kingsley Martin discussed the story in *The Political Quarterly*, VII, No 4 (1936): it was possible, Martin thought, that pressure had been applied to Blum; yet Blum had good reason – mainly that he was sitting on his own powder keg of Fascist opposition – to initiate Non-Intervention.
[2] Cot, *Triumph of Treason*, p 345.

became in Britain rather wearily known as the 'Spanish question' dragged on, through a minor irresolution within Neville Chamberlain's grand plan of Four Power (Britain, France, Germany, and Italy) cooperation and accord in European affairs. Chamberlain ended it only in February 1939, when he announced in the Commons, after the fact, that he had given diplomatic recognition to the Franco regime – although the Loyalist resistance held on for another month. The Opposition in the House requested of Chamberlain that he at least attach conditions to the British overture to Franco, especially a demand that the Nationalists prevent the spread of a 'Black Terror' against Spanish Republicans. Chamberlain replied that recognition was granted unconditionally because he did not want to 'embitter our relations with the new Government'.[1] Regard for the reactions of the Franco regime was demonstrated in other ways – for example, in British reluctance to assist the evacuation of Spanish Loyalist refugees without the consent of the Government. Franco's first statement after British recognition of the legitimacy of his rule was this: 'It would be unjust in these moments of triumph, when those who fought against us recognise us, if we did not remember those who from the first days believed in us. . . . To our sister nations, our neighbour Portugal, beloved Italy, friendly Germany, and the [Latin] American nations that encouraged us, goes our friendship and remembrance at this moment.' Chamberlain, however, was not disappointed by this Spanish coolness: he had it on the word of the 'prudent and ascetic dictator of Portugal' that, in the matter of British interests, Franco was 'well disposed'.

---

[1] *House of Commons Debates*, Vol 344, Fifth Series, p 117. *The Times*, naturally, approved the recognition of Franco, although the Editor felt it necessary to defend Chamberlain, particularly on the charge that he 'seemed indifferent to moral issues'; it was true, wrote Editor Dawson, that Chamberlain was not a man for 'any parade of idealism. He does not wear his heart on his sleeve'. But that the Prime Minister had 'deep and humane feelings' was demonstrated by his unending search for peace. See *The Times*, 1st, 6th March 1939. Even Editor Garvin of *The Observer* (who had since 1937 been demanding recognition of the Rebels) hoped that the British diplomatic gesture would prod Franco to clemency for the Loyalists. *The Observer*, 7th November, 26th February 1939.

PART THREE

ACTORS ON PERIPHERY
Fringe-Area Appeasers

8
The
Individuals

By 1937 THE leaders of the West waited anxiously for the next crisis in the fearfully difficult European world. There was no mistaking now the commanding figure of that troubled world: Hitler held the stage, and the bombast of his aggressive rhetoric was given substance by the mobilised might of the German nation.

It was at this 'critical juncture', Namier wrote, that 'the Western appeasers became active, as if intent on proving to Hitler that he had nothing to fear from them'.[1] 'As if' intent? British appeasers were *positively* trying to soothe the Germans, to placate the Fuehrer with vows of friendship and promises of British aid in the achievement of his foreign desires. Appeasement, in 1937, became the object of the organised efforts of politically minded individuals and groups, the publicised goal of pro-German, pro-Fascist elements within British society.

Who were these appeasers and what were their motives in demanding a pro-Fascist foreign policy? We can put aside for the moment the inner Cabinet group around the new Prime Minister, Neville Chamberlain – by the power of decision, the chief appeasers of them all. Here, the subjects are individuals and groups peripheral to the decision-making levels of government – although people hardly powerless. They constituted to a great extent the 'public' to which the Government listened; most were opinion-moulders, people of practised ability in reaching and influencing the thought of their countrymen. These were the voices trying to teach, in Great Britain, total understanding and sympathy for the goals of Hitler's Germany.

Consider, then, cases of solitary appeasers, individuals who

[1] Lewis Namier, *In the Nazi Era*, p 125.

enlisted in the cause of appeasement. One chooses models for this examination with some difficulty – there were, after all, so many friends of Fascism in Britain in the last three years of the interwar period. Members of the aristocracy, of the business community, literary circles, Press, military, clergy – among all of these the problem is one of discrimination, of selection of sample individuals, people characteristic of the type.

In any pro-Fascist field, however, Douglas Jerrold, grandson and namesake of the nineteenth-century playwright, stands as a first-rate candidate. Jerrold was a number of things: intellectual of the Right, Catholic crusader, Political Man – he possessed, that is, a complex of qualities that insured his passionate engagement in the ideological struggle of the 1930s. Jerrold the intellectual was a writer, author of *The Necessity of Freedom* and the autobiographical *Georgian Adventure*, and editor of *The English Review*, a journal which had the assistance of congenial friends, including T S Eliot, Hilaire Belloc and Wyndham Lewis. In all of his publications Jerrold worked over a familiar set of themes: disgust with modern Western society, distrust of both the activities and goals of monopoly capitalism, contempt for parliamentary politics – and for political types like Stanley Baldwin, who alternately deceived, cajoled, and crawled before an uneducated mass electorate. He lived in a world, thought Jerrold, without room for individual initiative or excellence, in a society in which even the ruling Conservative Party was drifting, against its own historic will, to 'Communism', to a social structure polarised between a leviathan government and a regimented mindless citizenry.[1]

Jerrold's Catholicism filled in the lines of his social pessimism – this, too, part of a familiar pattern. The European heritage precious to him stemmed from the centuries of common culture under the universal Church, the ancient legacy of authority and faith that had informed men's lives, given them purpose and place within society. Jerrold measured the

[1] Douglas Jerrold, *Georgian Adventure*, pp 332–334.

decay of Europe by the historical distance from that one-time age of Catholic uniformity: the English, for example, had been lost in the sixteenth-century rejection of the True Church, had succumbed to 'selfish and provincial nationalism' and a 'crude and naive materialism'; for a time, the English had valued the substitute creed of capitalist Liberalism, but now, in the twentieth century, with the exposure of Liberalism as hollow, comfortless materialism, came the inevitable moment of emptiness and despair. England – the Western democracies – 'frightened and solitary' relics of the capitalist nineteenth century, shivered in the new age, with no place to go – except, by the whole force of their materialistic logic, into Communism. And with this would come the final collapse, the termination of the West: European civilisation, Jerrold said flatly, 'stands or falls with the Church'.

So, driven by his analysis of the modern reality, the Catholic intellectual became a political activist, preaching not religious revival but a vague authoritarianism. He wanted a return, Jerrold wrote, to 'true Conservatism', which would 'turn its back on the present parliamentary system in favour of a system which will restore the reality of self-government in the appropriate spheres and enable a strong central government to speak for the nation, and not merely for a class, on national issues. This means the adoption of functional and not regional representation.' Jerrold was much concerned with 'public opinion', which, he thought, despised the 'present system', the class direction of Britain, 'with its denial alike of status, security and equality'; public opinion might, as a desperate alternative to the present class system, accept Socialism, 'with its denial of status, its doctrine of universal submission to the state' – but, given the proper instruction, public opinion would wholly approve the state which saw as its task 'the creation of conditions for independence, the secure ownership of property, and the corporate direction of industry by those engaged in it'.

Was this a call for Fascism? Jerrold avoided the word (just

as he avoided Sir Oswald Mosley's British Fascist Party, a movement, he said, that lacked the 'creative impulse'). Jerrold found more creative political company in the Tory Right-wing, with men like Sir Charles Petrie, biographer of the Chamberlains, Leo Amery, the ex-High Commissioner for Egypt, Lord Lloyd, or the financier – a director of Lloyds Bank – Sir Robert Horne,[1] all of whom were guest speakers for meetings sponsored by *The English Review*. And he worked with such people in organising in 1935 a political party, a splinter group of Tories calling themselves the Independent Conservatives, with Lord Lloyd as their candidate against Stanley Baldwin in the electoral campaign of that year.

But to a man of Jerrold's energy and commitment the British political arena was a dull place, especially so when exciting things – events demanding his creative impulse – were happening abroad. Early in the 1930s Jerrold had met that 'good democrat', the exiled King Alfonso of Spain, from whom he had obtained detailed information on the 'revolutionary conspiracy' preparing that country for Communism. Alfonso told him of the methods with which Spanish Socialists and Communists – and foreign agents as well – worked behind the unconvincing blind of the Spanish Republic, of the ways they incited the masses to class hatred and even to atrocities against the Catholic clergy and to desecration of churches. Jerrold reacted to these stories with the fury – and the fervour – of a Jesuit; the destiny of Spain became an obsession with him, this sacred land in which the future of 'religion and freedom in Europe' would be resolved, this home of the counter-Reformation, where the 'Last Crusade' had begun. Jerrold's emotional attachment to the cause of traditional Spain was so marked that it was he who was chosen to arrange the preface to the revolt of July 1936 – the airplane flight that returned General Francisco Franco to Morocco from his exile in the Canary Islands. His role in this cloak-and-dagger

[1] The last three men were Churchill's chief allies in his opposition to the Conservative Governments.

episode was to Jerrold the highlight of his European experience, his contribution to the 'counter-revolution' against the Communist plotters and the atheistic masses who would destroy the glory of Catholic Spain.

Douglas Jerrold was not, obviously, concerned about clarity or consistency in his thinking. He knew well enough what he was against. He despised the sham politics of the Baldwin Tories, indeed *in toto* the language and behaviour of middle-class democracy; and he was absolutely convinced that, in some subterranean way, a Moscow-directed conspiracy ruled the world. The force of his negativism – and the emptiness of his own positive ideas – brought him to Fascism; Fascism was *there*, established and strong, and Fascists were straightforward warriors against Bolshevism, spokesmen for the Christian tradition, and enforcers of social order and authority. But it was one thing for the Catholic fanatic to see the Rebels in Spain – where the Church and its hated clergy were under battering attack from the masses of people, where the Church was a pillar of Franco's power – as inspired crusaders against irreligion and militant atheism and quite another to enshrine Hitler and Mussolini on the same pedestal. Mussolini had, of course, made his peace with the Pope, but he was still the same man who had written – as it was pointed out with heavy irony in a House of Commons debate – that religion was 'scientifically absurd', and 'immorality' in practice, a 'disease of the mind among men'. And in Germany the drive to make religion an adjunct of Nazism proceeded relentlessly – even though the Catholic Church had publicly offered its help to the Third Reich 'in its historic campaign of repelling Bolshevism'.[1] Jerrold, the Catholic pro-Fascist, could explain it all away. Mussolini was the protector of Christian verities, courageously fighting the good fight against both visible and invisible enemies (in Ethiopia, for instance, where 'sinister forces . . . had tried to engineer the ruin of Italy'). And all the talk of German persecution for race and religion was the

[1] See *The Times*, 4th January 1937.

product of Leftwing exaggeration – besides, even if it were true, would it not be analogous to the English persecution of Catholics until the recent past?[1]

Jerrold was one kind of pro-Fascist activist and propagandist. Moving higher on the British social scale, to the pinnacle of the aristocracy, one finds, not unexpectedly, other types, in fact a good portion of the Lords of the Realm,[2] busy in the Fascist cause. It was among the aristocracy that Ribbentrop and his successor as Ambassador to Britain, Herbert von Dirkson, worked most profitably and found their most credulous listeners; and among the aristocrats few were more receptive to Nazi persuasion than Lord Londonderry. A man of few and simple ideas, Londonderry was attracted to Nazi Germany for reasons as uncomplicated as he. The Seventh Marquess of Londonderry was heir to a noble name – and to an uncompromising Tory tradition. He was owner of vast estates in England and Ireland, some of which were rich in coal; in consequence, he was a mine-owner, chairman of Londonderry Collieries, Ltd, who had done stalwart service on behalf of private ownership of Britain's turbulent coal industry.[3] Londonderry had deep admiration for the Nazi chiefs[4] – who were, he felt, misunderstood in Britain, where there was overemphasis on the rigorous rule of his Nazi friends, 'too much stress on Nazi dictatorship' and not enough on 'the great social experiment' that these men were conducting. Nor did the British properly appreciate the German toughness on Communism, the 'robust attitude' of the Nazis in condemning Bolshevism (and Bolshevism, Londonderry would add pedagogically, 'is a world-wide doctrine which aims at the internal disruption of all modern systems of Government with the ultimate object of what is termed World Revolution').[5]

[1] Jerrold, *Adventure*, p 353.
[2] See Chap 9, p 148 ff.
[3] See Simon Haxey, *Tory MP*, pp 151–152.
[4] See *Manchester Guardian Weekly*, 28th February 1936, 'An Innocent's Return', which tells of a Londonderry trip to Germany, where he 'sat at the feet (for two hours) of Herr Hitler'.
[5] Londonderry, *Ourselves and Germany*, pp 20–21.

In letters to *The Times*, and in a book he called *Ourselves and Germany*, Londonderry earnestly explained his approval of the Germans. The Nazis promised the salvation of Londonderry's world, and under the dispensation of this overarching consideration they could incur no blame. Was Germany unreasonably touchy, and its leader irrational in his hostility? For this, Britain and France were directly responsible: Germany had been unjustly tarred with fault in setting off World War I, and even more unfairly treated by the Peace of Versailles; these injustices had been compounded by the French policy – in which Britain acquiesced – of keeping Germany in the 'depths of degradation', in a pitiful state from which impoverishment, crushing economic humiliation, and finally social revolution had resulted. Was it not to be expected, then, that the Germans, a 'strong and virile race', would rebel against such inequity, that they would be 'driven to take the law into [their] own hands', that they would follow a leader who promised to restore both their self-respect and their equality with other peoples? And Londonderry understood the difficulties that Hitler had met and overcome during Germany's 'period of chaotic impotence', the perilous years of near-Communist revolution; the roots of the so-called 'excesses' of Nazism lay in the experience of that period, which had taught the Germans – if not the British or French – the necessity of dealing ruthlessly with internal subversion. In the same way, Hitler's aggressiveness, his defiance and hostility toward the outside world, was the sign of his superior perception of the gains of international Communism since 1936. The Fuehrer saw himself surrounded by Communist countries, 'militarily and economically hemmed in' – and with sound reason: France was Russia's ally, Belgium was 'showing signs of Bolshevism', and the condition of Spain was mainly due to 'Red machinations'.[1]

All this was a build-up to Londonderry's main point. Since he admired the toughness of the Nazis, the dynamism of their

[1] *The Times*, 10th March 1936.

methods, and the goals of their domestic and foreign policies, why should his countrymen not feel the same admiration? Why should there not be an agreement between Britain and Germany, nations which assuredly had a 'racial connection' and a 'primary friendly feeling'? An Anglo-German alliance would make peace a certainty, would pacify Germany – and confound the 'prophets of World Revolution'.

Douglas Jerrold, political journalist, Lord Londonderry, Minister of Air from 1931 to 1935 (and a continuing power on the Conservative Party) – beyond these, a score of others might be identified as notable propagandists of the extreme Right. One could as well select Francis Yeats-Brown, soldier, aviator, hero of World War I, and author of the book, *The Bengal Lancer*, which was made into a popular film, or the distinguished naval officer, Admiral Sir Barry Domvile,[1] or Sir Arnold Wilson, Conservative MP for Hitchin, whose views appeared regularly in 'Letters to the Editor' columns of the national Press or in articles contributed to journals like *The Observer*, *The Spectator*, or *Time and Tide*. All of these spokesmen eulogised the Fascist nations, and especially Nazi Germany, and held up the Fascist system as a contrast to – and a model for – the disorderly societies of the decadent democratic West. Sir Barry Domvile celebrated 'the great work done by Herr Hitler and his associates . . . one of the greatest – and most bloodless – revolutions in history'.[2] To Yeats-Brown, the 'great, disciplined, industrious' German nation had been restored to its true self by Nazi leadership, had been magnificently led from the sick despair of the Weimar period into the proud present of '*Ein Volk, Ein Reich, Ein Fuehrer*'.[3] It was precisely the totalitarian aspect of Nazism that appealed to these writers, the primary Nazi insistence on national discipline, national harmony and cooperation, achieved by a

[1] See Chap 9, p 150
[2] In the preface to Arthur P Laurie, *The Case for Germany*.
[3] Francis Yeats-Brown, *European Jungle*, pp 139, 172. See too the series of three articles on Germany and Central Europe by Yeats-Brown in *The Observer*, 27th March, 3rd April, 10th April 1938.

governing group unafraid to use force. 'What we are witness-
ing,' wrote Yeats-Brown, 'is a general readjustment in the
ideas of government in Europe. The Russians began it, but
their methods (to say the least) were unsuitable to Christendom.
Then Italy, then a dozen other countries evolved their own
methods and found them good. Now (besides Italy) Germany,
Spain, the Baltic States, Poland, Rumania, Yugo-slavia,
Albania, Bulgaria, Turkey, Greece, and Portugal – say
258,500,000 people in Europe alone, many of them admittedly
of high culture and intelligence – have come to the conclusion
that they have discovered political systems superior to the
British. . . . The world . . . is redefining its ideas of liberty.
Political liberty is a delusion in great modern States.' And,
according to these propagandists, the Fascist nations were
every year proving the superiority of their way of life. Sir
Arnold Wilson saw in vital statistics a clear contrast between
the dynamism of Fascism and the dwindling strength of the
democracies: Britain, he warned, was losing the 'élan vital',
with her birth rate falling far behind the swelling of that of
the German population; this demonstrated, Wilson argued, that
'Western parliamentary democratic systems are . . . co-existent
and co-terminous with conditions unfavourable to national
survival'. He concluded that the disintegrating democracies
were trembling targets for Communism – unless they attached
themselves to the totalitarian nations and searched, as well,
for some approximation of the German or Italian solutions to
modern political and social problems.

The monotonous sameness, the repetition and similarity,
in the views of these individual volunteers for Fascism suggests a rather simple packaging of their typical ideas. A summary of the responses of these ultra-appeasers would begin,
certainly, with their conspiratorial view of modern history –
that is, pro-Fascist spokesmen typically saw behind all things
that distressed them the sinister forces of Bolshevik-Com-
munism. Thus Douglas Jerrold wrote with heavy sarcasm
that 'the technique of the Revolution in Europe today is . . .

to create disorder and challenge decent and Christian people to put it down . . . then the forces of disorder became "the people struggling to be free" '. Their anti-Communism was, too, a catch-all negativism, covering their aversion to a variety of things within Britain – democracy and the mass electorate, social welfare legislation, materialistic values and, in the case of writers like Jerrold or Yeats-Brown, monopoly capitalism, 'Big Business, Big Finance'; all of these, in the logic of the Right, were pushing the nation to Socialism-Communism, or playing into the hands of the Communists. Creeping Communism at home, the international Communist conspiracy abroad – here, to the ultra-appeasers, was the danger-reality of the world, against which traditionalist countries – that is, the Fascist nations and a Britain wavering in indecision – must hang together in quintessential unity. One crack in this Fascist-led front would open the way for the ready forces of destruction; for example, 'if we were to isolate Germany and therefore prove to the German people that Herr Hitler had failed them, deluded them, betrayed them, eventually they will discard him and seek another God . . . there is only one, the anti-Christ of Communism'.[1]

Upon this basic structure of world-analysis Rightwing extremists nailed other predictable attitudes. They were nationalistic – their nationalism the deliberate antithesis of Marxist internationalism ('I dislike any sort of internationalism,' Yeats-Brown declared, 'I often feel inclined to heave half a brick at the foreigner'). And they were anti-Semitic. Nazi persecution of Jews worried Londonderry – because the Western Press so criticised Germany on the issue. He wrote to his friend Ribbentrop on this score, urging more discretion, and suggesting a rationalising principle by which the Germans might soften their understandable antipathies:

As I told you, [*Londonderry concluded*] I have no great affection for the Jews. It is possible to trace their participation in most

[1] Sir Thomas Moore, MP, quoted in Haxey, *Tory MP*, p 236.

of these international disturbances which have created so much havoc in different countries, but on the other hand one can find many Jews strongly ranged on the other side who have done their best with the wealth at their disposal, and also by their influence, to counteract those malevolent and mischievous activities of fellow Jews.

Yeats-Brown did not even attempt to blunt his straight-forward racism; he explained that Jews were 'unbalanced people', mentally of a 'revolutionary temperament', of a 'distinct, and instinctively disliked, race'. Further, Yeats-Brown observed that . . .

> . . . anyone who suggested that the Stud Book was of no importance in racing would be rightly considered a lunatic. Yet the Germans and Italians are ridiculed by our highbrows for taking measures to see that their future leaders shall be of what they consider sound stock! . . . I cannot think why it is considered so absurd, unsocial and unscientific of the Germans to attach importance to preserving the integrity of their blood.

Anti-democratic, anti-Communistic, anti-Semitic, pro-Fascist, pro-order, pro-force – these were the guidelines of the views of Rightwing propagandists, attitudes which they equated with traditional and Christian values, the core-meaning of 'Western Civilisation' which they, the Germans, Italians, and Spanish Rebels, were courageously defending.

9
The
Organisations

UNDERSTANDABLY, IN BRITAIN in the 1930s, individuals of Rightwing persuasion came together in various associations, enlarging their activities and their effectiveness through joint operation. The organisational efforts of pro-Fascist elements ranged from informal groups of like-minded persons to the action-centred cadres of Sir Oswald Mosley's British Union of Fascists. In one sense it was a broad spectrum – in terms of the variety of endeavour in the Fascist cause – yet such organisations possessed a common denominator in the class origins of the leaders, if not always of the total membership; these groups constituted the more formal engagement of the upper classes in the purpose of Anglo-German understanding and alliance.

Mosley's British Union of Fascists was in a category by itself, openly totalitarian in its imitation of the Italian *Fascisti*. Mosley's aim was the conversion of his mass following – an estimated twenty thousand in 1934, the bulk of them middle-class youths whose expectations had been limited by the Depression[1] – into a disciplined army and a ready fist to support his programme for the construction in Britain of an Italian-model corporate state.[2] His methods centred on mass propaganda meetings which, Goebbels-like, were carefully staged and rehearsed, with Mosley in full uniform – and with undeniable charisma – exhorting his howling disciples to hatred of 'Reds' and Jews. Mosley's jackbooted troops, parading by torchlight to huge well-publicised rallies, made the ideological war a reality to astonished Londoners, for the Marching cadres were irresistible targets for Leftwing hecklers and

[1] Mowat, *Britain*, p 473.
[2] See Sir Oswald Mosley, *The Greater Britain*, for an outline of Mosley's programme; also Frederic Mullally, *Fascism Inside England*, Chaps 1, 2, pp 20–23.

Communist youth groups. Attacking the Fascist lines, however, was a risky undertaking; skirmishes between Left and Right developed into bloody riots, during which police, if they intervened at all, used their truncheons to silence and subdue the battlers of the Left.[1]

The most notorious incident provoked by the BUF occurred in London on 7th June 1934, at a scheduled Fascist rally at Olympia. This was a shocking, brutal and violent affair, which roused a furore in Britain – and even abroad. Overseas papers talked of the 'red terror in London', and of the bloody street fights exploding in the City (while in Berlin, Nazi sources were sharply approving of Mosley's techniques, and of his promises to invade Socialist meetings and smash the Communist Party). In the House of Commons, Conservative MPs were inclined to dismiss the whole thing, although they could not wave away the testimony of one totally reputable witness: Geoffrey Lloyd, Private Parliamentary Secretary to Stanley Baldwin, had been in the audience at Olympia, had seen the 'unmerciful brutality' of the Fascists; to watch it, Lloyd said, had made his 'blood boil', had revolted him 'as an Englishman and a Tory'.

From its formation in the early 1930s Mosley's movement had picked up powerful support. Lord Rothermere, owner of the *Daily Mail*, and the *Evening News* and *Sunday Dispatch*, declared in that then lurid journal his admiration of the BUF; silent partners were Sir Henri Deterding, Chairman of the international cartel of the Dutch Oil Company, and Sir William Morris, automobile manufacturer – giants, both of them, of the business community.[2] Yet Mosley's organisation was not the political vehicle to draw widespread upper-class approval. It was too raw, too crude in its propaganda against Liberalism and the parliamentary system, too fanatic in its hatred of the Left for the taste of most respectable Britons; after Olympia and the public revulsion against the BUF

---

[1] Mowat, *Britain*, p 474; Mullally, *Fascism*, p 54.
[2] Mullally, *Fascism*, p 60; *The Spectator*, 27th July 1934.

even his business friends drifted away from Mosley, who was now, as *The Spectator* put it, a 'losing cause'.

Yet the upper classes did not turn their backs on Sir Oswald Mosley – who was, after all, one of their own. By his first marriage Mosley was son-in-law of Lord Curzon; his second wife was Lady Diana Guinness, daughter of Lord Redesdale and sister of Hitler's good friend, Unity Mitford. In his own circles, Mosley's erratic political career – he had travelled from the Conservatives to Labour before the inception of the BUF[1] – seemed a piece of eccentricity, and his espousal of authoritarian doctrines an odd turn that at most had, as Harold Nicolson observed, deprived the nation of a 'great Parliamentarian'. An apt fictional counterpart is Aldous Huxley's Everard Webley – regarded by his peers as a bit of a fanatic, headstrong, and impatient in the quite creditable campaign to avert 'the dictatorship of the stupid', but unquestionably accepted as a member in good standing of the national élite.

The type of organisation more to the liking of Fascist sympathisers of the second half of the 1930s was the *ad hoc* society, the single purpose group, in which a number of prominent people would declare themselves a committee for a cause, ready to accept subscriptions and to direct propaganda – the latter typically confined to frequent news releases and Press interviews and to occasional glittering society dinners. A spate of such groups sprang up in 1937 in response to the Spanish Civil War, pro-Franco organisations like the Friends of National Spain, the United Christian Front, the Spanish Children's Repatriation Committee. These groups recruited in Parliament, among the aristocracy, in wealthy Catholic and Anglican circles[2] for sympathisers and subsidisers anxious

---

[1] Mosley's political course thus bore a superficial resemblance to that of Mussolini and Pierre Laval; both were initially men of the left. Mosley's ambition and his impatience to get things done took him out of the plodding Labour Party of Ramsay MacDonald and Philip Snowden when the latter refused to listen to his plans to meet unemployment in 1930. Mosley, Clement Attlee said dryly, possessed 'considerable dynamic force'. Attlee, *As It Happened*, p 105.

[2] See Haxey, *Tory MP*, p 214; also *Church Quarterly*, April–June, 1937, p 115.

to engage in what had become in Spain a holy fusion of social and religious issues, 'the cause of Christianity against anti-Christ'.[1] Douglas Jerrold lent a hand in the formation of these groups for Rebel Spain, as did Sir Arnold Wilson who was quoted as saying, 'I hope to God Franco wins in Spain, and the sooner the better'.[2] Important people, influential people, people close to members of the Government were affiliated, too – Viscount Castlereagh, MP, and son of Lord Londonderry; the Earl of Glasgow, brother-in-law of Sir Thomas Inskip, Minister for the Co-ordination of Defence; Lord Home, whose son[3] was Parliamentary Private Secretary to Neville Chamberlain; Alan Lennox-Boyd, who became Parliamentary Secretary to the Minister of Labour.

There were, then, a number of upper-class pressure-and-propaganda groups, of which the most notable, both in effectiveness and for descriptive purposes, were the Anglo-German Fellowship and 'The Link'.

The Anglo-German Fellowship was a replacement of an older association of that name which had existed to build relations with the Weimar Republic. The new society was organised in early 1935, after the Nazi assumption of power, with a sister group founded at the same time in Germany. Its stated purpose was 'to promote fellowship between the two peoples', a goal 'non-political [in] its fulfilment', although the secretary of the Fellowship made this observation to the Press: 'It isn't numbers that matter. We want "Names", otherwise how can we have any influence with the Government or the Foreign Office.'[4] And 'names' the Fellowship got, by the scores, then hundreds – 'distinguished representatives of British Big Business', Members of Parliament, and of the aristocracy, a list splendid in its eminence.[5] Lord Mount Temple, President of the Fellowship, Lord Londonderry,

[1] Haxey, *Tory MP*, p 216.
[2] *Manchester Guardian*, 11th June 1938.
[3] Subsequently Lord Home, Foreign Secretary in the Macmillan Government (1962) and Sir Alec Douglas-Home, Prime Minister (1963).
[4] Quoted in Haxey, *Tory MP*, p 199.
[5] For a full account, see *ibid*, pp 198–202, 207–209, 230–232.

Lord Lothian, Lord Redesdale, Sir Arnold Wilson, Sir Thomas
Moore, Admiral Sir Barry Domvile, Major Francis Yeats-
Brown, Douglas Jerrold, Sir William Morris, ex-President of
the Board of Trade, Walter Runciman, a grandson of Queen
Victoria, the brother-in-law of Defence Minister Sir Thomas
Inskip, directors of banks and giant industries – an account-
ing of the individual members of the Anglo-German Fellowship
could be far extended: there were, besides, corporate member-
ships of the Fellowship, by which financial and industrial
firms – their directors in most cases already individual members
– could affiliate with the organisation. At the second annual
dinner of the Fellowship in December of 1937 – an affair
covered by the British and German Presses (and even in
diplomatic dispatches)[1] – the President, Lord Mount Temple,
could boast of the society's seven hundred members, 'citizens
of weight and influence, occupying responsible positions, and
drawn from all parts of the British Isles'. The enthusiasm for
the work of the Fellowship, Mount Temple added, showed
'that public opinion considered understanding with Germany
the most important object of British foreign policy'. Lord
Halifax was guest speaker at this social occasion which Ribbentrop attended – carefully noting details that would be included
in his report to Berlin – and honoured visitor of the evening
was the representative from the German 'sister organisation',
the Duke of Saxe-Coburg and Gotha. This anniversary dinner
indicates some of the activities of the Fellowship: it provided
a platform for Nazis and for British pro-German spokesmen
to publicise the German position on a variety of matters, the
importance of the people involved ensuring them coverage in
depth from the Press. At other functions, the Fellowship
sponsored the showing of German films, the advertisement of
German political tracts, or speaking tours for German 'edu-
cationalists'. Further – and a very important point – the
Fellowship gave to upper-class Britons the opportunity to know,

---

[1] See *Documents on German Foreign Policy, 1918–1948* (hereinafter cited as *German Documents*), Series D, Vol I, No 89, p 157.

to entertain, and to visit eminent German officials. Social exchanges constituted a valued part of the schedules of Fellowship members, with many of them travelling to Germany, and a lucky few – Mount Temple, Domvile, Lothian and Londonderry – granted the supreme honour of interviews with Herr Hitler; on the British side, hostesses competed briskly for the company of visiting Nazis – witness Tom Jones' report of Lady Astor 'chaffing' Ribbentrop about the frequency of his social evenings with Lord and Lady Londonderry.

'The Link' was an organisation akin to the Anglo-German Fellowship, its existence indicating, perhaps, the eagerness with which wealthy pro-Germans strove to outdo one another in setting up such groups. Its founder and chairman was Sir Barry Domvile, who retired in 1936 after distinguished service in the Royal Navy, as an Assistant-Secretary, Director of Naval Intelligence, Vice-Admiral of the War College. Besides Domville, *all* of the members of the committee of 'The Link' were members as well of the Anglo-German Fellowship,[1] although in spite of this peculiar overlapping of groups 'The Link' was the more extreme of the two. An interviewer writing in *The Observer* had this to say about the society: '[The Link] has begun to spread in this country [and] a corresponding movement has been founded in Germany. . . . Herr Hitler himself is very keen on the movement. . . . Twice Sir Barry Domvile has been Herr Hitler's guest. Recently he went chamois shooting for a week in the company of Herr Himmler, head of the SS detachments.' The organisers of 'The Link' were a voluble team, especially on the subject of British weaknesses and the comparative strength of Nazi Germany. They published a journal, *The Anglo-German Review*, in which contributors ridiculed the Government and Government policy, and denounced critics like Winston Churchill – 'the biggest war-monger in the world today' – or Anthony Eden – 'probably the most unfortunate choice of a Foreign Secretary within living memory.' Coupled with the editorial tone of the

[1] Haxey, *Tory MP*, p 204.

journal, these expressions added up to a demand, by *The Anglo-German Review*, for the total subordination of British policy to the wishes of the German Fuehrer.

One of the members of the committee of 'The Link', Professor A P Laurie – a man in his seventies, a retired principal of Heriot-Watt College in Edinburgh – expanded his opinions to book-size, with a tract (published in Berlin) called *The Case for Germany*. The book carried a preface by Sir Barry Domvile, lauding Professor Laurie as a 'brilliant scientist', and a main text that played upon every note in the Nazi propaganda refrain. One can select examples almost at random: 'We need to return,' Laurie declared, 'to a conception of the state as an organic living entity demanding service and sacrifice of individual gain from its members, and ending class war and spoliation'; Hitler's great work had been in 'stamping out all class war'; admittedly, the Nazis persecuted Jews, but 'every revolution has its excesses' – besides, Western critics failed to realise that Jews had monopolised the best positions in the old Germany, had been a foreign element depriving true Germans of economic opportunity, although even now they were not ruthlessly ejected by the Nazis but permitted to 'retire on pensions'. It was Professor Laurie, too, who wrote in *The Anglo-German Review* after Munich in 1938 – obviously out of the 'admiration and gratitude' he felt for the 'great work' done there by Hitler – that Czechoslovakia had been a 'tumour in the heart of Europe ruled by the Communist Benes, which required a surgical operation to prevent it poisoning the life-stream of Europe'. This type of Nazi patter, and this type of Nazi enthusiast, made up the organisation of 'The Link' – which attracted 'nearly a thousand direct members', by Domvile's count, including, of course, businessmen, Conservative MPs, and Peers of the House of Lords.

There remains for consideration one group, a special kind of group, very unlike the Anglo-German Fellowship or 'The Link', and one that received, probably, more publicity than the latter two in combination. In a 1936 issue of *The Week*, its editor, Claud Cockburn, identified a pro-Nazi influence in Britain, a powerful pressure group that he dubbed the 'Cliveden Set'. Cockburn described as core members of this group the regular company at the Astor estate of Cliveden: the host and hostess themselves, Lord Astor ('genial, vague') and Lady Nancy Astor ('opinionated, prejudiced'), and constant visitors like the editor of *The Times*, Geoffrey Dawson, or Lord Lothian.[1] These people, the Astors and their guests, said Cockburn, were 'an easy and obvious target' for German propaganda. Although they had shared, in 1933 and 1934, the general aversion to Nazi thuggery, their attitudes – an obsessive fear of the Soviet Union, suspicion of France and resentment of French dallying with the Soviets – opened the way for the emissaries of the New Germany; Ribbentrop and his colleagues had had little trouble convincing the Astor crowd that the French, with their Soviet ties, were unreliable and dangerous, and that safety for Britain lay in close relations with Germany. Thus, concluded Cockburn, the Cliveden Set had become, and not unwittingly, a conduit for German interests and designs; these influential people meeting at the Astor estate, where on any weekend the guest list might be headed by Chamberlain or Halifax or Inskip, were using their high social position to bring British policy to heel behind the Nazi Third Reich.

The phrase, 'Cliveden Set', became an accepted reference term for pro-Nazi forces in Britain, the opposition Press regularly reporting proof of its existence and power and the scope of its activities. Labour leader Hugh Dalton flatly called the Set a treasonous element, like groups in Spain or in France an upper-class underground for Nazi subversion; the Astor people, charged Dalton, were 'traitors of Printing House Square, this residue of the Cliveden Set, Hitler's Fifth Column

---

[1] *The Week*, 17th June 1936. Lothian (formerly Philip Kerr) was a member of Lord Milner's 'Kindergarten' in South Africa, and from 1910 to 1916 was editor of the Milnerites' journal for Imperialist ideas, *The Round Table*. After Milner joined the Lloyd George Government in 1916, Lothian was employed as a secretary to the Prime Minister.

in London'. Dalton substantiated this indictment with a record of a conversation in 1938 with Lady Astor, in which she had told him: 'You really ought to meet [Charles] Lindbergh. He said the German Air Force is the most terrific thing there ever was. No one can stand up to it. He says we ought to make our peace with Hitler as soon as we can.'

Was there, then, a Cliveden Set? The question persists because the accused dismissed the whole subject as the work of the irresponsible Left. That interested source, Thomas Jones, denied, as the Astors did, 'an organised or conscious group'. Weekends at Cliveden were famous, Jones pointed out, for the variety of the guest list:

> It is impossible to find any precise or consistent principle which decided the selection of the guests. . . . Neville Chamberlain and Anthony Eden enjoyed separate weekends. Bernard Shaw . . . dominated the scene with his wit and his brogue and out-talked every competitor, including that other torrential Irishman, James Louis Garvin [editor of *The Observer*], if he happened to be present. Meanwhile, Harold Nicolson would be alone on the terrace conscientiously conning a book. Other guests went walking in the woods or played tennis or went to see Lord Astor's yearlings in the paddock not far off. You might meet Mary Pickford or Charles Chaplin, Litvinoff or Maisky. Such was the variety and individuality of the persons gathered together that the notion of their forming a Cliveden Set was as grotesque as it would be to expect unity among the passengers of a Cunarder.[1]

On the other hand, Jones is the witness who has informed us that at Cliveden 'the talk was inexhaustibly political . . . always of the problems which exercised Parliament, Whitehall, the Foreign Office, the Empire, France, Germany, America; everlastingly of the rise and fall of Parties and leaders and reputations, the competents and the disappointments'.[2] We have seen what Jones himself did with this political conversa-

[1] Jones, *Diary*, p xxxvi.
[2] *Ibid*, p xxxix.

tion, the constant pressure he put on Prime Minister Stanley Baldwin, the ways in which he tried to turn the ideas developed at Cliveden into concrete policy. And the things Jones remembered from his frequent Cliveden excursions, the items he considered important enough for entry in his diary, were remarkably uniform bits of these political discussions. The group concensus of the Cliveden regulars, as Jones recorded day after day, was in absolute favour of rerouting British foreign policy away from alliance with the distrusted French and into cooperation with and appeasement of Hitler's mighty New Germany. Again and again in Jones' diary there is evidence of the unanimity of the group on crucial matters: the fear of Communism (which had developed into the propensity for seeing the moving hand of Bolshevism all about),[1] and the inclination to trust the Nazis precisely because their 'social experiment' was resolutely anti-Communist.

Further, the habitués of Cliveden were, indeed, people of power and influence. The hostess of the house was MP for Plymouth, and the pages of the House *Debates* reveal how she put her anti-Communist fears and her pro-Nazi preference into the public record. Lord Astor was owner of the Sunday *Observer*, and his brother, J J Astor, was part owner of the great London *Times*, both journals voices of tremendous persuasive ability in the cause of appeasement; to complete the family involvement, Lord Astor's son, the Honorable W W Astor, was Parliamentary Private Secretary to Sir Samuel Hoare, the Home Secretary – and a member of the Anglo-German Fellowship. The Astors' constant companion, Geoffrey Dawson, as editor of *The Times*, was one of the most influential men in England, an equal, according to his biographer, of a cabinet member or an archbishop of the Church.[2] Were such people talking idly in their 'inexhaustible' political discussions?

With the answer so clear, controversy about the existence or

[1] Lord Astor displayed such perception in explaining American dislike of Nazi Germany as the result of propaganda spread by 'Jews and Communists', Jones, *Diary*, p 390.
[2] Sir John Evelyn Wrench, *Geoffrey Dawson and Our Times*, p 366.

non-existence of a Cliveden Set seems decidedly pointless. Certainly there was, from the mid-1930s, a group of intimate friends, wealthy and influential people, meeting socially at that estate or the city, their consuming interest, in conversation as in occupation, the burning political questions and the critical foreign events of the decade; their views on these matters were uniformly pro-German; that is to say, Cliveden regulars, members of the aristocracy and the upper-middle classes, unhesitatingly chose, in the ideological polarisation of the 1930s, the anti-Communist side – that side manned with obliging zeal by the Fascists.[1] But the Cliveden Set, with its shifting personnel, had no monopoly on enthusiam for Fascism; they were one circle among many, all of them made up of people of similar social status and public prestige.

A postscript to the Cliveden Set(s): in 1939 Lord Lothian went to Washington as Ambassador to the United States, where New Dealers quizzed him about British partiality for Nazism. Lothian himself reported that President Roosevelt had twitted him about the way in which 'the wealthy class' placed its trust in Hitler, and that Felix Frankfurter – deadly serious – had observed that the 'bogey of Bolshevism' had seemed to blind Lothian and his friends to 'the immediacy of the threat of Hitlerism to everything we value in civilisation'.

---

[1] United States Ambassador to Spain Claude Bowers' experiences with the international set (social and diplomatic) are not irrelevant. On the Basque coast during 1937–38, among people from democratic nations, Bowers was amazed by 'the incessant beating of the tom-toms in glorification of the Fascist cause', amazed that he found 'the ideology of democracy most unfashionable'. In the cocktail bars of Biarritz, or at formal dinners in St-Jean-de-Luz, Bowers heard much of this 'partisanship of the fashionables'. He recorded this incident: 'One night at a party I was approached by a bubbling lady with the question:
' "You are a Fascist, aren't you?"
' "No."
' "Then are you a Communist?" she screeched, with a look of horror.
' "Have you, by any chance, ever heard of a democrat?" I asked.
With a supercilious lifting of the eyebrows she turned away, no doubt to whisper that the American Ambassador was a "Red"!' Claude Bowers, *Mission to Spain*, pp 297, 298.

10
The
Institutions

INDIVIDUALS, FORMAL AND informal groups – those elements within Britain were pressuring, demanding, working for an open declaration of a policy of appeasement. The identification of pro-German forces, however, leads to still another area, to what might be called the institutional weight in favour of appeasement. To talk of institutions as appeasing elements admittedly runs into wide difficulties: it would be impossible to say, for example, that the Army or the Navy or the Foreign Office – especially the Foreign Office – were institutions operating in total support of an obsequious line toward Nazi Germany; but it is perfectly valid to state that individuals within these institutions were, in their official capacities, enthusiastic and very effective appeasers. Further, by mid-1937, when Neville Chamberlain moved to the Premiership, this institutional assistance was of invaluable aid in his avowed attempt to placate the dictators.

Let us begin with the appeasers of the national Press. British journalism did not, of course, speak with one voice. Critical of the Government policy were the *Daily Herald* and the *New Statesman and Nation*, the *Manchester Guardian*, and even, to some extent, the Conservative weekly, *The Spectator*; these were important units, which reached and influenced millions of Britons. But on the appeasing pro-German side was the bulk of the large-circulation papers, notably *The Times*, Lord Rothermere's *Daily Mail*, Lord Beaverbrook's *Daily Express*, Lord Astor's *Observer*; in sheer volume this group was a formidable journalistic force, well able to drown its critical opponents.

Propagandists for appeasement, then, were *The Times, Daily Mail*, and *Daily Express* – but the greatest of these was *The*

Times. Just how great was it? It was 'one of the chief glories of English journalism',[1] holding an 'unchallenged position as the best-informed and most independent journal in England . . . accepted as gospel . . . a semi-official journal'.[2] Or it could be described this way: 'The power of *The Times* will remain just as long as England continues to be ruled by the intelligent upper-middle class which has been dominant since the Reform Bill. It exactly reproduces the merits and defects of the British governing class. It is as safe as that class, as safe as the monarchy with which *The Times* has been so often compared, as safe as the British Empire, as safe as, and no safer than, the capitalist system in England.'[3] It was this daily institution, with its tradition of speaking to and for the solid middle classes of Britain, that was prostituted to the cause of appeasement, an easy – a windfall – conquest for the Nazi persuaders.

That this was a particularly unfortunate misuse of the power of the Press became apparent even – belatedly – to *The Times* itself. After World War II the editorial staff of the paper published a massive history which (like Stanley Baldwin) was sometimes almost indecently honest in its detailed account of journalistic surrender to the Nazis. These confessions from the staff-historians are an interesting addition to the story of appeasement, in that the writers tried, with as much insight as they possessed, to explore the reasons for the *Times* era of pro-Nazism, and that their explanations at least opened a pathway to the heart of the matter. There were, wrote the staff-historians, primarily two reasons for the paper's policy toward Nazi Germany. First, it was because this journal of the middle and upper classes, so 'representative of the interests and tastes of a confident and complacent governing class', became a prisoner of those classes; whereas, before World War I *The Times* 'habitually led public opinion', in the decade

---

[1] William L Shirer, *The Rise and Fall of the Third Reich*, p 287.
[2] Robert Graves and Alan Hodge, *The Long Weekend: A Social History of Great Britain, 1918–1939*, p 46.
[3] *New Statesman and Nation*, 5th January 1935.

of the 1930s 'it habitually followed it'. And this public opinion
– the middle- and upper-class opinion that *The Times* now
followed – was pacifistic and appeasing; the proof was, as
cited by the staff-writers, the 1933 by-election in the heavily
Tory district of East Fulham, in which the Conservative
candidate had been defeated for 'warmongering'. Thus,
after East Fulham, *The Times* (like the Government, the views
of which the paper 'faithfully' reflected) was haunted by the
power of 'average' opinion, the 'one authority on foreign
policy' to be respected. The second cause of the *Times'* appeasement lay in the professional personality of the editor, Geoffrey
Dawson, and his chief assistant, Robert Barrington-Ward.
Dawson, presiding over a paper which had lost its independence
and autonomy, was the dictator of the *Times'* policy; it was he
who quaked before pacifist public opinion, and he who was
certain that the Government, in moving into deliberate
appeasement, was responding to the pro-German 'trend in the
constituencies'. And it was Dawson who welded *The Times*
to the Tory Government; 'the permanent principle of his
editorship,' wrote the staff-historians, was support of the
Baldwin and Chamberlain Governments, support that 'was
the more inevitable since he was a Conservative of the Right
with a loyalty to Party', and since he was 'intuitively' convinced that the men fit to rule Britain necessarily came from
'the hereditary English governing class, the middle class
gentry and their ennobled off-spring'.

This was, on the part of the *Times'* editorial staff, very
plain-speaking, the kind of firsthand testimony that deserves
respect, if not absolute credence. The claim of the staff-writers
that the paper was driven by fear of public opinion to appeasement, with its implication that if the *Times'* former independence of judgment had prevailed there would have been no
softness on Fascism, can be dismissed out of hand. One would
doubt the reality of that former independence of *Times* policy;
how could a journal be 'representative of the interests and
tastes of a . . . governing class' and yet maintain autonomy

and critical judgment? Clearly, *Times* policy was formed and always had been formed within the framework of the ideas and interests of the British governing classes; existing between the two was a tight bond of social kinship. For this reason *The History of the Times* repeated statements of the change in the interwar period, both in *Times* policy and in the body of *Times* readers, are most useful in a corroborating way. *The Times* presents a story within the story of appeasement, is a kind of miniature model for the era, precisely because it was so very much the journal of the governing class. If the paper had changed since World War I, it was not that the editor and writers had forgotten how to guide the opinions of the solid stratum of *Times* readers – far from it – but that the attitudes of both journalists and readers had been drastically transformed. The old-fashioned aggressiveness, the 'commercial jingoism' of the early years of the century, had faded away, leaving the governing classes, as Keith Hutchison said, 'as unbelligerent in the thirties as at any time in British history'.[1] Contrary to *The History of the Times*, those classes were no longer 'confident and complacent' but, rather, struggling to patch up a decaying social and economic structure, and of that desperate effort *The Times* was inevitably a part.

The staff-historians contributed solidly to an understanding of *The Times'* years of appeasement in pointing to the responsibility of the editor, Geoffrey Dawson. We might add a few facts on Dawson's background, a story that perhaps carries an explanation of his work as an appeaser. As a young man, Dawson was one of Lord Milner's secretaries in South Africa, a part of 'Milner's Kindergarten', the band of talented and dedicated people Milner selected for training in Imperial administration. It was a lasting reciprocal relationship Milner set up with Dawson – as with others of his promising followers: as editor of the *Johannesburg Star*, a post that Milner obtained for him, Dawson did his first journalistic service in the Imperial cause; back in Britain, he joined a clique of Milnerites –

[1] Hutchison, *British Capitalism*, p 225.

including, besides Milner himself, men like Leopold Amery, Philip Kerr (Lord Lothian), Lionel Curtis, and Waldorf Astor[1] – a group which held regular meetings ('moots'), founded a journal, *The Round Table*, to propagate ideas on Imperial unity, and acted in the political world as a pressure lobby in the interests of the Imperial idea; in 1912, when Dawson was first appointed editor of *The Times*,[2] the Milnerites rejoiced at his success – and the fact that the singular prestige of that paper would buttress their views and their causes.

Milner put a permanent stamp on his young men, who remained faithful after his death in 1925, created his myth (the *Religio Milneriana*) – and, it would seem, repeated within their own career-circumstances versions of his ideas and attitudes. In the words of Milner's biographer, the master had, for one thing, 'affected' his followers with 'his dislike of the ordinary methods of English political life': 'His experiences in South Africa served to convince him that the English system of government was inefficient and worthless. . . . He despised English politics. . . . He believed that the parliamentary system, based upon the necessities of Party and the whims of a "rotten public opinion", was totally unfitted for the rule of a great Empire.' And Milner's ideas of British post-1918 policies in Europe, especially towards Germany and Bolshevik Russia (ideas which we have seen),[3] bear unmistakable similarity to the proposals and programmes for appeasement in the 1930s – fervently presented by ex-Milnerites like Geoffrey Dawson.

Thus, we concentrate on editor Dawson, enlisting *The Times* in a prolonged campaign for friendship and understanding with the efficient dictatorship of Nazi Germany. According to *The History of the Times*, Dawson and his assistant, Barrington-

---

[1] Amery was beginning his parliamentary career at the time; Kerr and Curtis – who subsequently was elected a Fellow of All Souls – founded *The Round Table*; Waldorf (Lord) Astor was proprietor of *The Observer*. Gollin, *Proconsul*, 166 ff.

[2] Dawson was editor from 1912 to 1919, when his differences with *Times* owner Lord Northcliffe forced him out. At Northcliffe's death in 1922 Dawson was reappointed and remained editor until 1941.

[3] See the Introduction.

Ward, both Commonwealth men and informed only in the area of Commonwealth relations, 'relied for their knowledge of the Continent less upon . . . correspondents than upon certain personal sources, and thus the foreign policy pursued by *The Times* after the crucial year of 1936 became increasingly indebted [to] the Editor's ministerial friends, Baldwin, Chamberlain and Halifax'. That assertion might be revised: extreme Conservative that he was, Dawson was close to governments of the Right but, still, his ministerial friends were politicians, bound to some extent by the 'necessities of Party and the whims of a "rotten public opinion" '; perhaps Dawson felt Baldwin, Chamberlain and Halifax were indebted to *him* and *The Times* for injecting into their efforts the stiffening element of detached Milner-like statesmanship. At any rate, to explain the case for Germany, and for a British understanding with Germany, became Dawson's special objective (this, a contemporary observed, 'without any knowledge of European history, still less of German history, without knowing one word of the language or having the slightest insight into the German mind').[1] Dawson started with the fact that Germany had been badly mistreated by the Versailles peacemakers and contemptibly handled by a France bent on revenge and 'encirclement'; thus, in the name of international morality, the British should grant German demands for justice, equality, even of armaments, and for 'living room'. Hitler was a man of peace, and his Nazi movement was a factor for order and stability – witness the 1934 purge of Captain Ernst Roehm and his followers in the SA (which eliminated in one swift bloodbath the Leftwing rank and file of the Nazis, as well as selected, irritating opponents of the new Fuehrer). 'Whatever one may think of his methods,' ran a Dawson editorial, Hitler 'is genuinely trying to transform revolutionary fervour into moderate and constructive effort and to impose a high standard of public service on National-Socialist officials.' German Fascism, anyhow, was a clean variety of revolution: 'Nazism,

[1] Rowse, *All Souls*, p 6.

as a form of government, is . . . a domestic preference and has no mission (as Bolshevism has) to export its system to other countries.' And Nazi Germany was, above all – in the stock phrase, used over and over again – the 'bulwark of European discipline against Bolshevism'.[1]

From the mid-1930s to the late 1930s Dawson and *The Times* preached editorially 'the advantages of coming to terms with Germany before Germany became exasperated', that is, of giving the Germans what they wanted before they took it. The paper gave prominent play to communications from like-minded notables: 'Letters to the Editor' from Lord Lothian or Lord Londonderry or Sir Arnold Wilson, all of them applauding the editorial line of *The Times*, all of them urging 'justice' for Nazi Germany and insisting upon the sincerity of Hitler's pledges of peace. The interesting thing is that Geoffrey Dawson had different information, that he was regularly informed of the aggressive truth of Nazi intentions by *The Times*' Berlin correspondent, Norman Ebbutt – who was detested by the Nazis for the blunt honesty of his views. But Dawson deliberately suppressed Ebbutt's reports, 'doctored his dispatches', and finally, intimidated by Nazi fulminations against Ebbutt, withdrew him from Berlin.[2] The essential point was, Dawson explained privately, to ingratiate the touchy Germans with all possible means, 'to keep out of the paper anything that might hurt their susceptibilities'.

The highest accomplishment of Dawson toward his goal of ingratiation of the Nazis came in a lead article of *The Times* on 7th September 1938. The moment was one of looming crisis, when the West was about to be involved – to the brink of war – with Hitler's determination to grab the Sudetenland from the Republic of Czechoslovakia.[3] In that early September issue of *The Times* – the semi-official journal of Britain, the

[1] *The Times*, 6th July 1936, 28th October 1937, for the editorial argument for Germany's special interests in Eastern Europe, and against those who would ring Germany with 'hostile alliances'; *ibid*, 2nd July 1934, 6th July 1936, 1st January 1937.
[2] Shirer, *Third Reich*, pp 287–288; Rowse, *All Souls*, pp 10–11.
[3] *See Chap* 12, pp 207–216.

paper with international prestige and authority – the Editor
made an astonishing suggestion; in effect, he offered to the
Nazis a British acquiescence to the dismemberment of Czechoslovakia and the incorporation within the Third Reich of the
Sudetenland – and he did this before Hitler had even demanded
it! It was an embarrassing blunder; Dawson's too-eager
appeasement disconcerted the British Government, anticipated
Chamberlain's policy, and threatened the negotiations. Perhaps
in their postwar explanations the staff-historians of *The Times*
were still feeling the awkwardness of the incident: 'We felt
confident,' they wrote, 'that Hitler was going to say something
pretty violent about the Sudetens on the last day of the Nurem-
berg Conference [12th September] . . . we quietly and tentatively put forward the suggestion [to separate the Sudeten
from Czechoslovakia] before he did . . . we considered it best
to say so *before* Hitler spoke rather than after he had demanded
that there should be a revision of the frontier.'

It was, indeed, an incredible era, with the great, grey *Times* of
London politely offering to help the Nazi barbarian in his
subjugation of Europe. It was so incredible that even Geoffrey
Dawson blocked, in the aftermath, on some of its details. A L
Rowse told of two conversations which he had with Dawson,
the one during the height of appeasement, the second in 1939,
after the start of the war. In the first discussion, replying to
Rowse's argument that Nazi Germany, with all its formidable
might, would sooner or later turn upon Britain, Dawson had
said, 'if the Germans are so powerful as you say, *oughtn't we
to go in with them?*' When the men talked again, with Britain
facing the German juggernaut, Rowse reminded Dawson
(not without malice) that he had so recently wanted to throw
in with the Nazis. He got an answer that, Rowse reported,
'flabbergasted' him: 'Oh no,' Dawson replied, 'I can never
have said that.'[1]

The Times was an important voice for appeasement because
it occupied a unique position, and because it had such enor-

mous prestige. Measured against those qualifications, *The Observer* is a lesser example of the appeasing Press – although there are special features about its story in the 1930s that make it an even more intriguing case study. In its own way *The Observer* was as respected as *The Times*; it was the journal for the literate and urbane, for patrons of the theatre and the arts – or for readers as involved in the cricket score at Eton as in the latest news from abroad. We focus, however, upon one page of its weekly edition, upon the three- or four-column spread filled with the urgent thoughts of the editor, J L Garvin. Garvin conducted a one-man show as editor of *The Observer* – a post he had held from 1908 – almost every week contributing, under his own name, an impassioned plea for his personal causes in politics and foreign affairs. And his chief personal cause from 1936 to early 1939 was the conclusion of a Pact with Germany, 'a lasting settlement and friendship with Germany'.

The ideas that Garvin developed almost weekly – in a prose style that was both elaborate and didactic – were offered with evident honesty and deep concern. What, he asked his readers, were the most important matters in all the world? He answered: British interests, position, and welfare. And what was the main threat to Britain? Obviously, Communism, the 'one challenge of British systems and liberties' – Communism, with its 'seditious propaganda', its promise of world revolution that would be 'fatal to liberty for ever'. As Garvin saw it, Britain's course would be hard and dangerous: to counter the perils of the age, the nation had to maintain its internal strength, exploit the advantages – economic or financial – that it possessed, and join in alliance with other powers equally determined to be strong and equally aware of the Communist enemy.

In each crisis of the European *status quo* Garvin found fresh evidence of the Communist conspiracy – just as he saw ever more clearly Britain's necessary path. No journalist was as forthright and blunt, or even perhaps as consistent; none was as thorough in explaining his successive reactions. His readers were never in doubt, for example, about his feelings during the Italian campaign against Ethiopia. 'Despite sanctions,' he exulted in early 1936, 'the Italians are sweeping into the heart of Abyssinia proper'; it was 'a wonderful tale', a 'staggering drama', this conquest which the Italians had conducted with 'consummate political direction and military leadership'. When Garvin wrote in such terms, when he extolled Mussolini as 'a man who is among the most determined and inspiring leaders in modern history', it was not primarily that he had a particular regard for Italians and their Duce. Rather, devout nationalist that he was, Garvin was convinced that Britain needed the Italians as friends and allies and that safety for the British lay in recognising Mussolini's ambitions in Africa – as the Hoare-Laval Pact had done. The contrary policy of cooperating with the League of Nations made Garvin frantic – with fear for Britain. The League was 'an inadequate ark', boycotted as it was by two major European nations; it was a 'lunacy of the Left', which, on pretext of resisting the aggressor, was pulling Britain into a coalition against Fascism and risking the horror of a 'general war'.

The point is that Garvin said more plainly than anyone else in the public eye what, one would guess, many Conservatives were thinking. His position was rigidly defined by mid-1936, after the official announcement of the Franco-Soviet Pact and after the outbreak of the Spanish Civil War, two events that were to him major moves by Communist conspirators. The plot of the Left – in which Britain was involved through her ties with France – was to check and encircle Germany, dynamic, expansive, anti-Communist Germany; this was a policy (for Britain) of certain disaster. 'Are we to identify ourselves with Russia against the Reich?' asked Garvin. 'Are we to throw ourselves across Hitler's path? It is not in the interest of this country nor in any interest of civilisation that Britain and Germany should destroy each other to establish Bolshevist supremacy over Europe and

Asia.' Rather than war, there had to be understanding and alliance between Britons and Germans – understanding that could be extended, too, to the allies of the Germans, the Italians and Japanese, who were 'uniting to resist the spread of Bolshevik revolution and drive Russian influence out of the East'. Note, however, that Garvin did not suggest that Britain participate in any way in a holy war against Communism; 'general war' of any kind was the thing above all to be avoided, for 'war and the economic sequel of war' would 'throw to the ground the whole fabric of our welfare'. If Hitler, then, had his own plans for the East of Europe, that was 'no affair of ours'. The British affair was an agreement that would approve Germany's just aims and ambitions: 'We are asked not to join in tying Germany's hand in the East; not to bind ourselves against her in that quarter; and not to block her there and everywhere.'

Garvin watched with enthusiasm as the Germans made their initial moves in Central Europe. The necessary thing, he knew – or was told[1] – was to break the French security system, what Garvin described as 'the whole system of Soviet pacts between Moscow, Paris and Prague, which seeks to hold Germany in a vice'; Hitler needed room for readjustment in the area, room for the 'creation of a united "Middle Europe" under German headship'. Garvin applauded as the Germans incorporated Austria – a 'wholly Germanic land', in which, in any case, a 'large majority' wanted union with the Fatherland – and positively crowed when the fate of Czechoslovakia (the 'artificial State', the 'abcess in the body of Europe') was settled to Hitler's satisfaction. In the latter event the editorials of *The Observer* grew a trifle more shrill than usual, due to the tension of the affair, and the machinations of those who would commit Britain to the 'French Left and the Kremlin, and guarantee Czech domination of Bohemia'. When the Munich agreement ended the Czechoslovakian crisis (largely

[1] Garvin was a regular at Cliveden (as Tom Jones tells us) where he met and talked with Ribbentrop. See Jones, *Diary*, p xxxvi; also the reference to Ribbentrop in *The Observer*, 1st November 1936.

because of the 'healing statesmanship' of Hitler) Garvin was
so pleased – or relieved – that he indulged in what was for him
a rare comment on the human aspects of the situation: Hitler's
consent to an 'orderly' ten-day occupation of the German-
speaking sections of Czechoslovakia meant that 'many
humanities, decencies, and conveniences [were] thus preserved
instead of savage conquest and panic flight – fire and sword
and *sauve qui peut*'.

One has doubts, perhaps, that this was taken seriously – not
so much the message, but Garvin himself.[1] Week after week
he wrote at white heat, piling up thousands of words – the
same words on the same subject, over and over warning of
Britain's peril if she procrastinated before Hitler's expansive
needs, if she hung on to alliance with the French whose
policies would 'divert German force from the Soviet frontiers
to the west'. Yet it is not difficult to imagine that Garvin had
a faithful band of readers who considered him a sound fellow,
a journalist without cant and verbal trickery, a level-headed,
plain-speaking patriot. For openness was Garvin's special
quality, and nationalism the key to his foreign views. These
things were consistent even in his great inconsistency – his
break with appeasement. When the Nazis overran the rump
of Czechoslovakia in March of 1939, Garvin turned as violently
against Hitler as he had been for him: the Fuehrer, who had
once been the restorer of Germany, became the 'tyrant' who
had not only 'trampled a free people', but had in direct
challenge to Britain made a 'Bid for the World'.

The British response filled Garvin with pride: the 'Gold
Pledge to support Poland against attack' was 'as momentous an
engagement as ever was proposed by a British Government or
solemnly sanctioned by the Mother of Parliaments', and by
their refusal to surrender to further threats from Germany
the British had 'whatever happens, escaped for ever the
smirch and ruin of that shame, folly, and disaster'. Garvin

[1] See Malcolm Muggeridge, *The Sun Never Sets: The Story of England in the
Nineteen Thirties*, p 12, for the comment that Garvin continued through the
decade, 'not appreciably less noisy and incoherent' than before.

even became – and this was irrefutable proof of the power of his patriotism – a journalistic leader for alliance with Russia against the German evil; as the Government dragged its feet in negotiations with Moscow, Garvin remarked sternly that 'hedging influences', 'reluctance and prejudices', were 'out of date'. Aware of the reversal of his field, Garvin met the issue as truthfully as he could. *The Observer*, he wrote, had admittedly supported appeasement, but it had also called for rearmament and increased vigilance; thus, its aims had never been *'incompatible'* – that is, both had been part of Garvin's view of what was best for Britain.

Perhaps, we repeat, Garvin did have a following of readers and admirers, although that is conjecture. What is sure is that this voice of *The Observer* was an infrequent type – an appeaser who explained carefully and publicly his reasons for appeasement, and his reasons for abandoning it when, in his own terms, it had been proven an error.

From the appeasers of selected sections of the national Press let us turn to a set of actors even more basic to the plot, to groups for appeasement within the British world of business. To this point, we have had little direct confrontation of the subject of the relations of the business community with Fascist nations and, in particular, with Nazi Germany, although it had been suggested repeatedly that this is a crucial area of exploration. It is, too, a murky area; the shadows lie not so much over the facts of broad economic developments – which have been opened by other investigators – but over the matters that are most of all intriguing – the propelling ideas of the directors of British finance and industry in their contacts with Nazism.

Our institutional focus on the subject is – together – Montagu Norman and the Bank of England. The Bank of England was, of course, the banker's bank, the centre of the international money market that was London, with special powers to pass on all foreign loans emanating from the city market; it was, too, the private yet semi-official financial organ which controlled the credit system and thus the financial policy of Britain, standing to the Treasury like 'Tweedledum to Tweedledee', as its governor, Montagu Norman, is reported to have said.[1] And Montagu Norman presided over this great institution, a uniquely powerful man, with responsibilities and opportunities that had built his reputation as 'the currency dictator in Europe'.[2]

First, however, a digression is in order: the necessary preface to Norman's and the Bank's activities in the 1930s is a (long-delayed) survey of the world of British business in the interwar period. The following summary will serve – not as a technical economic analysis, but as a generalised statement of outstanding economic developments in Britain in the 1920s and 1930s.

After World War I, British capitalism – it has been said before – quaked under multiple unprecedented pressures. The awful truth had dawned: the war had proved an 'unmitigated disaster' to private enterprise. The ubiquitous appearance of governmental regulation was only the first of the brutal truths. Largely because of inadequate tax policies during the war – the war that had been costly beyond all expectations – Britain was left, in the aftermath, with a national debt of billions of pounds, a load of taxation that 'greatly depleted the fund of available capital', that 'permanently hindered the effective functioning of private enterprise'.[3] Further, with even more seriously damaging effects on an economy geared to foreign commerce, the war had disrupted international trade and credit – a wholly unexpected calamity: in 1914 British capitalists had warmed to the fact of war with the thought of padding their trade supremacy, eliminating the German rival and capturing German export markets and investment opportunities; the blasting of such hopes brought bitter disappointment. In explanation, the British economy was incapable of supplying both the needs of the national war machine and

[1] John Hargrave, *Montagu Norman*, p. 118
[2] *The Wall Street Journal*, 11th March 1927.
[3] *The Economist*, 20th November 1937; Hutchison, *British Capitalism*, p 133.

the demands of overseas markets and, under increasing governmental supervision as the war dragged on, the former was decidedly the priority area; coveted overseas markets, then, went to the supplier that could fill their needs – mainly to the United States. In a similar way, the British were over-taken as the chief creditor nation of the world, and by the 1920s were at a growing disadvantage in lending and invest-ment abroad before the top contender-nations, the United States and France.[1]

The net result of the war, and the reality of the economic situation of the 1920s, was the permanent loss of British commercial supremacy, and a British capitalism faced with these hard facts of economic life: the volume of exports and the British share of the world's total falling steadily; the volume of imports, into a nation incapable of self-sufficiency, just as steadily rising – and promising the day of reckoning for such an imbalance of trade; the decline in the volume of foreign investments, those 'invisible exports' that had for more than half a century buttressed the British economy; and, to cap it, industries that were cramped by their own backwardness and by 'technological and managerial' inefficiency.[2]

The Depression compounded the difficulties of business classes already economically and psychologically threatened. In the crises of the early 1930s international credit collapsed, international markets sank into inactivity – and ahead the prospects were even more bleak. British business adjusted to protective tariffs, sought preferential treatment from Common-wealth nations (which were infuriatingly inclined to consider first their own commercial advantage), negotiated bilateral trade agreements on the Continent, and accepted more and more governmental assistance in a joint public-private effort to raise exports and halt the rapid progress of the unfavourable balance of trade. And in this disintegrating economic situation

[1] John H Richardson, *British Economic Foreign Policy*, p 61.
[2] Alfred E Kahn, *Great Britain in the World Economy*, pp 134–140; Hutchison, *British Capitalism*, pp 132–134; *The Economist*, 20th November 1937; R Palme Dutt, *Britain's Crisis of Empire*, pp 42–50.

emerged the characteristics we have noted previously: the British businessman remarkably lacking in belligerency, and anxiously bent on the quest for peace, at any price – and this in an economic world that still operated on the principles of cut-throat competition. It was a dramatic change in the British lion. Compare, for example, the reasonableness of Neville Chamberlain, that prime product of capitalist industry, with his father, Joseph Chamberlain, who one generation before had joyfully plunged into pugnacious Imperialism: Neville Chamberlain was a young businessman when Britain had staked out the African continent as her own and thwarted the ambitions of the German challenger; yet in the 1930s he 'would not hesitate for a moment' in handing Tanganyika to the Germans, if Britain could thereby 'purchase peace and a lasting settlement'.[1]

Among the efforts of British business to hold its own in the cold commercial atmosphere of the 1930s the one of relevancy here is the continued search for opportunities for foreign investment – to rebuild the invisible export that was, as the respected voice of *The Economist* put it, still the 'nation's greatest single industry', a 'vast national asset'. Financiers could and did invest within the Commonwealth area, but the popular spot was Germany, a Germany engaged in fast industrial recovery after defeat in the war. With the stabilisation of German credit in 1924, Germany offered tempting investment possibilities, dangling the promise of high interest rates and higher profit rates before what immediately became a hotly competitive field.[2] The greater share of the German capital market was taken by Americans, but British financiers moved in too, with long-term loans and even more profitable short-term loans.[3] 'From 1924 onwards,' one economist explained, 'the financial authorities and the financial community of Great Britain plunged themselves wholeheartedly into an effort to assist Germany financially. . . . International banking

[1] Feiling, *Neville Chamberlain*, p 300.
[2] James W Angell, *The Recovery of Germany*, p 190.
[3] Allen Thomas Bonnell, *German Control over International Economic Relations*, p 15.

houses in London and other financial centres were engaged in reckless competition in the issue of loans for German States, municipalities, industrial undertakings.'[1] It was the beginning of a long relationship, which persisted despite the risks involved with Nazi autarchy – risks with Dr Schacht's 'State-controlled economy', or with the Four-Year Planning of General Goering, or with Germans who would simply announce, with bland audacity, their intention of defaulting on their debts.[2] British capital, then, was not only available, but eagerly available, put at the disposal of the Nazi state, of what was – and the fact was unmistakable after 1934 – the planned rearmament of a war economy.

The summary of economic affairs comes here to a crucial – if speculative – point. How can this interest in German redevelopment in British business circles be assessed? Was it merely, as the editor of the *Yorkshire Post* saw it, that 'big business thought there would be a better chance of business prospering if good relations with Hitler were maintained'?[3] Was the operating factor the sound business sense that profits were profits no matter what their source – and especially so when depressed business conditions prevailed? Certainly, this would be understandable: self-interest and national interest made absolutely necessary the balancing of trade, which might well have been achieved by increased earnings from capital investment abroad; in a matter so important to both the individual and the national welfare, British financiers would hardly examine the character of their customers. But the German relationship perhaps involved more than a commercial transaction – entered, rather, into the category of political economy. If the Germans were rearming, an obvious assumption might have been that those armaments would be somewhere put to use. Perhaps it occurred to British businessmen

[1] Einzig, *Appeasement*, pp 47–48.
[2] See an account by a German economist, W F Bruck, *Social and Economic History of Germany from Wilhelm II to Hitler*, pp 216, 255–256.
[3] Arthur Mann, quoted in Tom Driberg, *Beaverbrook: A Study in Power and Frustration*, p 148.

to ask themselves where the German warhead would be aimed? Perhaps, actually, they had an answer ready at hand. In 1936 the editor of *The Week* (whose sources were both anonymous and phenomenally well informed)[1] printed a story of financial manipulations going on in London. Bankers with 'enormous volumes of frozen credits in Germany', said *The Week*, were putting out rumours of a big loan to be made to Germany by the City, the purpose of the tales being to revive confidence in German credit and unload the bonds which the bankers already held; yet the same bankers, in spite of their sore experiences, were still giving short-term commercial credits to Germany, 'all of them going into armaments'. The Bank of England, *The Week* claimed, could by its simple fiat stop these questionable transactions, but the smaller bankers kept them going by playing a game called 'making Monty's flesh creep – that is, by activating 'Mr Montagu Norman's well-known phobia about Bolshevism'. This was an uncorroborated story, but its implications may be put into the record. The support of Germany by British financiers was, besides a hopeful way to quick investment profits, a contribution to the right side in European politics. A prosperous Germany meant a non-Communist Germany; even more, a prosperous, militarised Germany meant – the familiar refrain, a Germany that was the 'one effective barrier against the domination of Europe by Russia', the 'bulwark of European discipline against Bolshevism'. Speculation, to be sure, but it fits: the cry of Conservative politicians against British commitments in Central and Eastern Europe and for a 'free hand' for Germany in the East reflected the businessman's hope that Germany's profitable militarism would find a perfect outlet in the destruction of European capitalism's Public Enemy Number 1 – the Soviet Union.

By way of reference, the Bank of England and Montagu Norman have entered our story – the two together forming an institution, and together giving institutional assistance to

[1] See Claud Cockburn, *A Discord of Trumpets*, pp 226–229, 233–234.

the reality, as well as to the climate, of appeasement. Norman, who had been Governor of the Bank since 1920, longer by far than any predecessor, was not a man for personal publicity; he cultivated, in fact, and apparently delighted in his reputation as a figure of mystery and reserve. The screen about him and his tenure at the Bank is a misfortune; the knowledge we have of his affairs or his views is circumstantial – the bare facts of the policies of the Bank – or based upon the second-hand reports of critical (Leftist) observers, or an off-hand revelation from a contemporary, like that of Hjalmar Schacht, Hitler's economic 'wizard', who maintained from the early 1920s such close relations with Norman that the Governor was godfather to a Schacht offspring.[1] Still, imperfect as they are, bits of evidence of these kinds suggest something of this powerful man and of the supremely powerful institution he headed.

There is one biography of Montagu Norman, written in the early 1940s by John Hargrave. The book is, clearly, a part of a mission of exposure – of Norman and of the banking power which, Hargrave felt, had duped and exploited the masses of people with the magic of financial hocus-pocus, with the mysterious, and thus intimidating, manipulation of the symbols of high finance. According to Hargrave, Montagu Norman lived totally with such symbol manipulation: it was not enough that he controlled the economy of Britain, with the power of the Bank of England to issue or withdraw the credit-facilities for the industry of the nation; Norman's great dream, his life goal, was the creation of a superbank system, a towering structure of intertwined central banks which would exercise the same control over the credit and finance of all of Europe. Of this banker's empire that Norman envisioned, German financial agencies were, most naturally, to be a part (from Dr Schacht we have the story of his contacts with Norman from 1924, when he obtained a loan from the Bank of England for the capitalisation of a Central Bank of the Rhine). And when the Nazis eliminated the 'chaotic nonsense' of the

---

[1] Hjalmar Schacht, *Confessions of 'The Old Wizard', Autobiography*, p 185.

Weimar Republic and 'stabilised' the German nation in 1933,
Governor Norman and the Bank of England were even more
interested in Germany as a partner. Montagu Norman's
initial reaction to the Nazi regime developed – in Hargrave's
version – into this positive action:

> Early in 1934 a select group of City financiers gathered in
> Norman's room behind the Windowless Walls [of the Bank of
> England]. Those present included Sir Alan Anderson, partner
> in Anderson, Green & Co.; Lord (then Sir Josiah) Stamp, Bank
> of England Director, and Chairman of the LMS Railway;
> the Hon Alexander Shaw, Chairman of the P & O Steamship
> Lines; Charles Hambro, banker; and P C Tiarks, head of
> J Henry Schroder & Co.[1]
> Governor Norman spoke of the political situation in Europe.
> A new power had established itself, a great 'stabilising' force,
> namely: Nazi Germany. The Hitler regime was the only real
> bulwark against Soviet Russia and the spread of Communism.
> 'Hitlerism' was no temporary nightmare, but a system of Planned
> Economy with a great future before it. Norman advised his
> co-workers to include Hitler in their plans for financing Europe.
> There was no opposition.
> In May 1934, a private conference took place between Dr
> Schacht [German Minister of Economic Affairs and Governor
> of the Reichsbank in 1934] and Governor Norman. Then came
> the 'secret conclave' at Badenweiler, in the Black Forest, on
> 11th June, when Norman again met Dr Schacht for an 'un-
> official discussion'. They were both on their way to a meeting
> of the [Bank of International Settlements] at Basle. Nazi Ger-
> many needed a big loan. Early in October, the two met once
> more at the same Black Forest rendezvous, and again the secret
> negotiations for the support of Hitlerism were discussed and
> carried a stage further.

The last point of Hargrave's passage is the arresting allegation.
'It is a fact', wrote Franz von Papen, 'that after the Hitler
Government had been formed, Dr Schacht collected a cam-

---

[1] Sir Alan Anderson was Conservative MP for the City of London, as well as a
director of the Bank of England. (Lord) Stamp and F C Tiarks (and the J Henry
Schroder Bank) affiliated with the Anglo-German Fellowship. See Haxey, *Tory MP*,
pp 56, 230–232.

paign chest with subscriptions from various industrial and commercial firms.'[1] Was Montagu Norman on Schacht's list as a possible foreign contributor to the Nazi regime, or at least a willing creditor? British economist Paul Einzig offered in his own context – the economic details of appeasement of Nazism – a story that bears directly on the subject. Montagu Norman used the power of the Bank of England from the 1920s, Einzig explained, to sustain unsound financial deals with Germany: 'It was because of the lack of discrimination on the part of the banks in accepting German bills irrespective of whether they represented genuine trade transactions, and because of the Bank of England's unwillingness to discourage the practice and thereby to cause inconvenience to Germany, that the London banking community was caught in 1931 with unsecured credits amounting to over £40 million.'[2] Then the Nazis came to power, and 'it was widely felt in British political and financial circles that such a useful bulwark against Communism as Hitler deserved sympathy and support'. The first gesture of sympathy and support, Einzig found, was made in 1934, when the Bank of England saved Nazi Germany from British creditors: spending 'millions on public works and rearmament', the Germans decided to default on their commercial debts, and duly announced through the Reichsbank the suspension of debt payments. With relations thus strained between Germany and British creditors, Governor Norman brought the resources of the Bank of England to the German rescue and 'granted a credit to the Reichsbank in order to tide over the difficulties'. 'It would have been very easy at that stage', wrote Einzig, 'to strangle financially the Nazi regime and to compel Germany to revert to a more moderate foreign policy . . . the Bank of England's action in coming to the rescue of the Reichsbank and of the Hitler regime was certainly uncalled for.'

There is still another comment on Governor Norman's early

[1] Franz von Papen, *Memoirs*, Brian Connell, tran. p 233.
[2] Einzig, *Appeasement*, pp 53–54.

reaction to Nazi Germany. Leaked reports of the special generosity shown by the Bank to German debtors brought the Labour opposition bolt upright into critical posture. In the *Daily Herald* the financial editor wrote: 'In these circumstances, Mr Montagu Norman's financial support of the Nazi regime raises questions of the utmost political importance, particularly as this is the first time on record that the Bank of England has ever used its influence in this way to support any foreign bonds or has actually advised a purchase.'

In 1939 there occurred a proper climax to the story of the pro-Nazi activities of Montagu Norman and the Bank of England, and a made-to-order episode it is for a glance at financial appeasement. The main details of the story are to be found in the sterling source of the *Parliamentary Debates*, where Mr Norman's name, along with that of the Bank of England and the Bank of International Settlements, appeared with interesting frequency for more than two months. (The Bank of International Settlements was a prototype of Norman's dream of a superbank, although it was set up only as a clearing house for international – and reparations – payments; Governor Norman and Sir Otto Niemeyer, a director of the Bank of England, sat on its board of directors, among fellow bankers or industrialists from Germany or France or the United States or Italy, all of them there as private individuals and not as official representatives of their various governments.) The situation that aroused the Commons to concern for the affairs of this usually undisturbed financial structure was this: in March of 1939, immediately after the Nazis – in violation of their pledge at Munich – had marched into Czechoslovakia and claimed the whole of that nation as a conquest of the Third Reich, the Bank of International Settlements received a request from the management of the National Bank of Czechoslovakia that Czech gold on deposit with the BIS be turned over to the German Government; the request came from Czechs, yet it was clearly, obviously, absolutely certain that they were acting under duress, under pressure from their new

German masters. Nevertheless, the BIS promptly agreed to comply and ordered the Bank of England, which held the Czech gold, to transfer the deposits – some £6 million – to Germany. It was a simple story of cold finance – but it became complicated when the British Press and the members of the Commons was told of it.

The story was first brought to the House by David Lloyd George, and the aging crusader against Vested Privilege was jumping with old-fashioned Liberal indignation. Lloyd George had heard that the transfer of the Czech gold had already been made, or at least arranged for, and that officials of the Treasury department – who were meeting then with representatives of the Reichsbank – were in on the deal. What particularly incensed him, Lloyd George said, was that governmental concurrence in the transfer would appear to be *de facto* recognition of the German subjugation of Czechoslovakia, the British stamp of approval given to this atrocious act of the German 'brigands'; and it was the more intolerable because after the German occupation of Prague on 15th March, the Chamberlain Government had seemed to be reconsidering its appeasing ways, had even moved swiftly to block certain official Czech assets held in Britain. (The Restrictions on Banking Accounts Act.) The Liberal Lloyd George opened the matter; it was then picked up by a roster of outraged MPs, passed from Conservatives – Boothby, Macmillan or Churchill – to Clement Attlee and the Labour back-benches. What, demanded these critics, was going on? Why should the British Government and the Bank of England obey the orders of the German thieves and 'hand over the property of the Czech people, the savings of twenty years'? What, in any case, was the authority here of the Bank of International Settlements, and what was the relationship of Mr Montagu Norman – both to that bank and to his own Government?

The Government's response to these questions from the House shifted from flat denial to tortuous evasion to legalistic hair-splitting. Prime Minister Chamberlain dismissed Lloyd

George's initial charges with the remark that the whole thing was a 'mare's nest', but this, he admitted next day, was because he had been misinformed. The case for the Government was handed to its legal genius, the man who was supposed to be informed, Sir John Simon – at this point in his versatile ministerial career, Chancellor of the Exchequer. Simon was in top form in countering the sharp questions that rose repeatedly in May and June of 1939. He was, he said, terribly anxious to prevent the transfer of the Czech gold but, unfortunately, he could not do so. It was, in the first place, a legal matter; as he understood the statutes involved, it would seem certain that the BIS and the Bank of England could not refuse to comply with the orders of a depositor. Further, how could the Members expect the Treasury or the Government to have influence in the affair? As Chancellor of the Exchequer Simon had no authority with the BIS, and no responsibility for its actions; the Bank had been deliberately created in 1930 as an autonomous financial organisation, and its directors, sent from private businesses in each country – to conduct business, not politics – were specifically to be independent of their Governments. And then, as the Members of the House well knew, the Treasury could not interfere with decisions made by the Governor and directors of the Bank of England; the Government could not prevent the Bank from transferring the Czech gold because the Bank was not a governmental agency and because Governor Norman was not required to consult the Government about such decisions – witness the fact that neither the BIS nor the Bank of England had informed the British Government about the transaction from the initial order to the agreement to turn over the gold.

Simon stuck to the few facts of his explanation as his critics scored both the immorality of thus rewarding the Nazi conqueror and the practical stupidity of helping to fill the German war coffers with stolen gold. Members of Parliament could only fume helplessly about Simon's 'miserable legal quibbles', or turn in their frustration on the absentee culprit Montagu

Norman. To Labour MPs, the information that Governor Norman sat on the Board of the BIS as the private representative of the Bank of England, without responsibility to the Government, was the best argument they had heard for the nationalisation of the Bank and for making Norman 'the servant of the British people'; still, said the Labourites, they doubted that the Treasury was as remote from the Bank as Simon protested – in the past, when they criticised the independence of the Bank, they were told that it was, actually, 'an agent of the Government'. For their part, Lloyd George and Conservative Members knew the real position of 'the Threadneedle Street department of national financial affairs'. Lloyd George observed that in his experience the bank was not a private institution, but always maintained close contact with the Government, especially on matters that touched upon foreign policy. Robert Boothby explained that, in the relationship between the Governor of the Bank and the Chancellor of the Exchequer, the 'Governor tenders technical advice and the Chancellor decides on policy and between them they must make the thing work'. How then, asked the House critics, could the Czech gold have gone to Germany without the Government's knowledge?

But in the end the Commons was left with the facts that interest us here. Montagu Norman, Governor of the Bank of England and director of the Bank of International Settlements, had made the decision to turn over to Germany the deposits held for the National Bank of Czechoslovakia, and the British Government had accepted his decision, although under attack in the House of Commons, Government ministers were relieved to let the Governor have the sole responsibility. As one Member angrily concluded, 'the difficulty arose from the fact that the Governor of the Bank of England want[ed] Germany to get this money'. And another MP summarised the episode with this statement – properly an expression of total disgust – 'Really, this is the most squalid form of appeasement.'

PART FOUR

'THE GOVERNMENT . . . IS SET FOR THE APPEASEMENT OF THE WORLD'

Neville Chamberlain:
Second Son

NEVILLE CHAMBERLAIN SUCCEEDED Baldwin as Prime Minister in May of 1937. There is a clear record, in his letters and comments on the transition, that he considered it none too soon. Chamberlain was an energetic administrator, impatient of governmental drift, and harsh in his judgment of fumbling colleagues of the National Government. Winston Churchill called him the 'packhorse' of the Cabinet, and Chamberlain's own self-estimate echoed the description: 'I am more and more carrying this Government on my back,' he would complain, or again, 'by constant prodding I have got things moving at last'. He loyally supported Baldwin as leader and friend, but his private views of the Prime Minister revealed both contempt and frustration. Baldwin, he would peevishly observe, 'wavers backwards and forwards', he 'dallies', he will not 'apply his mind to problems'; a discussion of policy with Baldwin, he once noted, was almost impossible, for 'every time one attempts to begin a conversation on such lines one is baffled by a break-off, and a remark about the beauty of the scenery'. There could be no doubt, then, that he, Chamberlain, would improve on Stanley Baldwin: after the disaster of the Hoare-Laval deal on Ethiopia, in which, as Chamberlain admitted, British prestige abroad had 'tumbled to pieces like a house of cards', he wrote, 'if I had been Premier, the discredit would have fallen on me instead of on SB. That is true, if the same things had happened. But I affirm, with some confidence, that they would not have happened.'

Few writers have been tempted to do a serious study of Neville Chamberlain. He is an austere and unattractive subject: the accomplishments of which he was inordinately proud seem inconsequential, and the failures of his life – and failure dogged him – seem the predictable outcome of the goals of a narrow self-deluded man. True, a biographer has found undeserved misfortune, and thus a kind of tragedy, in Chamberlain's early family life, in his position as second son of a famous father: 'Here is a man over whom deep and seemingly obliterating shadows have lain. At the outset of his career he was arbitrarily condemned to obscurity.'[1] The reference is to Joseph Chamberlain's plans for his two sons – half-brothers actually, Austen older by six years than Neville. Brilliant, fluent, politically involved, Austen was chosen by his father as the Chamberlain successor in national affairs and given proper preparation at Cambridge, as well as apprenticeship in political campaigns, foreign tours, and intercourse with the great of Europe. Neville, on the other hand, 'pale, quiet and shy', lacking both aptitude and interest in politics, was sent from Rugby to Mason College, Birmingham, there 'to learn something of science, metallurgy, and engineering'.[2] Perhaps his father *was* an 'obliterating shadow' over Neville Chamberlain. There is much about Neville to support the theory that he withdrew early from what he felt to be an impossible competition with his father and brother. His record at Rugby was undistinguished, 'disappointing' (after Austen's record at the same school?) to Joseph Chamberlain. Neville liked quiet, solitary pursuits: he spent his free time with music or Dickens, entomology or botany, was a 'silent member' of the school debating society, who would sometimes explode that he 'hated' politics and public speaking; at home, he avoided gatherings of his father's friends and associates – the kind of people with whom Austen cut his political teeth – disappearing from such occasions 'to chase moths, not men'. Certainly, the effects of unfavourable family comparisons could produce a crippled ego: at the age of twenty Neville was judged to be of 'extreme immaturity'[3]; the normal sequence

---

[1] Duncan Keith-Shaw, *Neville Chamberlain*, p 62.
[2] Feiling, *Neville Chamberlain*, p 11.
[3] *Ibid.*

of adult choices he delayed until almost mid-life – significantly, perhaps, until after his father's death; he was forty-two when he married and forty-nine when he finally decided upon a national political career. And the irritating vanity which he displayed as Conservative leader might well have been the cloak of self-reassurance with which he covered still-painful early wounds. Criticism worried and upset him – witness his inability to let Leo Amery's estimate of him ('humdrum, commonplace and unenterprising') pass without a note to himself that the charge was, of course, 'groundless', or what Mowat called the 'secretive and autocratic methods' with which he protected himself as Prime Minister from possible hostility from his own Tory back-benches.[1] His father's political image, it seems certain, hung over Neville's career. Sir Charles Petrie wrote that Joseph Chamberlain was 'the pioneer of a new generation' in the late Victorian political arena, a man who 'brought with him from the world of business and of municipal life a freshness of outlook, a directness of purpose, and a certain impatience of conventional and circuitous methods'.[2] It was his son's self-comforting illusion that he, Neville, was another such Chamberlain, and that his own story would be given similar conclusion: 'I must be content to do my duty as I see it,' he would sigh, 'and trust to recognition in the future.' Or one can find evidence of his identification of his political accomplishments with those of his father. In 1903 he wrote concerning Joseph Chamberlain's (heretical) crusade for the imposition of tariffs in Liberal, free-trade Britain: 'Don't you think it is pretty plucky of my father, after coming home in a blaze of popularity from South Africa, to risk it all by starting this great controversy?' Compare this with a diary entry in 1937, when Neville, Tory businessman turned Chancellor of the Exchequer, proposed to solve the Government deficit by raising the rate of the income tax and by a graduated tax on profits: 'I reckon it to be the bravest thing

---

[1] C L Mowat, 'Baldwin Restored?', *Journal of Modern History*, XXVII (1955).
[2] Sir Charles Petrie, *The Chamberlain Tradition*, p 8.

I have ever done since I have been in public life, for I have risked the Premiership.' No doubt, many of Chamberlain's traits were rooted in his early experiences; his family did much to produce this cold and critical man, who was yet so pathetically eager for warmth and approval, delighted to get a rare, affectionate 'goodbye, old boy' from Stanley Baldwin – or for that matter, a report that Adolf Hitler, that most important European, considered him, Chamberlain, 'a man'.

But such explanations of the personality of Neville Chamberlain can be pushed too far. A renowned and intimidating father, the position as the second less-favoured son, the business career chosen for him – these things, although psychologically punishing, perhaps were not the controlling factors. Keith Feiling, author of the one substantial biography of Chamberlain, regarded Chamberlain's entry into the business world with the same sort of attitudes that, one would imagine, had decided the matter for Joseph Chamberlain. Business, after all, was the solid base of the Chamberlain tradition. For generations, Chamberlains – Unitarians they were, and proud in their public ostracism as Nonconformists – had risen steadily in the merchant world of London; in the nineteenth century the dazzling promise of the new industrial production had brought them to Birmingham, to be part of the 'master class' of the coal and iron centre of the 'second British renaissance'. From the small-screw manufacturing business of the 1840s the family assets had soared in thirty years to near-monopoly of the field; Joseph Chamberlain's spectacular successes in politics, in national and imperial affairs, had brought opportunities for wide-flung investments in the metal industry and in armaments and munitions – until it was quipped, in the opposition parlance of the day, that 'as the Empire expands, the Chamberlains contract'.[1] Neville's job, then, was one of immense importance – and prestige: Joseph Chamberlain well needed two sons, the one to follow him in directing the

[1] See Lloyd George, *House of Commons Debates*, Vol 88, Fourth Series, p 397; *Punch*, November 1900.

proper course of national policy, and the other to manage his share of the family industrial and financial empire.

And it would seem that Neville Chamberlain gained both power and self-confidence as a Birmingham businessman, filling a role firmly structured by family tradition. He was moved into directorships of a number of companies: Elliots', a 'substantial limited company' producing copper, brass and yellow metal and a subsidiary of the giant monopoly of Imperial Chemical Industries; the Birmingham Small Arms Company, manufacturers of military and sporting goods; and Hoskins' and Sons, which made cabin berths 'on Admiralty or private contract'. And he got political experience of a sort: he was liaison man for his father and Austen, their link with their base in Birmingham industry; the honour of local political position came to him 'as by hereditary right' – a city councillor in 1911, an alderman in 1914, a 'progressive' Lord Mayor in 1915, part of the process of becoming, like other Chamberlains before him, First Citizen of Birmingham.

These experiences, too, set the mould of the later Chamberlain, created the man that contemporaries assessed in the 1930s. One biographer (a laudatory one) described him as a 'shrewd and far-sighted business man' sought by company after company 'to strengthen their boards by his long-headed counsel'; the writer evidently saw no contradiction in the information, a few pages later, that 'it is typical of Chamberlain that he looks no further than the work immediate to hand', that 'sufficient unto the day is the evil thereof' might 'sum up Chamberlain's whole life',[1] Keith Feiling is more believable in his blunt remarks:

As a business man, those well fitted to speak would not put him in the absolutely front rank, though recalling many good speeches to his boards, tireless energy and administrative zeal. He was reckoned 'a good seller', knowing the value of money, ready to take a night train at any notice to clinch a contract, just as his men remember him flying up the stairs three at a

[1] Keith-Shaw, *Chamberlain*, pp 27, 43–44.

time, punctual to the minute at 8.30 or 9, and away, bolt upright, on his tall bicycle at 5.30 or 6.

This is the best that Feiling, the official apologist, could do – this sketch of a second-level executive, precise, exacting, unimaginative; Chamberlain's opponents in national politics chose their words with much less care. Lloyd George, under whom Chamberlain was a decided failure as a wartime administrator in 1916, observed that 'Mr Neville Chamberlain is a man of rigid competency', although he was 'lost in an emergency or in creative tasks at any time', possessing besides 'a vein of self-sufficient obstinacy'. To Winston Churchill, Chamberlain was 'alert, businesslike, opinionated, and self-confident in a very high degree' – although Churchill could show more cutting flash, as in his remark that Chamberlain looked 'at world-affairs through the wrong end of a municipal drain-pipe'. Political writers concentrated on Chamberlain-as-businessman: he was 'the unashamed spokesman of the new Birmingham industrial crowd',[1] a politician who carried with him the dictates of a business community that 'preferred short-term peace to risks for long-term security'.[2] Thomas Jones remarked that Chamberlain was 'much more prejudiced against Labour than Baldwin; there is also the Russian complex and I suspect that both Chamberlain and Simon are against thorough-going rearmament because of its effects on our foreign trade'.[3] Jones was right about all three things – the Russian complex (well put), the cautious concern for trade, the antipathy toward Labour. And on the last point, the Labour Left hated Chamberlain as the capitalists' capitalist, the 'Edgbaston Parrot' – doubtless a more satisfying feeling than they had for 'Earl Baldwin the wobbler', whose Conservatism was 'hampered by a distant and hazy humanitarian idealism'.[4]

[1] *The Week*, 17th February 1937.
[2] Audax, *Men in Our Times*, p 49.
[3] Jones, *Diary*, p 418. Jones' influence at Number 10 Downing Street went out with Stanley Baldwin. He was no particular friend of Chamberlain's.
[4] Sir Stafford Cripps, *Dare We Look Ahead?*, p 108.

Still – if many people thought him wholly unqualified, that he had a 'retail mind in a wholesale business'[1] – Neville Chamberlain moved into the coveted top position of national Leadership (an attainment missed by both his father and brother), apparently sure in his awareness that he was 'undeniably superior'[2] to his Conservative colleagues and arrogant in the certainty that the knowledge and experience he had gained from business, from municipal administration, and from the late-Victorian political environment of his father's home would carry him through as Prime Minister of the British nation.

[1] Lloyd George, quoted in Jones, *Diary*, p 422.
[2] Audax, *Men in Our Times*, p 49.

The Climactic Capitalisation
of Appeasement

AND SO IT is Neville Chamberlain whom we will watch in
following the last chapter of the era of appeasement. Chamberlain was quite correct in his belief that appeasement needed
him. The drift and blunder of the Baldwin years would have
continued in any case; but it Chamberlain who made what
Churchill called 'drift and surrender' into a purposeful planned
foreign policy – clearly a most peculiar individual undertaking.
Indeed, as he transformed appeasement into Appeasement
(the capitalisation due to a deliberately developed historical
phenomenon), Chamberlain became a most peculiar individual.
He went through a process of identification with his policy of
Appeasement that reached a peak in late 1938, an identification
that was not destroyed by the disillusioning events of 1939. In
a real sense, the necessary condition for the end of the era of
Appeasement in Britain was the end of the power of Neville
Chamberlain.

The story began in the summer of 1937, when the new
Prime Minister set with will and energy to the problems of
foreign affairs, holding, as his good friend Sir Samuel Hoare
said, 'the most definite views as to what was needed'. What
was essential, Chamberlain was convinced, was firmness and
strength in adherence to a declared clarified policy; if he
could make it terribly clear to the dictators that Britain meant
them no harm, then there would be peace and stability in the
Western world. The businessman-son of Joseph Chamberlain
told Conservative groups when he took office that 'he meant
to stop the drift' and 'to face facts as he found them, not as
he would have wished them to be'; 'the Government, of which
I am at present the head,' he promised, 'intends to hold on to
its course, which is set for the appeasement of the world'.

Do we overstress the business mind of Neville Chamberlain? A close reading of Feiling's pages would deny it. Getting 'on terms' with Germany was his 'first thought', for 'as he told some of the many who volunteered advice', Germany was 'a rising market'. It need hardly be said that Chamberlain was not a Nazi, not even pro-Nazi (although one could leave open the question of the applicability of the more generalised term of pro-Fascist); it was simply that on the evidence of his life experience he believed that representatives of European nations – except Russian-Bolsheviks – were people to be met over the bargaining table, that if he had insulting and pugnacious (but important) customers like Mussolini and Hitler, the proper action was not to call in the police nor club them over the head, but to hear their grievances and make what adjustments he could. In what other way could he keep their business?

Chamberlain's first task in enunciating the policy of Appeasement was to achieve unanimity in his Government, to ensure that Cabinet, Commons, and Civil Service spoke with one voice in foreign affairs. The Cabinet was easiest to tighten for Appeasement. Chamberlain was 'too masterful', wrote Feiling, 'to look much for policy to others', although he did value the opinions of those 'whose precision of expression he found congenial'. Within his Cabinet there were a few who could be trusted to be congenial – 'Neville's bodyguard', Halifax, Hoare, Hailsham, Kingsley Wood – or the even smaller circle, the 'Big Four', Chamberlain with Halifax, Simon and Hoare; this became the Inner Cabinet, the effective, operating Government, compatibly composed of like-minded ministers.

As he shaped the Government to his satisfaction Chamberlain took a line toward the Commons that was particularly revealing of his nature. His problem, apparently, was to anticipate and block criticism from the House, first from the Conservative members, that body of votes essential to his power. A Tory revolt was extremely unlikely – for years observers had noted the 'almost complete docility' of the Party rank and file[1] – but the Prime Minister was a cautious man; in 1937 the already highly developed discipline of Tory MPs was solidified into absolute control, with Chief Whip Captain David Margesson seeing to it that the Party back-benches – filled with men eager for advancement – obediently approved the Government line.[2] And, in his handling of the full House, Chamberlain deemed other measures essential to the great service he was performing for his country. No one expected perfect frankness from a government in parliamentary debate, but Chamberlain treated the Commons like an enemy, with whom subterfuge, evasion, and dishonesty were not only expedient but proper. Underlying the debate on the transfer of the Czech gold,[3] for example, was the hostility and distrust of MPs who had learned that Neville Chamberlain could deny, in answer to their questions, an action that he planned or had already set in motion. Winston Churchill marked this dis-function of the parliamentary system with grave misgivings and finally spoke, in 1938, after Munich – the negotiations for which had been held while Parliament was in recess. It was, said Churchill, a serious error that Parliament had adjourned in 'this period of very rapid daily change in Europe'. It was, he continued,

> derogatory to Parliament . . . that it should be thought unfit, as it were, to be attending to these grave matters. . . . I know that there is a certain undercurrent of derision of Parliament even among its own Members, and a feeling no doubt among Ministers, 'What a relief it will be when we have got them sent about their business and we can get on with our work.' That is exactly the idea which in other countries has led to the institution of dictatorship, the same process of impatience with the parliamentary machine which has swept it away and has led to its replacement by one-man rule.

[1] *The Spectator*, 3rd November 1934; see also the review of Chamberlain's domination of Party and Government in *Manchester Guardian Weekly*, 17th May 1940.
[2] 'Cato', *Guilty Men*, pp 91–95.
[3] See Chap 10, pp 178–181.

THE CLIMACTIC CAPITALISATION OF APPEASEMENT

Neville Chamberlain, dictator – it is an incongruous thought; but Neville Chamberlain, autocratic old man, his ego staked to the only policy he could believe would save his kind of world – that, perhaps, is not too far-fetched an explanation.

There was a special unit of officialdom to be reconstructed before the Government could be declared fit and ready for Appeasement. Chamberlain's battle with the Foreign Office occupied the better part of the first six months of his Premiership – testimony to the stubbornness of its officials – but he finally won a clear victory, and an important one it was, with immediate consequences on the Continent. The showdown with the Foreign Office, where 'the German game was too well understood',[1] was foreshadowed in Chamberlain's earliest remarks as Prime Minister, his private observation that better relations with Italy and Germany were possible if that department would only 'play up'. And since he was determined that those foreign relations would be bettered, it became necessary to get rid of the British officials who would not play up. Some of them were eliminated without fuss or public fanfare: that steady Germanophobe, Sir Robert Vansittart, was lifted from his post as Permanent Under-Secretary of State and deposited on an (honorarily-speaking) higher rung, with the harmless title, and function, of Chief Diplomatic Adviser to the Government; Sir Eric Phipps, whose rigid observance of traditional diplomatic ways irritated the Nazis, was recalled as Ambassador in Berlin, and Nevile Henderson, a younger, malleable man – who watched Hitler or Goering with wide-eyed admiration and told his countrymen that sometimes dictators could be 'extremely beneficial for a nation' – was installed in his place. These changes, however, were only a preface to the main objective: the removal of the Foreign Secretary, Anthony Eden.

Perhaps the dismissal of Eden was in Chamberlain's mind from the start. His friend, Sir Samuel Hoare, wrote that in his policy of reaching a 'reasonable understanding' with the

[1] Namier, *Nazi Era*, p 90.

Fascist nations, Chamberlain intended to approach Mussolini first – this was known as 'separating the dictators' – and that if Eden demurred, he would be quite willing to sacrifice his Foreign Secretary.[1] Thus, Chamberlain chose the one area certain to emphasise his differences with Eden. The two agreed on essential points of appeasement – non-intervention in Spain, the conciliatory approach in Berlin, even the reopening of the Stresa Front, with Britain, Italy and Franco standing together in a kind of friendly warning to Hitler against irresponsible moves in Central Europe. But Eden's sticking point came at the preparation of new negotiations with the Italians; he was reluctant to conduct fresh discussions with a government that had repeatedly broken pledges in Spain, tired of concluding 'Gentlemen's Agreements' with leaders who gleefully refused to be gentlemen.[2] He balked, then, at a reaffirmation of understanding with Italy until Mussolini had demonstrated his good faith by some positive compliance with British conditions – the withdrawal of some of the Italian troops from Spain, for example. Chamberlain, however, had a timetable of his own: warm Anglo-Italian relations by July 1937 – with no conditions required – and, from there, an all-out effort to win the friendship of the Germans:[3] if Eden stood in the way of this plan, he would have to go.

The Prime Minister held a clear edge in this conflict within his Cabinet, with most effective ways to undermine the authority of the Foreign Secretary. From early summer of 1937 he simply went around Eden and relied on his own sources for contact with the dictators. He set up a channel of communication with Mussolini through Italian Ambassador

[1] Hoare, *Nine Years*, pp 258–259. The pro-appeasement Press had been sniping at Eden for months before Chamberlain's differences with him became public. See *The Observer*, 24th January 1937, for the Editor's annoyance with Eden's suspicions of Germany and his failure to see Hitler as an 'extraordinary historic person'.
[2] The final chapters of Eden's memoirs are devoted to his break with Chamberlain and his resignation as Foreign Secretary. See Eden, *Facing the Dictators*, pp 628–689 and Appendices A–D.
[3] See Hoare, *Nine Years*, p 258. Eden noted in his diary during this period, 'I fear that fundamentally the difficulty is that Neville believes that he is a man with a mission to come to terms with the dictators'. Eden, *Facing the Dictators*, p 635.

Count Grandi, and sent letters of goodwill to the Duce – without, of course, consulting Eden. And for service on the Italian front, he had even an emissary in his family, Lady (Ivy) Chamberlain, widow of his brother Austen, whose long-standing friendship with Mussolini could be used to convince the Italians of British willingness – eagerness – to talk. (Lady Chamberlain departed at this time for a 'long stay' in Rome, where, wrote Feiling, her 'footing in Fascist circles differed from that of other British subjects; she had always known Mussolini at his simplest and best, in his genuine affection for Austen and his kindness to their children'.)[1] Chamberlain displayed his lack of trust in Eden, too, by open preference for more pliable friends and colleagues – for example, Lord Halifax and an ex-civil servant, 'chief industrial adviser', Sir Horace Wilson, whose 'amateur advice' on foreign affairs was so indispensable to the Prime Minister that he was moved, a kind of unofficial consultant, into an office in Downing Street.

To his credit, Eden delayed his resignation until February of 1938, although he was directly affronted by Chamberlain's insulting arrogance.[2] Lady Chamberlain's presence in Rome 'embarrassed' the Foreign Office, admitted Feiling with typical understatement. While Eden tried to maintain a firm line with the Italians, Lady Chamberlain 'sang a very different tune' of 'understanding, agreement, friendship' to Ciano and

---

[1] See *Ciano's Hidden Diary, 1937–1938*, trans Andreas Mayor, p 47: 'Lady Chamberlain wears the Fascist badge,' Ciano wrote (with contempt – he disliked the British appeasers as well as the tough variety); also, *House of Commons Debates*, Vol 211, Fifth Series, p 1547 (1927): MPs wondered aloud about Foreign Secretary Austen Chamberlain's relations with the Italian Fascists – their curiosity aroused by 'a photograph of the Foreign Secretary giving the Fascist salute in Italy'. In the late 1930s, incidentally, Lady Chamberlain made other visits to Fascist lands. The pictorial section of a journal published by the Spanish Nationalists showed her in various moments of her tour of Franco-held Spanish territory, during which she was met and fêted by Franco and his associates. *Spain: A Semi-monthly Publication of Spanish Civil War Events*, 1st October 1938.

[2] See Eden's account of his disagreement with the Prime Minister about a message from President Roosevelt, the latter offering (for the first time) the moral support of the United States in dealing with the dictators. Chamberlain resented this interference from abroad – to Eden's dismay. Eden, *Facing the Dictators*, pp 621–645.

the Duce.[1] In early February 1938, Lady Chamberlain had an appointment with Mussolini, a visit which Ciano described:

> I took Lady Chamberlain to see the Duce, and she showed him an important letter from Neville Chamberlain. Two points: Great Britain is coming round to the idea of a formal recognition of the Empire [*conquered Ethiopia*]; conversations can begin at the end of the month. Mussolini approved and agreed. Lady Chamberlain will write to her brother-in-law to inform him of the Duce's reactions, which were definitely favourable. He showed himself in full sympathy with the project of an agreement and said that he intends to make one which will be complete and durable and able to serve as a basis for cooperation between the two Empires. He dictated to Lady Chamberlain the terms of her letter.

Lady Chamberlain's letter, delivered to her brother-in-law, became the basis of intensified negotiations for Anglo-Italian agreement, conducted by the Prime Minister and Ambassador Grandi – in blatant intervention in matters properly belonging to the Foreign Office.[2] Eden decided he had had enough after a meeting with Chamberlain and Grandi on 18th February, a meeting which was actually a two-way conversation between friends, with Eden treated as a fractious interloper. Eden's resignation was a Chamberlain coup: German dispatches to Berlin delightedly detailed the Foreign Secretary's 'humiliation', the Italians crowed, and Ciano, who had been saying that an attack from Britain was possible if Eden ever became 'the head of a Labour-Liberal Government', noted in his diary, 'I have authorised Grandi to take any step which may add an arrow to Chamberlain's quiver'.[3]

---

[1] *Hidden Diary*, p 47.

[2] Eden, *Facing the Dictators*, Appendices C and D; Feiling, *Neville Chamberlain*, pp 337–338. Chamberlain circumvented, too, the British Ambassador in Rome, Lord Perth, even though Perth was eager to please the Italians. See Sir Robert Vansittart, *The Mist Procession*, p 516, for an account of the peculiarities of the British Embassy in Rome.

[3] See Eden, *Facing the Dictators*, pp 661–663, for Eden's notes of the meeting. Also *German Documents*, Series D, I, No 127; *Hidden Diary*, pp 69, 78. The British Press divided on now predictable lines on Eden's resignation: *The Observer* (27th February 1938) stated that the Cabinet count had been twenty to one against

The tale of conflict with Anthony Eden adds, again, an insight into Neville Chamberlain. Chamberlain felt, wrote Feiling, that the difference between him and Eden were, 'and always had been, fundamental'. There was the basic separation of their ages, twenty-eight years, which inevitably meant a divergence in outlook and feeling. But there were other things, as Feiling summed them up, matters of 'temperament'. The interpretation could be pushed further: his Nonconformist, bourgeois background was strong in Chamberlain; the man trained to repress and despise emotion, the man of business, the practical realist, found in Eden qualities he disliked and mistrusted – an emotionalism of a sort, 'natural vibrations' which could interfere with his performance of a given assignment. Rightly or wrongly, Chamberlain believed that Eden was prejudiced against Fascists, and that it was on the basis of this feeling that the Foreign Secretary tried to prevent accord with the rulers of Italy and Germany. Chamberlain did not make judgments on ideological abstractions, nor would he let his personal feelings enter into public affairs; if Anthony Eden could not conceal his private 'sensibilities', his antipathy for dictators, to be precise, he had no further effectiveness as a minister of the Crown.

With Eden disposed of, Chamberlain could proceed with an Italian understanding – although, it now appeared, an Anglo-Italian agreement was only a subsidiary preoccupation, a first step toward a new system of peace-insurance in Europe. 'If only we could get on terms with the Germans,' said Chamberlain, 'I would not care a rap for Musso.' And, indeed, it became the 'destined purpose' of Neville Chamberlain to assure peace through trust with Germany, to convince the wary Germans (with their rising market) of enduring British friendship and British assistance in solving the problems that

Eden – that is, the 'weight of wisdom and judgement' was with Chamberlain in his move to end the 'furious nonsense' of Eden's distrust of the dictators; the *Manchester Guardian Weekly* (4th March 1938) regretted Eden's loss – and Chamberlain's methods: Chamberlain who 'cultivates a certain ruthlessness and directness . . . is, for a Prime Minister, uncommonly insensitive to political atmosphere'.

most vexed German national existence. In Berlin, Adolf Hitler and the Nazi high command, making plans in late 1937 for the conquest of Austria and Czechoslovakia, were beginning to feel the point of the Chamberlain policy[1] – aided by enlightening episodes like the transformation of the British Foreign Office. But certain that there were still German doubts about his sincerity, Chamberlain made it clearer. He declared his disinterest in the League of Nations and in a 'collective security which this country was being asked to carry alone'. He added that 'we must not try to delude small nations into thinking that they will be protected by the League'. He let it be known to German officials that he desperately wanted a Four-Power-Pact – which would break the Franco-Soviet alliance, exclude the Soviet Union, and settle European affairs through the joint action of Britain, France, Germany and Italy. He confided, too, according to German diplomats, that he considered the Rome-Berlin Axis the 'pillar of European peace'[2] – this, if true, a most interesting admission of his real attitude toward the Anti-Comintern Pact. And Chamberlain sent Lord Halifax in November of 1937, *before* Halifax succeeded Eden as Foreign Secretary, on a supposedly unofficial visit to Germany, there to sound out the Fuehrer, to learn first-hand of Nazi desires, and to see if some way might be arranged to satisfy them. The message that Halifax transmitted was of the purest essence of Chamberlain's Appeasement. Hitler was informed that Britain was willing, of course, to discuss the granting of overseas colonies to Germany – that was the cheap way of buying German friendship – but the main thing was this: the British Government would willingly, too, accept German-made changes in the 'European order', changes, that is, in the status of Austria, Czechoslovakia, and Danzig that, in any case, 'sooner or later would probably take place'. In this meeting with Hitler, Halifax made it explicit and official that

[1] See *German Documents*, D, I, No 19, for the meeting of the Nazi chiefs at which the conquest of Austria and Czechoslovakia was planned – for 1938, if possible, but not later than 1943–45.

[2] *German Documents*, D, I, Nos 126, 130.

the Chamberlain Government consented to a 'free hand' for Germany in the heart of Europe – upon the one condition that any reconstruction in Central Europe be 'effected by peaceful evolution'.[1]

What could the Germans make of this firm Appeasement? They were surely aware that there were other Britons for whom Chamberlain could not speak – Churchill or Eden, not to mention Attlee, Cripps or Bevin. But Chamberlain held the front line, with assistants who were certain to echo his ideas (a governing group which, the once pessimistic Ribbentrop predicted from London, would never go to war to block German expansion). Halifax, who was Foreign Secretary, had told Ribbentrop that war between Britain and Germany would mean 'the end of civilisation'; behind him were sympathisers like Defence Minister Inskip, who had 'always been one to understand German views', or the unofficial adviser, Sir Horace Wilson, with his 'decidedly pro-German' attitudes;[2] or, in Berlin, new Ambassador Nevile Henderson, though only a transmission wire, was being helpful in scurrying about telling people that 'Germany is to dominate Europe, and England and Germany must come into close relations, economic and political, and control the world.'[3] The Nazis made the obvious estimate of the import of Appeasement – and revised their blueprint for the subjugation of Central Europe. Thus, the *Anschluss* was consummated, and Austria made a part of the New Germany, with German troops enforcing the changed status by a victory march into Vienna on 13th March 1938.

The Chamberlain inner circle reacted with an odd ambivalence to the *Anschluss*, to the ending of Austrian independence.

[1] *Documents and Materials Relating to the Eve of the Second World War*, I, 34. Halifax's visit, said Garvin in *The Observer*, opened a 'new book' in Anglo-German relations (21st November 1937).

[2] *German Documents*, D, I, Nos 24, 149, 128. 'The truth was,' wrote Anthony Eden, 'that some of my seniors in the Cabinet, like Inskip, could not believe that Mussolini and Hitler were as untrustworthy as I painted them. After all, had not Mussolini defeated the Reds and made the trains in Italy run on time?' Eden, *Facing the Dictators*, p 636.

[3] Quoted in *Ambassador Dodd's Diary, 1933–38*, William E Dodd, Jr and Martha Dodd, eds, p 421.

They had known it was coming – from the time of Hitler's first attempt against Austria in 1934, from Nazi spokesmen like Ribbentrop, who had been long appealing to his London friends to look kindly upon German ambitions in Austria,[1] even (a new note, in late 1937) from warnings of a secretly forming opposition inside Germany, anti-Nazi generals and civilian officials beginning, tentatively, to try to awaken the British appeasers to the fact of Hitler's war plans.[2] Yet, that the *Anschluss* was done by force, by the mechanised advance of the German Army, was a shock to the peaceful negotiators of the Chamberlain team. Lord Halifax was upset by it and perhaps here begun to internalise the doubts and disgust that would eventually take him out of the course of Appeasement.[3] In Ribbentrop's dispatch of the reaction of British leaders to the news from Austria, he described Halifax as 'excited' and talking of sending an international force to supervise a plebiscite that would ascertain the real feelings of the Austrian people. Claud Cockburn of *The Week* had heard a story of a frantic Halifax, 'clutching his head in his hands and moaning, "Horrible, horrible. I swear I never thought they would really do it" '. As for Chamberlain, only his second thoughts are available', conclusions that the *Anschluss* was, first, the fault of Anthony Eden and, second, a minor failure of his own: 'It is tragic,' he complained, 'to think that very possibly this might have been prevented if I had had Halifax at the Foreign Office instead of Anthony at the time I wrote my letter to Mussolini.'[4] It is clear

[1] See Jones, *Diary*, p 208. The *Manchester Guardian Weekly* (18th March 1938) printed a story of backroom diplomacy preceding the *Anschluss*: it was 'possible, indeed, that a conversation between Herr von Ribbentrop and Lord Halifax in London the day before the stroke finally decided Herr Hitler'. Still, thought the *Guardian*, the *Anschluss* was long-planned.

[2] General Ewald von Kleist informed the British Foreign Office of Nazi plans in 1937; subsequent warnings came from German Secretary of State Ernst von Weizsaker, Erich and Theo Kordt (Chargé d'Affaires in London), and Ulrich von Hassell, Ambassador to Italy until 1938. See, for comprehensive treatment, Hans Rothfels, *The German Opposition to Hitler*, Laurence Wilson, trans; also Erich Nordt, *Wahn und Wirklichkeit*, pp 113–114, 124–128; Ulrich von Hassell, *Diaries*; Hans Bernd Gisevius, *To the Bitter End*, pp 350–351.

[3] But not as long as Chamberlain held the reins of government.

[4] Feiling, *Neville Chamberlain*, p 342. The *Observer* – for one extreme Press example – saw nothing tragic in the *Anschluss*. 'This is a mighty event,' wrote Garvin,

enough what Chamberlain meant: if, he thought, he had
concluded an understanding with Mussolini in the summer of
1937, the two of them, with the French, might have persuaded
Hitler to come to a four-power conference, at which, like a
board of directors of international affairs, they would have
dealt sympathetically with German designs in Austria. Chamberlain saw only what he wanted to see; he would not perceive
that the Italian military fiasco in Spain had tightened the
Rome-Berlin Axis,[1] and more, that the strutting showman of
Rome would most certainly choose as the side of safety in
Europe, not the tired Conservatism of Britain, but the master-
race dynamics of Nazi Germany.

The chief thing that Chamberlain got from the lesson of
Austria was the reinforcement of his reliance on Appeasement,
the necessity now of hurrying to be nice to the Germans, in
order to keep the peace of Europe, in order 'to avoid another
violent coup in Czechoslovakia' – which, according to Keith
Feiling, the Prime Minister well knew was the next victim
on Hitler's aggression agenda.[2] One week after the *Anschluss*,
on 20th March 1938, Chamberlain set down these comments on
the European scene:

> With Franco winning in Spain by the aid of German guns and
> Italian planes [*!*], with a French Government in which one
> cannot have the slightest confidence and which I suspect to be
> in closish touch with our Opposition, with the Russians stealthily
> and cunningly pulling all the strings behind the scenes to get
> us involved in war with Germany (our Secret Service doesn't
> spend all its time looking out of the window), and finally with
> a Germany flushed with triumph, and all too conscious of her
> power, to be badgered and pressed, to come out and give a
> clear, decided, bold and unmistakable lead, show 'ordinary
> courage', and all the rest of the twaddle, is calculated to vex
> the man who has to take the responsibility for the consequences.

related to 'forces of race and history', and a 'removal', as well, of 'one of the
standing causes of war'. (20th February, 13th March 1938.)
  [1] See Chap 7, p 127.
  [2] Feiling, *Neville Chamberlain*, pp 342, 347. Mr Feiling does *not* say that Chamberlain might have known this from anti-Nazis like General von Kleist.

As a matter of fact, the plan of the 'Grand Alliance', as Winston calls it, had occurred to me long before he mentioned it. . . . It is a very attractive idea; indeed, there is almost everything to be said for it until you come to examine its practicability. From that moment its attraction vanishes. You have only to look at the map to see that nothing that France or we could do could possibly save Czechoslovakia from being overrun by the Germans, if they wanted to do it. The Austrian frontier is practically open; the great Skoda munition works are with easy bombing distance of the German aerodromes, the railways all pass through German territory, Russia is a hundred miles away. Therefore we could not help Czechoslovakia – she would simply be a pretext for going to war with Germany. That we could not think of unless we had a reasonable prospect of being able to beat her to her knees in a reasonable time and of that I see no sign. I have therefore abandoned any idea of giving guarantees to Czecho-slovakia, or the French in connection with her obligations to that country.[1]

From Chamberlain, this was an enormously revealing state-ment of Appeasement, of a policy that had become one of desperation, of near-paralysis before a German grown fright-eningly strong (not least because of the sustenance of appease-ment in the past). As the Prime Minister saw it, there was no hope in the encirclement of Germany through a Grand Alliance with France and – conspiratorial – Russia; to talk of Leadership with courage was 'twaddle', and Czechoslovakia would simply have to drop into the German lap. The *Anschluss* was a milestone, to be sure – in fear and demoralisation, which spread, moreover, from Chamberlain through the 'Government upper-world of London'.[2]

And so Czechoslovakia was lost – in the mind of the Prime Minister – even as the German pressure was turned on Presi-dent Eduard Benes and the Czech Government from the spring of 1938. Czechoslovakia was a rich prize for Hitler, with its strategic position, valuable mineral resources, heavy

---

[1] Feiling, *Neville Chamberlain*, pp 347–348. This passage was part of a letter to Chamberlain's sister. He wrote her weekly such frank and detailed accounts – most valuable documents.

[2] The phrase is Claud Cockburn's. *The Week*, 23rd March 1938.

industry, and magnificent fortifications along the border of Germany; it was, too, a specially selected victim – and specially detested by the Fuehrer – because of its mutual assistance ties with France and Russia, an alliance directly aimed at the containment of Germany. Chamberlain, then, was psychologically prepared to grant this prize to Hitler in early 1938; the game was conceded to the Nazis even as they began their agitation against the Czechs, as they declared their right to interfere in Czech internal affairs on behalf of the Sudeten German minority – who belonged by blood and race to the Third Reich.

Let us review in outline the facts of the five months of crisis over Czechoslovakia that ended at Munich in late September of 1938.[1] Hitler and the Nazis found the opportunity to manœuvre in Czechoslovakia because of the minority problems within that small republic, because in a nation of some fourteen million people there was a large minority group of Germans in the Sudetenland; this group, the Nazis claimed, and their Sudeten puppets echoed, were not at one with the Czech majority of Czechoslovakia, but were related, rather, to the Germans of greater Germany. From 1933 a Nationalist Socialist party of the Sudetenland had created trouble within the Czech state, with Party boss Konrad Henlein and his Sudeten Nazis – following the will of their Berlin masters – creating incidents to demonstrate that Germans in Czechoslovakia were a persecuted minority. By the spring of 1938, Hitler himself was ready to take up the case of the Sudeten Germans, planned pretext for invasion and subjugation of Czechoslovakia – although still, through the summer months, Henlein was the front man in the Nazi campaign. Henlein first demanded, as 'justice' for the persecuted Sudeten Germans, the status of autonomy within the Czech state; when, under pressure from the British and French, the Czech Government

[1] The following account is based on (the most impressive work) J W Wheeler-Bennett, *Munich*, pp 1–181; A Snejdarek, 'The Participation of the Sudeten-German Nazis in the Munich Tragedy', *Historica*, I (1959); Dr Eduard Benes, *Memoirs: From Munich to New War and New Victory*, pp 36–43.

granted this demand, Henlein shifted his ground, and asserted the right of 'self-determination' for the Sudetens – that is, the right to secede altogether from the nation. Behind the twisting Sudeten path stood the Nazi controller – and Hitler's plan, that hoped for no solution for the tension except what might be imposed by the roll of the German Army into the Sudetenland.[1]

Thus the crisis over Czechoslovakia was developing when Chamberlain privately announced his decision to refuse aid to or involvement with that nation in its peril from Germany. Strangely enough, however, in what looked like the first threatening Nazi move, the British Government was apparently lined up with the allies of Czechoslovakia, the French and Russians; on the weekend of 20th–22nd May 1938, rumours of German troop movement near the border of Czechoslovakia[2] brought a lightning countermobilisation of the Czech Army – the reaction supported by France and Russia, and by Britain, the Foreign Office stiffly informing the Germans that in case of aggression against Czechoslovakia they could not guarantee to stay uninvolved.[3] Had Chamberlain, then, reversed himself? Was he ready, that critical weekend, to be tough with the Germans about Czechoslovakia? Hardly. The details of the events of those two days are still cloudy, but their consequences are not. Apparently, the tension built so fast from the moment of Czech mobilisation that the Foreign Office was taken off-guard: Halifax did indeed transmit strong warnings to the German Government in the midst of frantic British activity to establish the facts of German military movement; but interwoven with his message were professions of his 'profound regret' at the damage being done to Anglo-German

[1] As readers of the *Daily Mail* might have perceived. See the interview of correspondent Ward Price with Henlein, in which the latter stated that the 'simpler' solution to Sudeten grievances would be war (26th May 1938).

[2] In the words of Wheeler-Bennett: 'Whether or not the Nazi leaders had actually intended to make a descent in force on Czechoslovakia during the weekend of 20–22nd May, is of secondary importance beside the fact that Europe at large seriously believed that they had harboured such an intention.'

[3] *German Documents*, D, II, Nos 184, 186; Henderson, *Failure of a Mission*, p 139.

relations, and pleas that the 'parties concerned' be 'stronger than fate', that the situation not be allowed to get out of hand, for 'then the only ones to profit would be the communists'. And the lesson the appeasers – specifically Prime Minister Chamberlain – learned from the incident was that the conditions which permitted such a brush with disaster must be abolished altogether; as Wheeler-Bennett put it, 'Mr Chamberlain, appalled at the chasm of war which had seemingly opened suddenly at his feet, became more and more determined that never again should he be placed in such an unhappy position'; in fact, 'instead of taking practical measures to strengthen the powers at the command of those who were opposed to the potential aggressor, he set about weakening still further the position of the victim of aggression'.[1]

Behind the events that followed in the betrayal of Czechoslovakia is the spotlight story, the decisive intervention of Neville Chamberlain. It was he who took the initiative in surrendering all to Hitler; and he who conducted a solitary and secretive policy, made decisions, and then informed the British Cabinet or the French or the Czechs, or – even more tardily – the House of Commons. Clearly, this is Chamberlain's story, but the intriguing thing is the way he felt it, and made it, his hour of 'destined purpose'. Chamberlain took charge of the crisis over the fate of Czechoslovakia, and he did it with a strange packet of inner convictions. He still had the old reasons for his actions: he wanted German friendship; he had no stomach for war under any conditions; he had accepted the idea that mighty Germany could not be stopped in her aggressive behaviour. But with an amazing capacity for self-deception he managed to channel those reasons into a new drive, into a mission for peace that was his duty and privilege to pursue. Through Appeasement *he* found the solution for the Sudeten

---

[1] Wheeler-Bennett, *Munich*, pp 62–63. The anti-appeasement Press chose to see, rather than this, the strength of the Government. *The Spectator* wrote that 'a rudimentary and emergency form of collective security' might have begun in the May crisis (27th May 1938). The *Manchester Guardian* (27th May 1938) was pleased – although cautious – that Britain had 'followed' the French and Russian action.

affair; *he* met Hitler face to face and *his* judgment of what would pacify the 'half-mad' dictator sufficed for his colleagues and allies. Appeasement meant Peace, and thus he was a 'symbol of peace' for hundreds of millions of anxious people; as for Britain, 'he believed he, in some sense, alone could save his country'. Almost seventy years of age, he wanted 'a few more years of it', for 'although I know the danger of thinking that one is indispensable, I do not see anyone to hand over to without undermining confidence'. Chamberlain, this narrow, limited man, found in the Sudeten crisis the chance to win a place in history, convincing himself that fear and weakness and personal doubts were the qualities of a great peacemaker. It might have been pathetic, had he not been delivering, in the name of peace, millions of Central Europeans to the trained violence of the Gestapo.

Chamberlain had marked out from the beginning the impossible approaches to the problem of the Sudetens. He would not promise to aid the Czechs in event of attack from Germany, for 'we could not always undertake to protect every small State against the bullying of a great one'; 'if we have to fight,' he added primly, 'it must be on larger issues than that'. He would not listen to a Labour proposal, made in the Commons, for the united action of Britain, France and Russia against the Nazis, because this would be a return to the 'alliance system' and would inevitably 'plunge us into war'.[1] He had decided that the French were totally unreliable as allies, people with whom he would not work; when Daladier (a 'taciturn peasant') came to London – in April 1938 – to discuss the conditions of an Anglo-French stand for Czechoslovakia, the consultation almost ended in an open break, and Daladier being told that they must 'press the Czechs to the

[1] *House of Commons Debates*, Vol 334, Fifth Series, p 61. For a résumé of Labour's stand on Czechoslovakia see *The Times*, 18th September 1938. Defeatism, however, was not a Conservative monopoly. Hugh Dalton reported that Kingsley Martin felt during the Czech crisis 'that things had gone so far that to plan armed resistance to the dictators was now useless'. Dalton, *The Fateful Years*, p 162. See, as an interesting analysis (and apologia), Kingsley Martin, 'British Foreign Policy in the Thirties', *New Statesman*, 26th April 1963.

limit of concession'. Chamberlain was adamant in his refusal of Soviet assistance or participation in any of the negotiations about Czechoslovakia; 'I must confess,' he said, 'to the most profound distrust of Russia,' a distrust he well demonstrated with the positive policy of excluding the Soviets from Western councils. He had no interest in preserving intact a national unity for Czechoslovakia, which he considered an unviable state, a nation of warring groups and, moreover, 'full of refugees, German Liberals and Socialists, and latterly of Austrian democrats' – the residue of European Leftism; there was no reason that Sudetens should not 'enjoy self-government' within this state, or even self-determination, if they chose to join with their kin of Nazi Germany. Thus, Chamberlain told Hitler at Berchtesgaden: 'My personal opinion was that on principle I didn't care two hoots whether the Sudetens were in the Reich, or out of it, according to their wishes.'

From the summer of 1938, then, Chamberlain's choice of action was easily made – since he had eliminated all alternatives. He would not fight for the Czechs, would not stand with France and Russia, would not insist on special formulae to keep the Sudetenland within the Czech nation. He would not, that summer of 1938, even consider exploring the overtures from the German generals – the German military clique that was alarmed now, foreseeing German disaster if the West and Russia should unite against Hitler's rashness.[1] Chamberlain knew better than those inclined to listen to General von Kleist's warning that the British must stiffen against Nazi demands: 'I take it,' he opined, 'that von Kleist is violently anti-Hitler, and is extremely anxious to stir up his friends in Germany to make an attempt at [Hitler's] overthrow. He reminds me of the Jacobites at the Court of France in King

[1] Churchill summarised what frightened the German generals: 'Between thirty and forty Czech divisions were deploying upon Germany's eastern frontier, and the weight of the French army, at odds of nearly eight to one, began to lie heavy on the Western Wall. A hostile Russia might operate from Czech airfields, and Soviet armies might wend their way forward through Poland or Rumania. Finally, in the last stage, the British Navy was said to be mobilising.' Churchill, *Gathering Storm*, p 311.

William's time and I think we must discount a good deal of what he says.'[1] Chamberlain could see only one course: to concede to Hitler, in business-like negotiation, whatever it was that the Fuehrer desired.[2] The clarity with which he viewed the matter accounts for his icy displeasure with the Czechs in September, stubbornly withholding, as they did, their concurrence in their own national dismemberment; it accounts, too, for his frustration with Hitler – Chamberlain was incapable of understanding Hitler's controlling desire to invade Czechoslovakia in fine military style – in the tension-filled days before Munich, when the Fuehrer seemed intent upon war. Was it not incredible, Chamberlain complained, that Europe 'should be plunged in a bloody struggle over a question on which agreement has already been largely obtained?'[3] What was the matter with Hitler? Had he not had Chamberlain's sympathy from the start? Why could he not take what was offered him and let Europe get back to the business of peace?

The last of his meetings – there were three of them – with Hitler, at Munich during 29th–30th September, was the pinnacle of Chamberlain's personal diplomacy. He arranged the meeting himself, through a letter which he drafted in hasty response to a slim hope held out by the Fuehrer: 'After reading your letter,' Chamberlain wrote, 'I feel certain that you can get all essentials without war, and without delay.' He came back from Munich vastly pleased with having invited Hitler to occupy the Sudetenland; it is, he said, 'my hope and my

[1] *Documents on British Foreign Policy, 1919–1939* (hereinafter cited as *British Documents*), E L Woodward and Rohan Butler, eds, Third Series, II, 686.

[2] The Runciman Mission was an important part of Chamberlain's negotiations for peace: Lord Runciman, ex-President of the Board of Trade, 'this puritan shipping-magnate', was sent by Chamberlain (the Czechs did not want him, nor did the French approve) in August 1938 as 'conciliator and mediator' between the Czech Government and the Sudeten Germans. Lord Runciman's impartiality, it has seemed to many observers, was a 'sham': 'He spent the weekends with German princes in the Sudetenland; he tended to listen to Czechs with Nazi leanings.' Martin Gilbert and Richard Gott, *The Appeasers*, p 130. These authors, however, believe that Runciman sought an 'honest compromise', which failed because neither Hitler nor Chamberlain was interested. *Ibid*, pp 130–131. For a contemporary view on the Mission, see *The Times*, 29th September 1938.

[3] The words are part of Chamberlain's speech to the nation. *The Times*, 28th September 1938.

belief, that . . . the new Czechoslovakia will find a greater security than she has ever enjoyed in the past.' He had, too, a paper which he cherished : Hitler's signed promise to negotiate all future differences between those pacific friends, the British and the Germans (and Hitler 'was a man who could be relied upon when he had given his word'). Munich was Chamberlain's moment of triumph, the justification and climax of his career; Appeasement, for him, had proved to be the magic formula, the device that had wiped away the years of disappointment and disregard, that had granted him – as intoxicating as peace – recognition in his time. Chamberlain was beyond understanding that people lacking his personal involvement with Appeasement might react to its accomplishments in a different way. Tom Jones, flitting about his usual London circles, reported that 'we are all filled with gloom and shame'; the message that Jones and his friends got from Munich was that Britain had abjectly surrendered – to terrifying German power. Jones talked again with Colonel Lindbergh, who told him that 'the air power of Germany is greater than *all the European nations combined*', that German planes would 'lay the great capitals level with the ground'; with London 'at Germany's mercy', Jones thought, it was to be expected that the Chamberlain group – 'a feeble lot anyway' – would capitulate at Munich. But this sort of talk was not for Chamberlain; for once he preferred the reactions of 'the people', the hysterical relief of millions, whose only knowledge of his secret diplomacy was that at Munich war had been averted.[1]

[1] Even the responsible Press tended toward hysteria in those final weeks of September 1938. The *New Statesman and Nation* (30th September 1938) as much as *The Times* (29th, 30th September 1938) offered grateful thanks to the Prime Minister, enthusiastically applauded the 'dramatic climax' of the Munich trip. And as the tension increased, the usually sober *Spectator* vacillated wildly: on 16th September, an editorial spoke of Chamberlain's 'momentous mission' to Berchtesgaden, not to 'settle the future of Czechoslovakia over the head of the Czechs', but to avoid war in Europe; by 23rd September, after Godesberg, the editors were outraged that the Czechs were 'surrendered', and 'without the knowledge of Parliament in Britain or France and without consultation with Czechoslovakia itself'. In the same issue (23rd September), columnist 'Janus' wrote that he was 'divided between cowardly relief and utter shame' with the news of Munich, then, on 30th September 'Janus' was 'proud of Chamberlain', and the editors certain that the Prime Minister had saved the peace.

Nor could Chamberlain understand that as Munich was the bottom of defeatism and fear, so it was the turning point, the crisis-moment after which British opinion steadily stiffened against further surrender to Hitler.[1] One wonders if Chamberlain even glanced at, for example, a most interesting memorandum sent him at Godesberg by his closest associate, Lord Halifax, a report of 'predominant public opinion': 'While *mistrustful* of our plan but prepared *perhaps* to accept it *with reluctance* as an alternative to war, great mass of public opinion seems to be hardening in sense of feeling we have gone to limit of concession.'[2] Halifax, too, had gone to his limit of concession, and he was aware, moreover, of the criticism against the Government and continuing Appeasement that was coming from the Press, from the Liberal and Labour Opposition, even from the ranks of the Conservative Party. Gently, he urged Chamberlain to enlarge the 'Big Four' of the Cabinet to bring in new men – perhaps Eden: 'I should not myself', he wrote to the Prime Minister, 'rate too highly the annoyance caused to dictators by the inclusion of some of those whom they dislike, because I think your own position is great enough in their eyes to carry it, and to make it plain that you had attracted those who might join you to your policy rather than abandoned your policy to attract them.' Unlike Halifax, other Conservatives were harsh in condemnation of a leader who chose his ministers to please the dictators; and, Keith Feiling writes, there were members of the Parliamentary Party demanding changes within the Cabinet because they feared that 'some senior colleagues wanted courage, and some junior ministers

[1] See, for example the 'Letters to the Editor' in *The Spectator*, 7th, 28th October 1938, for almost unanimous expression of shame and anger with the Government; also *The Spectator* editorial (7th October 1938) on the 'Price of Peace', which declared that Chamberlain had averted war only at gunpoint, and predicted that there would be no stability or certainty of peace in Europe as a result of an agreement that would merely increase Hitler's appetite. Similarly, the editors of the *Manchester Guardian* (7th October 1938) pointed out that not only had the Czechs been sacrificed, but the word of the British and French had been hopelessly compromised with the peoples east of the Rhine; furthermore, *The Guardian* soberly warned, Munich had so disgusted the Russians that they would now 'leave the Democracies to their fate'.
[2] *British Documents*, Third Series, II, 490 (italics are the author's).

lacked loyalty'. Duff Cooper, First Lord of the Admiralty, resigned immediately after Munich and explained his decision with a blistering attack on Appeasement in the House of Commons. Cooper jotted further in his diary: 'I hoped that when the Prime Minister saw Hitler he would say to him that he had done all and more than all that he had undertaken, that he was bringing him Czechoslovakia's head on a charger, and that further he could not go. He would prefer, if it were necessary, to go to war.' He had been sickened, Cooper wrote, by the details of Chamberlain's meetings with Hitler and by Chamberlain himself, 'obviously pleased at the reports he had subsequently received of the good impression that he had made'; 'he told us with obvious satisfaction,' Cooper added, 'how Hitler had said to someone that he felt that he, Chamberlain, was "a man" . . . but the bare facts of the interview were frightful'. With Cooper, Tory rebels gathered in the House, joining the Labour Opposition to condemn the humiliation of Munich, to demand an end to Appeasement and an all-out acceleration of British armament. Chamberlain coldly rejected both criticism and advice. He would, he said, continue to press the rearmament programme, but Appeasement was his steady aim; what his critics refused to see was that 'the conciliatory part of the policy is just as important as the rearming'.

After the partition of Czechoslovakia, what more could Chamberlain do with his Appeasement? He could do a number of important things. There were still a few loose ends to be tied – for example, the interrupted attempt to make a friend of Mussolini. Or he could please three dictators at once, a splendid opportunity that he grasped in recognising General Franco as the legitimate ruler of Spain, in February 1939.[1] Recognition of 'National Spain' was granted, Chamberlain told a House rumbling with revolt, because Franco's forces held most of the territory of Spain, certainly all that was valuable in resources and industry, because the Republican

[1] See Chap 7, p 132.

Government was 'no longer exercising settled authority', and because 'certain declarations' by Franco regarding his domestic policies afforded 'satisfaction' to the British Government. In the last analysis, Chamberlain said, recognition of Franco's Government was essential to 'secure that British interests not be jeopardised'. In the angry debate that followed the Prime Minister's statement, Clement Attlee made a provocative point. Chamberlain, Attlee said, 'is thinking all the time of the interests of British capital. What does it matter if Gibraltar is endangered if Rio Tinto Mines pay a dividend? What does it matter about the women and children if Spain is made a place safe for autocracy?' The same type of rhetorical questions could be fairly asked about the post-Munich course of Appeasement in Central Europe. What did Czechoslovakia matter if its partition was the concession that had brought peace with Hitler (had not the Fuehrer promised that the Sudeten was the last territory he wanted in Europe?). What did the Czech nation matter if the British now could settle down to mutually profitable economic relations with Germany? And so, as the Nazis prowled menacingly on the fringes of what was left of Czechoslovakia, Chamberlain – and the faithful Sir Samuel Hoare and Sir John Simon – talked brightly of planning for a disarmament conference, and predicted, even, a glorious future, a 'Golden Age' of peace with the dictators ahead.[1] In March 1939, a delegation of the Federation of British Industries met with representatives of the counter German organisation, the Reichsgruppe Industrie, at Düsseldorf – a 'non-political' meeting, so it was said, between industrialists of both countries, to iron out their trade differences and the difficulties of international trade competition.[2] It was a 'non-political' meeting – except that Chamberlain 'approved of discussions between British and German industrialists and

[1] See *The Times*, 11th March 1939; also the *Daily Express*, 2nd January 1939, for an isolationist's pleasure in the thought of the Chamberlain record. Halifax – more the realist – was not so certain of these hopes for disarmament and peace. See Feiling, *Neville Chamberlain*, pp 396–397.
[2] See the discussion of the Düsseldorf meeting in Einzig, *Appeasement*, pp 107–121; *The Times*, 15th–17th March 1939.

planned that in March the President of the Board of Trade [Oliver Stanley] should visit Berlin'. This, too, Chamberlain could do with Appeasement; he could give the blessing of the Government to the Düsseldorf conference, as a preface to a general commercial treaty with Germany. He told the House on 15th March that the discussions between the industrialists were 'proceeding in a satisfactory manner' – and indeed they were: the 'Düsseldorf Deal' was chiefly an agreement to future agreement among the industries represented, although a clause stated that one of the objects of the Agreement was to enable Germany to increase her foreign exchange resources;[1] it was signed, moreover, on 16th March, the day following Hitler's occupation of Bohemia-Moravia, and the triumphant German entry into Prague.

Chamberlain hung on with Appeasement after 15th March, after Hitler had torn up his guarantee of the shrunken borders of Czechoslovakia and had declared the whole of the Czech state a German 'protectorate'. Appeasement continued, even though Neville Chamberlain was a fading figure, increasingly out of touch with 'predominant public opinion' in the nation which he headed. In debates seething with anger, critics in the Commons battered at Chamberlain and his obdurate ways. The flat unemotional tone of the Prime Minister's announcement of the end of the existence of Czechoslovakia was horrifying to Members, his 'scant amount of feeling' on this 'day of humiliation and shame' for Britain. What Chamberlain had said was this: 'I bitterly regret what has now occurred, but do not let us on that account be deflected from our course.'[2]

---

[1] Einzig, *Appeasement*, p 117.

[2] *House of Commons Debates*, Vol 345, Fifth Series, pp 440, 441–443, 539. *The Times* or the *Daily Express*, *The Spectator*, *The Observer*—all were horrified at Hitler's move. Only the *Daily Mail* took it in its stride, although the Editor noted the 'swift and brutal manner' of the occupation : 'The final disintegration of Czechoslovakia was almost inevitable. . . . Britain has now no cause to interfere. The final split-up of Czechoslovakia was due to an internal aggression. One thing, and one thing only will save Britain—her own armed might' (*Daily Mail*, 16th March 1939). Lead articles in *The Times*, incidentally, reported on 18th March that the Gestapo was already at work in Czechoslovakia, news items that Editor Dawson caught up with three months later: in the editorial of 17th June 1939, Dawson wrote of the repression that was, he thought, only then beginning to appear in that con-

Under prodding from Halifax, and because strong elements of Press, Party and public opinion demanded it, Chamberlain somewhat toughened his tone after 15th March,[1] but hostile Members of Parliament knew their man. They scented a fresh act of Appeasement in the guarded manner of Government spokesmen in answering queries of official relations with the German-imposed puppet rulers of conquered Czechoslovakia. Chamberlain had intimated in March that his Government would not recognise the changed status of Czechoslovakia – now but an annex of the Third Reich – but in response to questions in the House in May, he revealed that 'the matter is being considered'. Sure enough, a few days later, that recognition was hurried through, to the disgust and shame of MPs, who extracted the additional information that British contact with the *de facto* masters of Slovakia has been established without French concurrence and without discussion with the Czech Legation in exile in London. It was done, the Government spokesman said, 'to facilitate the conduct of normal business and to protect British interests'. Were the Germans informed, a Member asked. The answer came: 'Well, they got to know.' The MPs leading the inquisition finally abandoned the matter, filled with contempt for such a Government.

Thus Chamberlain did not change after 15th March, and not even after 31st March, although on that latter date the great shift in British foreign policy occurred. To be sure, the proven worthlessness of Hitler's word was a shock to him, personally, just as the rape of Czechoslovakia was a direct affront to his self-esteem; he was terribly upset, as the Nazis trampled over Central Europe, that he had been deceived,[2] that his policy had been a failure – although he hoped, still, only temporarily.

quered country; because the Czechs are 'high-spirited' the 'Gestapo rules the land', although that was 'probably not the intention of the German authorities'. *The Times*, 18th March, 17th June 1939.

[1] See his speech to his constituents at Birmingham in *The Times*, 18th March 1939.

[2] Perhaps unconsciously, Churchill made an apt remark about businessman Chamberlain's reaction to Hitler's betrayal of his pledge at Munich: Chamberlain 'did not like being cheated'. *Gathering Storm*, p 344.

Keith Feiling's narrative brings out clearly the primary content of Chamberlain's sorrow:

> At moments he endured an intense loneliness. His policy, would they not say, had expired in ignominy, by his credulity he had destroyed the Czech democracy, as *he had destroyed the democracy of Spain*? And what was he to understand by the resolution set down on 28th March by Eden, Churchill and some thirty Conservative Members, which called for a National Government and prosecution of the policy lately pronounced by 'the Foreign Secretary'? . . . Sometimes he felt dumfoundered, as though there were two Neville Chamberlains. There was one whom the mass of people still flocked after and greeted wherever he went, 'and then I go back to the House of Commons, and listen to the unending stream of abuse of the Prime Minister . . . and I say to myself, "this is the real thing".' On his black days he allowed that events 'enable my enemies to mock me publicly', and confessed to feeling dispirited and alone.

What megalomania was this, this delusion of self as the great peacemaker, in his hour of trial mocked publicly by his enemies? In this time of disaster brought by Appeasement, Chamberlain could see only the crushing blow to his hopes, and that 'they', his historical judges, would preserve the ignominy of his failure.

Officially, Appeasement ended in March 1939, as Hitler prepared his next aggression, as the Nazis began the campaign for the conquest of Poland. Appeasement, in fact, ended in an amazing crashing reversal, in reaction to Hitler's demands that Germany be granted the free city of Danzig and a territorial right of way across the Polish Corridor. Clear-sighted, apparently – in seeing that Danzig and the issue of the Polish Corridor were only the Nazi pretext for invasion of Poland[1] – the Chamberlain Government stood up tall and pledged the

---

[1] A Poland ruled by a 'purblind oligarchy who preferred government by junta rather than by parliament'. Wheeler-Bennett, *Munich*, p 375. It was a Poland, too, in the grip of an 'oligarchy of landlords and colonels', run by an 'illiberal, vainglorious and impotent regime'. Fleming, *Cold War*, I, 88.

resources of Great Britain to maintain the territory and independence of the Polish nation. Not only that: when Mussolini seized Albania (on 8th April), additional guarantees were given by the British to Greece, Turkey and Rumania; the new policy took on muscle with the announcement of a speed-up in British armaments and, in April, with the decision for limited conscription. After Appeasement had permitted the Rhineland to be fortified, Spain to be smashed by the Fascists, Austria and Czechoslovakia to be swallowed by the Nazis – after all these positions of strength had been lost, Chamberlain declared his readiness to fight. In Winston Churchill's words:

> And now, when every one of these aids and advantages has been squandered and thrown away, Great Britain advances, leading France by the hand, to guarantee the integrity of Poland – of that very Poland which with hyena appetite had only six months before joined in the pillage and destruction of the Czechoslovak State. . . . History, which we are told is mainly the record of crimes, follies and miseries of mankind, may be scoured and ransacked to find a parallel to this sudden and complete reversal of five or six years' policy of easy-going placatory appeasement.

Yet, was Appeasement done with? Had the Chamberlain Government actually accepted the fact of an 'obviously imminent war' (and war 'on far worse conditions and on the greatest scale' than at any time before)? True, the reversal was evident in opinion sources, in weather vanes like Tom Jones, who talked of the great 'fight against tyranny today', and of 'people waking up' to the real motives of the Nazi deceivers.[1] But Appeasement died hard for Neville Chamberlain, this policy that had been so right – in the larger sense, cut to the measure of Conservative needs, and as a personal policy, carrying him to an apogee of political success. Chamberlain's lingering attachment to Appeasement was the expression, he told himself – and the public – of his unchanged longing for peace.

[1] Jones, *Diary*, p 425. And in the Press: see *The Times*, 3rd July 1939, for Dawson's resigned view that further German aggression would mean war.

Despite the new hard British line, he did not accept war as inevitable; he did not, in fact, mean to fight: 'I am no more a man of war today than I was in September . . . I trust that our actions, begun but not concluded, will prove to be the turning-point not towards war, which wins nothing, cures nothing, ends nothing, but towards a more wholesome era, when reason will take the place of force.' And Chamberlain was not alone in reluctance to bury Appeasement: 'High-pitched, or at least high-placed, voices' cautioned him against giving Hitler cause for alarm.

Strange things occurred in the Government upperworld of London in the summer of 1939, in the months of drift that would end in war. In July, Dr Helmuth Wohltat, sent as 'Goering's emissary', paid a visit to Sir Horace Wilson and Robert Hudson, Chamberlain's economic advisers. The story that emerged in explanation of the meeting of these gentlemen was summarised as this:

> Mr Hudson submitted to Herr Wohltat a proposal of a loan amounting to £1,000 million for the purpose of enabling Germany to convert her industries from war requirements to peace requirements. The offer was subject to a fundamental modification of Germany's foreign policy, an undertaking of partial disarmament under international control and the evacuation of Czechoslovakia.[1]

'Danegeld' it was called in the almost unanimously condemnatory Press; the big question was whether the offer carried with it the official word of the Government. In the Commons, the Government declared it a private and personal matter between Hudson and Wohltat, a matter in which, Chamberlain said, he saw no harm.[2] Chiefly, wrote Keith Feiling, Chamberlain regretted that these 'conversations

---

[1] Einzig, *Appeasement*, p 137.
[2] *House of Commons Debates*, Vol 350, Fifth Series, pp 1025–1027. Chamberlain's words are also in *The Times*, 25th July 1939. The story repeated Chamberlain's denial that the proposed loan was a last-ditch effort to get an 'ultimate settlement' with Germany.

regarding an economic solution somehow reached the Press:
privately, he judged this indiscretion severely, seeing that the
time for such discussion must depend on a change in Germany'.
Hudson's loan offer was dropped, given the reaction in Britain
– and Germany – but, official or unofficial, its details entered
the record: here was one more instance of the businessmen's
group attempting to buy off the gangster Nazis.

The end of Appeasement, then, was neither apparent nor
real, as Chamberlain proceeded carefully, Prime Minister of
a newly-resolved Britain. He was, he said, still working for the
same goal of peace – but with different means; consequently,
he defined with precision the new means he would use. He
would not have a warmonger like Winston Churchill in the
Cabinet, as enthusiasts were suggesting: 'If there is any
possibility,' he explained, 'of easing the tension and getting
back to normal relations with the dictators, I wouldn't risk
it by what would certainly be regarded by them as a challenge.'
And he did not intend to join with the Soviet Union in a
defensive alliance of nations, in what he considered a union
to persuade Hitler toward peace, for this act, an Anglo-
French-Soviet alliance, might prove the affront to the Fuehrer
that would provoke immediate war.

The issue of alliance with the Soviet Union was the revealing
matter – the crucial and decisive matter. In the crisis of
Czechoslovakia the Russians had unequivocally restated their
adherence to collective security, and their intention to stand
by their Pacts with the Czech Government and with France.[1]
The Soviet Union offered its participation again, in a united
front against the German threat looming over Poland and
Rumania, on 18th March 1939, with a proposal for a conference 'of the most interested States – namely Britain, France,
Rumania, Poland, Turkey, and the USSR'. The Chamberlain
Government, after considering this offer, deemed it 'prema-
ture'; then, less than two weeks later, Chamberlain announced
British (and French) guarantees to Poland in event of attack

[1] See *Soviet Documents on Foreign Policy*, Jane Degras, ed, III, 304–305.

from Germany.[1] This promise to send support to faraway Poland, without an understanding with the Poles' Russian neighbour, astounded Chamberlain's critics, Tories, Liberals and Labour men alike. Why have you done this? they demanded. Why commit the British to an action they could not possibly perform and at the same time refuse the only concrete aid that was available? It was still baffling to Sir Robert Boothby after the war: to guarantee Poland without alliance with Russia was madness, he wrote, 'an act of insanity. . . . To this day, I can't imagine why they did it – they who had always been so cautious and timid.'[2]

They – Chamberlain, Simon, Hoare and Halifax – did it precisely because they were so cautious, because they, the inner circle of government, were trying doggedly to sustain the policy of Appeasement. They guaranteed Poland because they hoped with that action to deter Hitler (the Fuehrer, that psychological puzzle, had responded to a pacific policy with threats of war – was it not possible to try the reverse process to persuade him to peace?). Certainly, this is the message which Ambassador Nevile Henderson passed to the Nazis. 'Chamberlain's policy was one of peace,' Henderson was quoted as saying, 'but Chamberlain believed that the best way of maintaining peace was for Britain to demonstrate beyond any doubt that in case of necessity she was ready to fight, and to defend herself against an attack. However, the British Government were, as always, determined to do everything in their power to maintain peace, and to seek a satisfactory solution to the existing difficulties without having recourse to war.' And the conclusive evidence that Chamberlain worked still to make a deal for peace with Hitler was that he

---

[1] It is an interesting insight into the abilities of Chamberlain and his colleagues that the pledge to Poland was made secretly earlier in March, that it was part of a diplomatic manœuvre managed by the wily Polish Foreign Minister, Colonel Beck—who convinced the British that Poland was safe from German aggression. See *British Documents*, Third Series, IV, No 518. Thus, the 'British offer of a guarantee to Poland was made on the assumption that Poland was in no danger'. Gilbert and Gott, *The Appeasers*, p 241.

[2] Lord Boothby, *I Fight to Live*, p 187.

rejected a Soviet alliance, the one action that could indicate to the Germans the untruth that he meant to go to war for the Poles.

There were other thoughts, certainly, that reinforced the reluctance to deal with the Kremlin in the last summer of European peace in 1939. If there was a basic rationale to the strategy of Appeasement, it was – as critics claimed from the mid-1930s (and since) – the 'free hand' granted to Hitler in the East, the deflection of aggressive Nazism toward the Bolshevik enemy.[1] The fate of Czechoslovakia demonstrated Hitler's fanatic bent for conquest; why, under any conceivable circumstances, should the Chamberlain Government commit itself to intervention in any part of Eastern Europe, try to prevent the surely cataclysmic conflict between the (now proven) unreliable Germans and the detested Russian communists?

(And in 1939, Russian policy was being reshaped to counter this clear Western analysis, moving away, after the collapse of collective security at Munich, from the policy – since 1934 carried by Foreign Minister Maxim Litvinov – of safety from German aggression through cooperation with the West. On 10th March 1939, Premier Stalin addressed the Eighteenth Congress of the CPSU on the 'new imperialist war':

> It is a distinguishing feature of the new imperialist war that it has not yet become universal, a world war. The war is being waged by aggressor states, who in every way infringe upon the interests of the non-aggressive states, primarily England, France and the United States, while the latter draw back and retreat, making concession after concession to the aggressors.
>
> Thus, we are witnessing an open redivision of the world and spheres of influence at the expense of the non-aggressive states,

[1] See *The Week*, 1st April 1936; Hugh Dalton, *House of Commons Debates*, Vol 310, Fifth Series, pp 1453–1458; Fleming, *Cold War*, I, 84–87; Wheeler-Bennett, *Munich*, pp 326–328. See also Salvemini, *World War II*, 509: British actions 'were the logical consequences of a basic assumption, ie, that Hitler, after swallowing Austria and Czechoslovakia, would go and meet his doom in Eastern Europe. If one ignores that assumption, British foreign policy after 1934 becomes a succession of absurd muddles. If one bears it in mind, the polices of the British Tories become clear and consistent.'

without the least attempt at resistance, and even with a certain amount of connivance, on the part of the latter.

To what are we to attribute this one-sided and strange character of the new imperialist war? . . . Is it to be attributed to the weakness of the non-aggressive states? Of course not! Combined, the non-aggressive, democratic states are unquestionably stronger than the fascist states, both economically and in the military sense.

. . . The chief reason is that the majority of the non-aggressive countries, particularly England and France, have rejected the policy of collective security . . . and have taken up a position of non-intervention, a position of 'neutrality'.

. . . The policy of non-intervention reveals an eagerness, a desire, not to hinder the aggressors in their nefarious work: not to hinder Japan, say, from embroiling herself in a war with China, or, better still, with the Soviet Union; not to hinder Germany, say, from getting bogged down in European affairs, from embroiling herself in a war with the Soviet Union. . . .

. . . take Germany, for instance. They let her have Austria, despite the undertaking to defend her independence; they let her have the Sudeten region; they abandoned Czechoslovakia . . . and then began . . . egging the Germans on to march farther east, promising them easy pickings [in] war on the Bolsheviks.)

The Chamberlain clique was guided, too, by built-in reactions against contact with the Russians. At base it was the cleavage between two worlds, the conditioned response of hostility and hatred between bourgeois and Bolshevik; it was this sort of rooted attitude that an MP identified when he charged that Chamberlain 'could not let a single friendly word pass his lips' in reference to the Soviet Union. On this foundation twenty years had piled distrust and suspicion – on both sides; for their part, Chamberlain and his associates pointed to 'Russian plots and intrigues', and cited evidence to prove that Stalin had consistently been 'exploiting for his own ends the differences between Germany and the West'.[1] And the Chamberlain group buttressed their long-standing negativism with the argument that the Russians, in any case, were worthless allies, that the

[1] Hoare, *Nine Years*, p 350.

purges in the Soviet Union from 1936, that had liquidated Marshal Tukachevsky and his fellow generals, as well as thousands of other top officers, had crippled the efficiency and striking power of the Red Army; the talk, said Conservatives, of Russians being able to send troops, munitions or supplies to Poland was the rankest nonsense.[1] Chamberlain expressed such attitudes in a note of 26th March:

> I must confess to the most profound distrust of Russia. I have no belief whatever in her ability to maintain an effective offensive, even if she wanted to. And I distrust her motives, which seem to me to have little connection with our ideas of liberty, and to be concerned only with getting every one else by the ears. Moreover, she is both hated and suspected by many of the smaller States, notably by Poland, Rumania and Finland.[2]

The British Government received from the Soviet Union, on 18th April, the formal proposal of alliance of Britain, France, and the USSR, which pledged the three powers to act together in case of aggression against any one of them and promised the aid of the three powers against aggression to Eastern European states 'situated between the Baltic and Black Seas and bordering on the USSR'. Churchill said in the House:

> Above all, time must not be lost. . . . There is no means of maintaining an Eastern Front against Nazi aggression without the active aid of Russia. . . . It could still be possible to range all the states and peoples from the Baltic to the Black Sea in one solid front against a new outrage or invasion. Such a front, if established in good heart, and with resolute and efficient military arrangements, combined with the strength of the Western Powers, may yet confront Hitler, Goering, Himmler, Ribben-

---

[1] Churchill knew better: 'A system of government,' he said, 'that is founded on terror may well be strengthened by a ruthless and successful assertion of its power.' *Gathering Storm*, p 289.

[2] Feiling, *Neville Chamberlain*, p 403. Dawson of *The Times*, trying hard to keep in step with the Government, wrote (2nd May 1939) that although the British might be 'indifferent' to the 'internal system' of the USSR, other states were not. On 4th May, however, Dawson was realistic enough to add that though Britain had 'no wish to join an ideological front', alliance there should be if the Soviets would 'stand against aggression'. *The Times*, 2nd May, 4th May 1939.

trop, Goebbels and Company with forces the German people would be reluctant to challenge.[1]

Despite pressure from the Commons – or Press – Chamberlain would not be pushed into alliance with the Soviet Union. He found his immediate counter-argument in the attitude of the Polish Government (and those of Rumania and the Baltic states) toward cooperation with the Russians. Chamberlain's hesitation in negotiating with Russia, wrote Feiling, 'was not derived from ideological prejudice', but 'it was at once made manifest that Poland would refuse contact with the Soviet, which alone was enough to prevent us taking up the Russian proposal'. The Poles felt – and Chamberlain confessed he very much agreed – that an understanding with Russia would lead to 'an immediate declaration of war on the part of Germany'. Here, then, was sufficient explanation of the 'considerable delay' which accompanied the Anglo-Soviet negotiations that Chamberlain reluctantly agreed to – as a sop to his critics in the Commons – during the summer of 1939. Quite deliberately, Chamberlain treated the discussions with the Soviet Union as a negligible matter: he would 'not consider Eden's offer to go to Moscow', and sent instead William Strang, 'an able official but without any special standing outside the Foreign Office'; to conduct military conversations an Admiral Drax travelled to the Kremlin, an officer with 'no written authority to negotiate'.[2] All of the negotiations 'wandered around the question of the reluctance of Poland and the Baltic States to be rescued from Germany by the Soviets[3];

[1] Churchill, *Gathering Storm*, p 365. Press experts shared the analysis. The Editors of the *Manchester Guardian* called for the end of 'our foolish policy towards Russia', and the conclusion of the alliance that would confront Hitler with a circling wall of nations determined for peace. *Manchester Guardian Weekly*, 31st March, 7th April 1939. Even Garvin of *The Observer* (14th May 1939), his energies devoted now to showing Hitler the British determination to resist aggression, demanded a 'full understanding with Russia' – which would guarantee Russian borders, if that were the condition – as the only way to 'uphold our pledges'.

[2] Churchill, *Gathering Storm*, pp 389, 390.

[3] Especially the *impasse* centred on the Soviet demands for military rights in the Baltic states in case of attack. What seems most likely, however, is that deadlock was inevitable – as the documents show. *British Documents*, Third Series, IV, Nos 479, 484; *ibid*, VII, Nos 70, 87, 90.

and here they made no progress' – nor were they intended, in Whitehall, to make progress. As Lloyd George acidly observed, there was no hope of alliance with the Soviet Union – 'this powerful gift horse' – while the Chamberlain hand guided the policies of the nation.[1]

On 3rd May it was announced from Moscow that Foreign Minister Maxim Litvinov had been dismissed, and that he had been replaced by Vyacheslav Molotov. The shift was portentious. Litvinov, champion of collective security, of Soviet cooperation with the Western democracies, was eliminated, and Molotov, reputedly Stalin's 'closest collaborator', substituted in the Foreign Office; the reason for the change, speculated the German Chargé d'Affaires in Moscow, was perhaps 'the deep distrust which Stalin feels for the whole capitalist world'. On 21st August a trade and credit agreement was concluded between Germany and the Soviet Union, and on 23rd August the two nations signed a non-aggression pact, pledging peace with one another, and neutrality should one become engaged in hostilities with a third power[2]; Stalin, quite clearly, had become impatient with half-hearted Western negotiators and had bought himself a moment of safety – and a more realistic ally. The German-Soviet non-aggression pact broke 'like an explosion' in the West[3]: with the Russians neutralised, Hitler was free to move

[1] Although the faithful Dawson supported Chamberlain in editorials (see *The Times*, 11th, 12th July 1939), the opposition Press condemned more strongly his hesitation to 'encircle' Germany through alliance with Russia. *The Spectator* voiced the suspicion that the Government was 'hankering after an early resumption of the policy of appeasement', that Chamberlain would 'make any concession in preference to war'. *The Spectator*, 19th May, 9th June, 17th July 1939.
[2] *Soviet Documents*, III, 359, 360. Rumours of a Russian-German agreement had been floating about during the summer of 1939. *The Observer* staff had heard them: in 'The World' it was reported from German sources that Litvinov's removal was the sign of Stalin's turning against alliance with the West, and from Japanese sources that a Russian-German deal was in the offing; such tips were ominous, thought the writer, for Russia was 'cardinal to the whole situation in Europe'. *The Observer*, 7th May 1939.
[3] Although the French knew it was coming, informed by their Ambassador in Moscow, Robert Coulondre. Coulondre told the story of his interview with Vladimir Potemkin of the Soviet Foreign Office, on 4th October 1938, immediately after Munich: 'He received me coldly and listened to me without a word.' Finally, Potemkin spoke, with these words: 'I would say simply that the Western powers deliberately excluded the USSR from these negotiations. . . . My poor friend, what have you done? For us, I see no other alternative but the fourth partition of Poland.' Robert Coulondre, *De Staline à Hitler, Souvenirs de Deux Ambassades*, p 165.

where he liked – nothing, as Churchill said, 'could now avert or delay the conflict'.[1]

And so, although it was only a paper pledge, the Chamberlain Government was held by the guarantee to Poland; with Hitler's troops smashing toward Warsaw, the Appeasers went to war – and without Russia as an ally.[2] (Perhaps they thought it better that way. In a last pleading interview, Ambassador Nevile Henderson tried to convince Hitler of the Chamberlain Government's unchanged longing for peace with Germany. He, personally, said Henderson, 'had never believed in an Anglo-French-Russian Pact' as a weapon against the Fuehrer; in any case, he personally preferred 'that it should be Germany rather than England who should have a treaty with Russia'.) But it was a strange entry into war, all quite consistent with the line of Appeasement. German troops invaded Poland on 1st September, whereupon the British Government, under its obligations, might immediately have declared Britain at war with Germany. But no – for two days the war declaration was held up, while feverish activity went on behind the public scene. Tory MP Leopold Amery related the feeling in the House of Commons:

> On 1st September we met again late in the afternoon expecting to be told we were at war. We were told, instead, that the British and French Ambassadors in Berlin had been instructed to present a memorandum demanding satisfactory assurances by the German Government that it had suspended aggressive action against Poland and was prepared promptly to withdraw its forces from Polish territory, failing which we should without hesitation fulfil our obligations to Poland. The absence of any time limit to these curious and obviously unfulfillable conditions,

[1] Churchill, *Gathering Storm*, p. 394.
[2] The tone of the responsible Press was impressive – both toward the Russian-German Pact and Britain's entry into war. See *The Times*, 26th August, 4th September 1939; *The Spectator* (25th August 1939) stated calmly that there was no use for regrets about the Russian action, urged that the nation face the consequences as it had other, past 'desperate perils'. Even Garvin aimed the brunt of his attack against Hitler rather than the Soviets – vowing to avenge the criminal acts of the Nazis and citing only the 'Realpolitik' of Russia. *The Observer*, 27th August 1939.

and a grateful reference by the Prime Minister to Mussolini's efforts to find a peaceful solution, left the House puzzled and deeply disquieted.

The House was puzzled and deeply disquieted because its Members could not quite believe that Neville Chamberlain was capable of leading the nation to war against Nazi Germany – or, no doubt, Members too had heard the kind of talk that an unnamed correspondent sent as a 'Confidential Report' from London to Berlin:

> Considering the obligations which they have undertaken, the British feel that they cannot avoid declaring war in the event of an attack on Poland, but they still manage to believe that it will be conducted on such a moderate scale that there would be no question of a life and death struggle between the Great Powers. . . . At all events the 'qualitatively limited war' is at present engaging the minds of quite a number of know-ledgeable people and the idea seems to have a certain attraction for various ministers. Even such a convinced 'supporter of Munich' as Sir Samuel Hoare is reported to have made the following statement immediately before the Cabinet meeting: 'Although we cannot in the circumstances avoid declaring war, we can always fulfil the letter of a declaration of war without immediately going all out.'

Inevitably, as long as Chamberlain remained as Prime Minister, Appeasement hovered in the air – much as he tried to dispel it, much as he tried to pretend to reflect the new spirit of resolve both in his Party and in the nation. It was a set of responses, for one thing, typical Chamberlain responses that kept it alive. His speech to Parliament on 3rd September, when he announced that Britain was at war with Germany, was a wail of personal tragedy, the shockingly bad taste of which he was, undoubtedly, totally unaware. With all Britain expecting the first attack of the enemy bombers, Chamberlain bemoaned the fact that

everything that I have worked for, everything that I have hoped for, everything that I have believed in during my public life, has crashed into ruins. There is only one thing left for me to do: that is, to devote what strength and powers I have to forwarding the victory of the cause for which we have to sacrifice so much. I cannot tell what part I may be allowed to play myself: I trust I may live to see the day when Hitlerism has been destroyed, and a liberated Europe has been re-established.

It was the same old Chamberlain, obsessed with his personal failure. The steady concentration on self would make him strain to stay in as Prime Minister – although he would admit that he 'was never meant to be a war minister'; through the long bitter debates with the House Opposition on the impotency of his leadership, he must surely have been telling himself: 'one more year, and I will justify my public actions, re-establish the name of Neville Chamberlain'. Arrogant, secretive – it was the same old Chamberlain, who was even more suspect now to those whom he called enemies in political circles: typical, for example, was the swift judgment in the House during the two-day delay in declaring war, the certainty among Members that the Government was attempting a surreptitious deal with the Nazis; Chamberlain himself was shaken by the reaction, noting with dismay that 'the House of Commons was out of hand, torn with suspicions, and ready (some of them . . .) to believe the Government guilty of any cowardice and treachery'. Trust and confidence in his leadership, in even the most stalwart Conservative circles, was fading rapidly during what Chamberlain was pleased to call the 'Twilight War'.

Others dubbed it the 'Phoney War' – the suspended status of European conflict from the fall of Poland to the German invasion of the Low Countries and France, during the last months of Chamberlain's premiership. Stories of peace feelers and top-level secret agreements persisted and circulated, stories from which Chamberlain carefully separated himself. His biographer will admit that the Prime Minister was over-confident: he thought that Hitler, 'faithful to his aim of

conquest without a total war, would not face the carnage of a
frontal attack on the Maginot Line'; he doubted also 'the
turning of that line by an armoured invasion of the Low
Countries', for even Hitler would shrink from 'the political
reactions of a breach of neutrality so flagrant and unscrupulous';
as for a great air offensive, 'that too he doubted', for an 'air
attack of this kind would entail retaliation, which might have
unexpected effects on morale in Germany'. He would use the
Navy, maintain the blockade against German shipping, and
exhort the nation to 'hold on tightly, keep up the economic
pressure, push on with munitions production and military
preparations with the utmost energy, take no offensive unless
Hitler begins it'; then, he thought, something would give in
Germany, depression or unpopularity of the war, that would
upset Hitler and his Nazis – in fact, he had a feeling that the
war would be over in the spring. Were there those who warned
of the striking power of the German Army and air force, so
frighteningly displayed in the blitz against Poland? Said
Chamberlain, 'I shall do as I always have done, go for what
I believe to be the right course, and risk the consequences.'

It was indeed a 'qualitatively limited' war (incredible,
bourgeois concept!) that Chamberlain waged, this leader
who, until May of 1940, was in 'effective control of the general
conduct of the war'.[1] Leo Amery's account of the course and
of the effects of the 'Phoney War' ranks as one of the best:

> The British and French Governments immediately on the
> outbreak of war issued a declaration 'solemnly affirming their
> intention to conduct hostilities with a firm desire to spare the
> civilian population' and to preserve historical monuments,
> and announced that they had instructed their forces not to
> bombard any but 'strictly military objectives in the narrowest
> sense of the word', providing always that the enemy did the
> same. I was not long in discovering how narrow was to be the
> interpretation put on the words 'military objectives'. On 5th
> September I saw Kingsley Wood, the Air Minister, with the

[1] Amery, *Political Life*, III, 328.

suggestion that, in view of Germany's shortage of timber, we should try and set fire to the Black Forest. I was quite prepared to be told that there were technical objections or that there were other, more worth while and militarily more important objectives. To my consternation he told me that *there was no question of our bombing even the munition works at Essen, which were private property, or lines of communication,* and that doing so would alienate American opinion. To my question whether we were going to lift a finger to help the Poles he had no answer. My diary says that 'I went away very angry'.[1]

Mr Amery got angrier as the 'Phoney War' progressed:

> While the hapless Polish Army was being overrun, mainly because all its communications were wrecked by the over-whelming German Air Force, which had no scruples about bombing Polish civilians, our only contribution to the battle was to send our bombers to drop leaflets telling the Germans how misguided they were to be at war! . . . Nor do Ministers seem to have seen anything inconsistent with our self-denying ordinance against attacking German communications or private property on land and the indiscriminate German laying of mines, the bombing of lightships, merchant vessels and even the machine-gunning of crews trying to escape in their boats.

Further during, the months of the 'Phoney War', while the British and French Air Forces refrained from action,

> A gigantic expansion of German munitions production was carried out in complete ease and comfort. Thousands of tanks, armoured cars and lorries rolled off the production lines. Airplane production was feverishly speeded up. All the material required for an immense increase of the Army was provided and distributed. All under conditions of perfect peace. By March, Hitler could claim, without undue boasting, that Germany's fighting power had increased more in the last five months than in the previous seven years. No doubt a more active war . . . would at least have forced the Germans to expend the petrol, rubber and other special metals and materials required for aircraft production, in all of which they were

[1] Italics are the author's.

short, while the Allies had all the world to draw upon. It is, indeed, doubtful how far the Germans could ever have mounted the great break-through in the spring, or the Battle of Britain in the autumn, but for the unexpectedly low rate of oil consumption during the 'Phoney War'.

The last five months of Chamberlain's term were a fitting climax to his career. Within this period came the Russian war against Finland, the German invasion of Norway, and the countering British campaign, the German *Blitzkrieg* on the Western Front – and all of these Chamberlain met in an entirely, rigidly, predictable manner. With the outbreak of the Russo-Finnish War, he became, suddenly, a veritable warlord – he and a well-nigh unanimous Conservative leadership, the rebels as well as the Appeasers (here was a war to believe in!): two British divisions, British bombers, fifty thousand French 'volunteers' and a hundred bombers were readied to send to Finland, and would have gone except for the refusal of the Norwegians and the Swedes to allow them passage. In view of the intelligence reports of German forces massing on the Western Front, the size of this force for Finland was, Winston Churchill admitted, 'far beyond what prudence would allow'. The campaign in Norway – and there was no inconsistency here – was from the start ill-conceived, ill-supported, and under-supplied, a 'ramshackle campaign', Churchill called it, for which he, as First Lord of the Admiralty, took his share of the blame. The German invasion, begun on 9th April, was a brilliant co-ordination of landing vessels, troops and air cover – 'surprise, ruthlessness and precision' – with the result that in 'forty-eight hours all the main ports of Norway were in the German grip'. The British annals were brief and disastrous: troops landed at two ports on 14th and 17th April, made no headway against German resistance and were evacuated on 1st and 3rd May. Leo Amery pointed to the clue to the British defeat: 'The airfields of Germany were the real bases of the campaign, as we knew both from commonsense and captured pilots; the official policy, however, was to take no action which might provoke, or help to touch off, retaliation against the British or French soil'. British pilots, Amery continued, 'were not given permission to bomb the Ruhr till 15th May. They were not even allowed to attack German-held aerodromes in Denmark and Norway till 11th April, and even then, for another two days only allowed to machine gun, but forbidden to drop bombs!' What Chamberlain-type madness was this? Fear of over-offending the Germans, fear of destroying 'private property', fear of the social effects of Nazi bombers over British cities – the fears of a handful of old men, crippled the war effort, poisoned the national spirit. And on 10th May, as Hitler's mechanised division cut through Holland and Belgium, Neville Chamberlain, proven incompetent, and self-declared minister of peace, manœuvred desperately (was he not 'indispensable'?) to stay on as Premier.

The sessions and debates in the House of Commons during which Chamberlain – and Chamberlainism – was, in the name of the nation, eliminated as a guiding force, stand among the most dramatic of British history. The debates opened 7th May with discussion of the debacle in Norway, but they stopped only briefly there; until 10th May, the Members were preoccupied with but one thing – to ensure that after their meetings Britain would have a government with courage and resolution to carry the nation through this grave period. Not that Chamberlain felt the profound matter at stake. Faced with the vote of censure, he was personally affronted: 'I accept the challenge,' he said. 'I welcome it indeed. At least we shall see who is with us and who is against us, and I call on my friends to support us in the Lobby tonight.' Chamberlain, a partisan politician to the end!

Leopold Amery held the historic spotlight of these momentous May debates – Amery, who had gone into the House prepared for 'open warfare', knowing, as he did, that Chamberlain would not give way gracefully. Amery knew, too, that he gave that day the speech of his life. He began with a review of the Government's lame explanations for the failure of its war plans, then passed to an analysis of the special qualities needed – 'vision, daring, swiftness and consistency of decision' – in wartime, qualities that were, in a representative political system, so very hard to find. Finally:

> In recent years the normal weakness of our political life has been accentuated by a coalition based upon no clear political principles. . . . Surely, for the Government of the last ten years to have bred a band of warrior statesmen would have been little short of a miracle. We have waited for eight months, and the miracle has not come to pass. Can we afford to wait any longer?
>
> Somehow or other we must get into the Government men who can match our enemies in fighting spirit, in daring, in resolution and in thirst for victory. Some three hundred years ago, when this House found that its troops were being beaten again and again by the dash and daring of the Cavaliers, by Prince Rupert's Cavalry, Oliver Cromwell spoke to John Hampden. In one of his speeches he recounted what he said. It was this: 'I said to him, "Your troops are most of them old, decayed serving men and tapsters and such kind of fellows. . . . You must get men of a spirit that are likely to go as far as *they* will go, or you will be beaten still".' It may not be easy to find these men. They can be found only by trial and by ruthlessly discarding all who fail and have their failings discovered. We are fighting today for our life, for our liberty, for our all; we cannot go on being led as we are.

At that point, Amery related later, he hesitated. Should he, he wondered, quote certain other words of Cromwell, phrases that would make here, in this moment of 1939, an apt and powerful conclusion to his own speech? True, he was not out for a 'dramatic finish, but for a practical purpose; to bring down the Government'. Yet, as he looked around the House he knew he had carried its Members with him. Thus:

> I have quoted certain words of Oliver Cromwell. I will quote certain other words. I do it with great reluctance, because I am speaking of those who are old friends and associates of mine, but they are words which, I think, are applicable to

the present situation. This is what Cromwell said to the Long Parliament when he thought it was no longer fit to conduct the affairs of the nation: 'You have sat too long here for any good you have been doing. Depart, I say, and let us have done with you. In the name of God, go!'

When he sat down Amery knew that he had done what he had meant to do.

And so Neville Chamberlain departed from public life, to be remembered by a nation learning piecemeal the details of the diplomacy of the 1930s, as the man who prepared the way for Hitler's aggression. He is a fitting symbol of Appeasement – this old Victorian, whose life spanned revolutions within British society, whose perceptions and attitudes and abilities might have distinguished him as the Lord Mayor of Birmingham at the turn of the century. He never admitted an awareness of the horror he had helped turn loose upon Europe, never admitted an awareness that the crimes of Nazism were on a lower level than disturbance of the peace. Chamberlain was sorry about the state of affairs at the end of his career (and his life – he died November 1940), unhappy about his political fall, truly distressed that war had come, but out of it all he managed to find one self-justifying point: 'I know', he wrote, 'that my persistent efforts have convinced the world that no part of the blame can lie here. That consciousness of moral right . . . must be a tremendous force on our side.'

13
A Conclusion
on Responsibility

IN HIS *Origins of the Second World War*, A J P Taylor proposes
Ramsay MacDonald, twice Labour Prime Minister in the
1920s and 'renegade' Prime Minister of the 'National' (Conser-
vative-dominated) Government until 1935, as the father of
the policy of appeasement of Germany, indeed as 'the patron-
saint of every contemporary Western politician who favours
co-operation with Germany'. Perhaps there is such a case for
MacDonald, who loved to pose as 'aristocratic charmer and
courtly society man',[1] who as Prime Minister was gradually
converted to 'the outlook of the city and "London Society" '.[2]
MacDonald was a sick man and a negligible leader in the
1930s (he died in 1937), but in his interwar career his attitudes
on basic matters of foreign policy, his hopes for a stable German
partner, his anti-Bolshevism,[3] were as staunchly Right as those
of any Conservative. On the other hand, this seems an unnecessary stretching of the historical imagination. If one
wants to select a 'patron-saint' of Appeasement, Lord Milner
is the most obvious candidate – Milner, whose Imperial vision
had shown him the clearest way to protect British interests
and world position in the dangers of the aftermath of World
War I.[4]

Possibly, even probably, Milner himself would have dis-
avowed the Conservative Appeasement of the 1930s. It was,
after all, the work of politicians, who operated within a
democratic system and had to take into account the erratic
and uninformed reactions of public opinion; Milner, we know,
'loathed the slipshod compromises, the optimistic "slogans",

[1] *Beatrice Webb's Diaries*, 1924–32, p 18.
[2] *Ibid*, p 283.
[3] See G D H Cole, *A History of the Labour Party from 1914*, pp 168, 257–258.
[4] See the Introduction.

the vote-catching half-truths with which democracy seemed to compromise the majestic governing art'.[1] His followers and disciples – Dawson, Lothian, even J L Garvin, who had been on the fringes of Milner's clique – were consistent and clear-headed enough in their efforts to adapt his ideas to the chief foreign problems of the 1930s. Leopold Amery was perhaps the most tough-minded (the most like Milner?) of them all: he would, apparently, have armed to the teeth, cemented an alliance along the lines of the Stresa Front – and then negotiated an understanding with the difficult masters of the New Germany. Dr Schacht is cited as a second-hand source for Amery's 'advice' to Germany: 'You can't have colonies,' Amery is supposed to have said, 'but Eastern Europe lies before you.'[2] The politicians were not quite cut to such Milnerite standards of statesmanship – Baldwin, with his inability to think consistently and for long on any diplomatic matter, forlornly wanted to forget the existence of the 'mad' outside world; Chamberlain, who certainly tried to apply a Milnerite blueprint to Europe, but embroidered it with his own personal needs and his own kind of unctuous moralism. (Amery, in a classic, Milner-like passage, commented on Chamberlain's inadequacies: 'Poor Neville. . . . If ever there was an essential civilian, a citizen accustomed to deal with fellow citizens on City Council or in Cabinet, and a man quite incapable of thinking in terms of force, or strategy or diplomacy, it is Neville. If he survives his efforts as a Foreign Minister I wonder how long he can survive as a war leader.'

Yet Conservative leaders did well enough with the Milnerite content of Appeasement that observers, then and later, recognised the shadow of its form. 'He had to ally himself,' Lord Boothby wrote about Chamberlain, 'to one or other of the military dictatorships which were engaged in mortal struggle for the hegemony of Europe. There was no other way of

[1] Lord Lothian's words, quoted in Gollin, *Proconsul*, p 48.
[2] Quoted in Butler, *Lord Lothian*, appendix, p 352.

preserving any kind of balance of power, or the values of Western Civilisation anywhere. Germany or Russia. Which should it be?' ('For my part,' Boothby continued, 'I had no doubt as to what the decision should be. I chose Russia because socialism was still their proclaimed goal, because in socialism there was still hope, and because Litvinov had espoused the cause of collective security; whereas the ultimate objective of the Nazis was racial domination, the total destruction of individual freedom, and the annihilation of culture and reason.' It was this kind of thinking, among younger men of his own Party, as well as the Labour Opposition, that contributed to Chamberlain's problems in 1938 and 1939.) A L Rowse, who from All Souls despaired over the course of Appeasement, observed elliptically that there was a 'fatal confusion' in the minds of the Conservatives 'between the interests of their social order and the interests of their country. They did not say much about it, since that would have given the game away, and anyway it was a thought they did not wish to be too explicit about, even to themselves, but they were anti-Red and that hamstrung them in dealing with the greater immediate danger to their country, Hitler's Germany.' Or – interesting episode – there is the example of one apologist for Chamberlain who did in fact 'give the game away' in an interview with the Press: in 1962, Sir Alec Douglas-Home (then Lord Home)[1] explained to his interviewer this about Appeasement in the 1930s, when he was Private Parliamentary Secretary to Neville Chamberlain:

> I think the main thing to grasp is that Chamberlain, like many others, saw Communism as the major long-term danger. He hated Hitler and German Fascism, but he felt that Europe in general and Britain in particular [*why, 'in particular'?*] were

[1] Sir Alec was then Foreign Minister in Harold Macmillan's Cabinet. His record as an appeaser was not forgotten by the editors of the *New Statesman* who were reminded of it by an incident that occurred during a state visit from Queen Frederika of Greece: Home's 'abasement' before the 'fascist-minded' Queen brought back the editorial memory that he had 'learned his diplomatic manners at the feet of Neville Chamberlain and Lord Halifax'. *New Statesman*, 3rd May 1963.

in even greater danger from Communism. Hitler was an evil man but in the short term one should—and possibly could—do a deal with him, and after that he could be controlled. He didn't realise till too late, you see, that the man was mad and his policy *aimed* at war.[1]

Sir Alec thus seemed to have had the last, or at least the latest, word in explaining the attempt to 'do a deal' with Hitler – as an earlier phase of Cold War statesmanship.

Ultimately, however, it was not Lord Milner but the Conservative leaders who were responsible for the policy of Appeasement of Nazism. Rowse, in discussing those leaders, remarked that they were only the most 'eminent specimens' of a 'class in decadence' – a perspective that would tend to diffuse their responsibility among the governing upper-classes of the nation. And Conservatives had occasional assistance in or assent to their Appeasement – perhaps, as Mr Taylor wrote, from an *ersatz* social democrat like Ramsay MacDonald, or positively, for a time, from the aging *enfant terrible* of Liberal politics, David Lloyd George.[2] There are obvious reasons, however, for insisting that the record of Appeasement be 'pinned squarely on the politicians and diplomats',[2] for refusing to let the Blimps of the 'thirties off lightly. As the politically ambitious of their society they offered themselves as symbols and agents; they were there, in the national spotlight, and prominent, as their nameless constituents were not, as

---

[1] 'The Foreign Secretary Opens Up', *The Observer*, 16th September 1962.

[2] Lloyd George, always unpredictable, was heard in the 1930s both 'singing the praises of Stalin' and loudly enthusing about Hitler – calling the latter a 'magnetic, dynamic personality'. In 1934, in the Commons, Lloyd George made a statement in favour of ignoring the war-like sounds coming from the New Germany – words that remind us that he was part of the 'secret appeasement plans' of 1918: 'I remember very well when the Russian army was a mere rabble, ill-equipped, and yet all Europe was trembling. It was just imagining hordes of Lenin's banditti tearing down and trampling over Europe. [Now the Russian army] is infinitely the best army they have had. [There is] no danger comparable to that of Red Russia. . . . In a very short time, perhaps in a year or two, the Conservative elements in this country will be looking to Germany as the bulwark against Communism in Europe. . . . Do not let us be in a hurry to condemn Germany. We shall be welcoming Germany as our friend.' *House of Commons Debates*, Vol 247, Fifth Series, pp 918–919.

[3] Salvemini, *World War II*, p 7.

examples of the kind. Further, they were leaders of a great nation, representatives of a proud tradition of leadership, and supposedly trained to responsibilities that were worldwide. Besides, the special contributions of the individuals were important; the qualities of character and mind of these Conservative leaders, almost immovable in their monopoly of the top positions of Party and Government, determined the dismal twist of the policy-choices that were actually made.

The 'Munichmen' stand identified as the Appeasers, and indicted, broadly, on the same two charges levelled against them by contemporary critics. The Churchillian opposition, people of their own Party or class, accused them of 'spineless concessionism' (although the phrase is Rowse's), and – most serious – of ineptness and incapacity, almost criminal negligence in their appointed tasks of protecting the national security. After the war against Germany had been won, Churchill was still feeling the shame of Appeasement: it still made him 'flush' to hear of the contempt and derision with which the dictators had regarded the pre-war British leadership – Mussolini's remark, for instance, that they were 'the tired sons of a long line of rich men'. The son of the house of Marlborough would not have knuckled down to the Italian adventurer or the Austrian corporal! Nor, Churchill insisted, would a government of his kind of people have been brought to the incredible disadvantage that was Chamberlain's position in 1939: the Grand Alliance would have been an early, and for Hitler an unmistakably restrictive, fact – and thus might have saved Britain and Europe from the immeasurable toll of the war. The maddening thing to Churchill was that even in 1939 it had not been too late: 'If Mr Chamberlain on receipt of the Russian offer had replied "Yes. Let us band together and break Hitler's neck . . ." Parliament would have approved, Stalin would have understood, and history might have taken a different course.'

From the Left in Britain came a different charge, although one of equal and lasting validity. The Conservatives, Leftists

said, had led the nation, with Appeasement, into a course of
utter political immorality, had in their pro-Fascism, or at least
preference for Fascism as a checkmate to the advances of
Communism, exposed as hollow and insignificant the British
commitment to constitutionalism and democratic progress.
With the paralysing contradictions of its own policies – its
insistence on collective action against aggression, to be achieved
without war and without 'unilateral rearmament'[1] – the
Labour Party had, certainly, inadequacies of its own in the
encounter with Fascism. But, in their increasingly bitter
opposition to Conservative Appeasement, Labour Members
made necessary points. The Appeasers *were* blinded by their
reading of the ideological issues of the age – in their favour
for Fascist nations that seemed to be 'run by people who
somehow stand for their own class, who know how to keep
their own working class in order'; at the very least, their
ideological blinkers gave them – as Eden discreetly phrased it
– an 'insufficiently clear view of whose side [they] were on'.
And Labour's lead in saying these things – the proper performance of the role of Opposition – was picked up by others,
by Liberal and/or democratic voices in Britain: the editor of
the *Manchester Guardian*, for example, discovered in 1938 'the
dangerous reactionary temper of large sections of the Conservative Party, to whom a virtual alliance with the dictators
would not be altogether distasteful'; or, in *The Spectator*, in 1940,
a writer sickened by the Conservative record of 'abandoning
Abyssinia, turning a blind eye towards Spain, or truncating
Czechoslovakia', flatly asserted that, through it all, Chamberlain and his supporters from the 'business community' were
'not sacrificing principles, but rather cutting their losses'.

The condemnation of Conservative Appeasement as a

---

[1] Even in 1939, Labour MPs, under leader Clement Attlee, were still opposing
military conscription in Britain – a sign, by this time, primarily of distrust of
Chamberlain's Government, fear that that Government would 'muddle into war',
or even that the Government would use the weapons of rearmament 'on the wrong
side'. For example, see Attlee, *As It Happened*, pp 114, 138–139, 146; G D H Cole
and M I Cole, *The Condition of Britain*, pp 441–442; Bertrand Russell, *et al, Dare
We Look Ahead*, pp 121–122 and *passim*.

betrayal of democratic – and humanistic – values leads to another aspect of Conservative deficiency in 'moral fastidiousness'. The charge that Chamberlain was 'blinded by his affection for the dictators, that dictatorship [was] dearer to him than democracy', was a sign of the political passions of the time – and no doubt, as close to reality as J L Garvin's outbursts in *The Observer*. Clement Attlee's accusation that Chamberlain was concerned only with 'the interests of British capital', that freedom, and even human lives, mattered little to the Prime Minister as long as 'Rio Tinto Mines [paid] a dividend', the historian, J L Hammond's charge that the Government was less concerned with British interests than with the successes of the 'Fascist trio, Hitler, Mussolini and Franco' – these were immoderate statements, to be sure. But behind the extremism of Leftists, one feels a special quality of frustration: they were deliberately trying to shock – to shatter the halo of propriety and *righteousness* with which Conservatives habitually surrounded their activities. All the while they pursued policies so agonising to democrats and socialists, the Appeasers (especially Chamberlain) spoke loftily of their preservation of peace, of their protection of the freedom of individuals and of the rights of 'small nations', of their unique contribution as defenders of the cherished values of Britain, indeed, of 'Western Civilisation'. Professor Rowse, whose insights on the Appeasers are well worth quoting, had this to say about official hypocrisy and, particularly, its effects: the Appeasers, Rowse wrote, 'came at the end of the ascendancy of the Victorian middle-class, deeply affected as that was by high-mindedness and humbug. They all talked, in one form or another, the language of disingenuousness and cant: it was second nature to them.' And this is the important thing: applied to the crisis-issues of the 1930s, that combination of high-mindedness and humbug 'was deeply corrupting, both to them and the nation'.[1]

---

[1] Rowse, *All Souls*, p 116.

Bibliography

As A J P TAYLOR has noted, it is quite true that in comparison with records on the causes of World War I the sources on the period of appeasement prior to World War II are peculiarly limited. The chief problem (although surely one not unique to this period) is to get to the heart of the matter of the Conservative policy, to find suggestive patterns of thought and action behind the bland narrative account, to locate reality beneath elaborate apology and self-justification. In both quantity and quality the sources are uneven. Memoirs of the major figures are few, although the literature from lesser officials and contemporary observers and participants is enormous. Documentary evidence is becoming massive – particularly Foreign Office records, which, however, are uncomplicated by explanation of motives behind British policy. In any case, the decisive area of policy-making, particularly in the Chamberlain years, was the Cabinet, ultimately the 'Big Four'; the only close account on the deliberations of these bodies is Anthony Eden's testimony in his *Memoirs* (1962) – far after the events and that ending in 1938. And yet the historian has workable and provocative material on the events and the men of Appeasement. For example, the story of that complex personality, Stanley Baldwin, may indeed remain to be done, but an informative figure emerges from a number of pages – from Baldwin's own speeches on political platforms or in Parliament, from Thomas Jones' *Diary*, or even from G M Young's slim biography. Similarly, few of Neville Chamberlain's personal records are available in the original; but his official biographer, Keith Feiling (a source in himself, as a staunch Conservative and Chamberlain defender), from his access to restricted material painstakingly reproduced dozens of personal letters, diary entries, and bits and fragments of both casual and official conversation. Or from others – Halifax, Hoare – who have told their own stories, one gets, if not a frank discussion of policy formulation, important insights into Conservative social and political ideas and attitudes. The point is that familiar and available sources contain essential outlines of the tale of Appeasement.

The books cited here are, then, for the most part, staple sources of the interwar period and, as such, represent a solid beginning bibliography for the general reader. At the same time, they are the sources that were most immediately useful, most directly valuable, to this study.

Memoirs, diaries, collections of letters, and biographies contain much information. In the first category the chief titles are these: Leopold S Amery, *My Political Life* (3 vols, London, 1955); Clement R Attlee, *As It Happened* (London, 1954); Eduard Benes, *Memoirs: From Munich to New War and New Victory* (Boston, 1953); Robert Boothby, *I Fight to Live* (London, 1947); Claude G Bowers, *My Mission to Spain* (New York, 1954); Duff Cooper, *Old Men Forget* (London, 1953); Robert Coulondre, *De Staline à Hitler: Souvenirs de Deux Ambassades, 1936–1939* (Hachette, 1950); Hugh Dalton, *The Fateful Years: Memoirs, 1931–45* (London, 1957); Herbert von Dirksen, *Moskau, Tokio, London: Erinnerungen und Betrachtungen zu 20 Jahre Deutscher Aussenpolitik, 1919–1939* (Stuttgart, 1950); Anthony Eden (Earl of Avon), *Memoirs: Facing the Dictators, 1923–1938* (London, 1962); Lord Halifax, *Fullness of Days* (London, 1957); Nevile Henderson, *Failure of a Mission* (London, 1940); Cordell Hull, *Memoirs* (New York, 1948); Douglas Jerrold, *Georgian Adventure* (London, 1937); Erich Kordt, *Wahn und Wirklichkeit* (Stuttgart, 1947); David Lloyd George, *Memoirs of the Peace Conference* (2 vols, London, 1938); Franz von Papen, *Memoirs*, trans Brian Connell (New York, 1953); Joachim Ribbentrop, *Memoirs* (London, 1953); Stanley Salvidge, *Salvidge of Liverpool: Behind the Political Scene, 1890–1928* (London, 1934); Hjalmar Schacht, *Autobiography: Confessions of 'the Old Wizard'* (Boston, 1956); Sir John Simon, *Comments and Criticism* (London, 1930); Lord Templewood (Sir Samuel Hoare), *Nine Troubled Years* (London, 1954); Lord Vansittart, *Lessons of My Life* (London, 1943); Lord Vansittart, *The Mist Procession* (London, 1958).

Diaries, collections of speeches and letters, and biographies that reprint diaries and letters are important sources, sometimes goldmines of information. The following were not of equal value, but all were useful: C F Adam, *The Life of Lord Lloyd* (London, 1948); A W Baldwin, *My Father: A True Story* (London, 1956); Stanley Baldwin, *Our Inheritance: Speeches and Addresses* (London, 1928); J R M Butler, *Lord Lothian, 1882–1940* (London, 1960); William Camp, *The Glittering Prizes: Lord Birkenhead* (London, 1960); Ciano's [Count

Galeazzo] *Diary, 1937–1938*, trans Andreas Mayor (London, 1946); William E Dodd, Jr, and Martha Dodd, eds, *Ambassador Dodd's Diary* (New York, 1941); Anthony Eden, *Foreign Affairs* (London, 1939); Keith Feiling, *The Life of Neville Chamberlain* (London, 1947); A M Gollin, *Proconsul in Politics* (New York, 1964); Ulrich von Hassell, *Diaries, 1938–1944* (New York, 1947); Thomas Jones, *A Diary with Letters, 1931–1950* (London, 1954); Maxim Litvinov, *Against Aggression: Speeches* (New York, 1939); Lord Lothian, *American Speeches* (London, 1941); Iain MacLeod, *Neville Chamberlain* (London, 1961); Harold Nicolson, *King George the Fifth, His Life and Reign* (London, 1952); Frank Owen, *Tempestuous Journey: Lloyd George, His Life and Times* (London, 1953); Sir Charles Petrie, *The Life and Letters of the Rt Hon Sir Austen Chamberlain* (2 vols, London, 1940); Lord Riddell, *Intimate Diary of the Peace Conference and After, 1918–1923* (London, 1933); *Beatrice Webb's Diaries*, ed Margaret Cole (2 vols, London, 1952–1956); Sir Arnold Wilson, *Thoughts and Talks, 1935–37: The Diary of a Member of Parliament* (London, 1938); G M Young, *Stanley Baldwin* (London, 1952).

Indispensable government publications and documents included *Parliamentary Debates; House of Commons Debates; House of Lords Debates* (Fourth, Fifth Series, 1900–1940). Of foreign policy documents, the following were most closely consulted: E L Woodward and Rohan Butler, eds, *Documents on British Foreign Policy, 1919–1939* (London, 1949); James W Gantenbein, ed, *Documentary Background of World War II, 1931–1941* (New York, 1948); *Documents and Materials Relating to the Eve of the Second World War, 1937–1939* (2 vols, Moscow, 1948); *Documents on German Foreign Policy, 1918–1945*, Series D, 1937–45 (10 vols, Washington, 1949–1957); *Les Événements Survenus en France de 1933 à 1945*, Rapport fait au nom de la Commission de l'Assemblée Nationale (6 vols, Paris, 1952); *Le Livre Jaune Français: Documents Diplomatiques, 1938–1939* (Paris, 1939).

A list of contemporary works on social and political affairs – in an age which most people recognised as a time of crisis – could be very long. The sources here are those most relevant to the present study, as well as a sample of a large selection of literature: Norman Angell, *Peace with the Dictators?* (London, 1938); H Page Arnot, *The General Strike, May 1926: Its Origins and History* (London, 1926); Audax, *Men in Our Times* (New York, 1940); Arthur Bryant, *The Spirit of Conservatism* (London, 1929); 'Cato', *Guilty Men* (New York, 1940); Lord Hugh Cecil, *Conservatism* (London, 1912); Claud

Cockburn, *In Time of Trouble* (London, 1956); G D H and M I Cole, *The Condition of Britain* (London, 1937); Duff Cooper, *Conservative Pamphlets* (London, 1925); Pierre Cot, *The Triumph of Treason* (New York, 1944); James Drennan, *BUF: Oswald Mosley and British Fascism* (London, 1934); Major Walter Eliot, *Toryism and the 20th Century* (London, 1927); Keith Feiling, *What is Conservatism?* (London, 1930); Captain Russell Grenfell, *Unconditional Hatred* (London, 1953); Simon Haxey, *Tory MP* (London, 1939); Sir Samuel Hoare, *Ambassador on Special Mission* (London, 1946); Quintin Hogg, *The Left was Never Right* (London, 1945); William Inge, *Labels and Libels* (London, 1929); William Inge, *Our Present Discontent* (London, 1939); Douglas Jerrold, *Georgian Adventure* (London, 1937); Duncan Keith-Shaw, *Neville Chamberlain* (London, 1939); Wyndham Lewis, *The Hitler Cult* (London, 1939); Arthur P Laurie, *The Case for Germany* (Berlin, 1939); Lord Lloyd, *The British Case* (London, 1939); Pierse Loftus, *The Creed of a Tory* (London, 1926); Lord Londonderry, *Ourselves and Germany* (London, 1938); David Low, *A Cartoon History of Our Times* (New York, 1939); Sir Oswald Mosley, *The Greater Britain* (London, 1931); Malcolm Muggeridge, *The Sun Never Sets: The Story of England in the Nineteen Thirties* (London, 1940); Harold Nicolson, *Small Talk* (London, 1937); Philip Noel-Baker, *The Private Manufacture of Armaments* (London, 1936); George Orwell, *The Road to Wigan Pier* (London, 1937); Sir Charles Petrie, *The Chamberlain Tradition* (London, 1938); J Henry Richardson, *British Economic Foreign Policy* (London, 1936); Stephen H Roberts, *The House that Hitler Built* (London, 1938); Bertrand Russell, *et al*, *Dare We Look Ahead* (London, 1938); R W Seton-Watson, *Britain and the Dictators* (Cambridge, 1938); Sir Osbert Sitwell, *Laughter in the Next Room* (London, 1949); Andrew Soutar, *With Ironside in North Russia* (London, 1940); *The History of The Times* (4 vols, London, 1952); Arnold Toynbee, ed, *Survey of International Affairs* (London, 1925); 'Unknown Diplomat', *Britain in Spain* (London, 1939); Sir Robert Vansittart, *The Black Record* (London, 1941); Colonel John Ward, *With the 'Die-Hards' in Siberia* (London, 1920); Francis Yeats-Brown, *European Jungle* (London, 1939).

Newspapers and journals – it is obvious in the text of this study – have a special kind of value, for they present an immediate, running commentary on both appeasement and the appeasers. Of consistent usefulness were the *Daily Express*, 1934–1939; *Daily Mail*, 1930–1940; *The Economist*, 1933–1938; *The Times*, 1926–1940;

Manchester Guardian, 1933–1940; *New Statesman and Nation*, 1931–1940; *Nineteenth Century*, 1930–1939; *The Observer*, 1930–1940; *The Spectator*, 1930–1940; and *The Week*, 1934–1939.

Monographs and later accounts are, again, voluminous. The following have direct bearing upon the present study: R Bassett, *Democracy and Foreign Policy: A Case History* (London, 1952); Allen T Bonnell, *German Control over International Economic Relations* (University of Illinois Press, 1940); W F Bruck, *Social and Economic History of Germany from William II to Hitler* (Oxford, 1938); Collin Brooks, *Devil's Decade* (London, 1948); Lord Camrose, *British Newspapers and Their Controllers* (London, 1947); E H Carr, *Britain, A Study of Foreign Policy from the Versailles Treaty to the Outbreak of War* (London, 1939); Randolph S Churchill, *Lord Derby, King of Lancashire* (London, 1959); Winston S Churchill, *The Gathering Storm* (London, 1948); Robert G Colodny, 'A Study of the Foreign Genesis of the Franco Regime' (unpublished Master's Thesis, University of California, 1947); Gordon A Craig and Felix Gilbert, *The Diplomats, 1919–1939* (Princeton, 1953); George Dangerfield, *The Strange Death of Liberal England* (London, 1936); R Palme Dutt, *Britain's Crisis of Empire* (London, 1949); Paul Einzig, *Appeasement Before, During and After the War* (London, 1942); Martin Gilbert and Richard Gott, *The Appeasers* (London, 1963); Robert Graves and Alan Hodge, *The Long Weekend: A Social History of Great Britain, 1918–1939* (London, 1941); Philip Guedalla, *Mr Churchill* (London, 1941); D L Fleming, *The Cold War and Its Origins, 1917–1960* (2 vols, New York, 1961); Keith Hutchison, *The Decline and Fall of British Capitalism* (London, 1951); Alfred E Kahn, *Great Britain in the World Economy* (New York, 1946); Compton Mackenzie, *Dr Benes* (London, 1946); Charles Mowat, *Britain Between the Wars, 1918–1940* (London, 1955); Herbert Muhlen, *The Incredible Krupps* (New York, 1959); Frederic Mullally, *Fascism Inside England* (London, 1946); Pertinax, *Gravediggers of France* (New York, 1944); Hans Rothfels, *The German Opposition to Hitler* (London, 1961); A L Rowse, *The Churchills* (London, 1958); A L Rowse, *All Souls and Appeasement* (London, 1961); Gaetano Salvemini, *Prelude to World War II* (New York, 1954); Frederick L Schuman, *Europe on the Eve: The Crises of Diplomacy, 1933–1939* (New York, 1948); Frederick L Schuman, *Soviet Politics, At Home and Abroad* (New York, 1946); D C Somervell, *British Politics since 1900* (London, 1950); A J P Taylor, *The Origins of the Second War War* (London, 1961); Hugh Thomas, *The Spanish Civil War* (London, 1961); E S Turner, *The Phoney War* (London,

1961); J W Wheeler-Bennett, *Munich: Prologue to Tragedy* (London, 1948); K Zilliacus, *Mirrors of the Past: A History of Secret Diplomacy* (London, 1944).

These articles were consulted: R Bassett, 'Baldwin', *Cambridge Journal*, II (1948); Henderson Braddick, 'The Hoare-Laval Plan: A Study in International Politics', *The Review of Politics*, XXIV, No 3 (July 1962); R Girardet, 'Notes sur l'Esprit d'un Fascisme Français, 1934–1939', *Revue Française de Science Politique*, V (1955); Harvey Glickman, 'The Toryness of English Conservatism', *Journal of British Studies*, No 1 (November 1961); Sir Samuel Hoare, 'Edens Bruch mit Neville Chamberlain', *Aussenpolitik; Zeitschrift für Internationale Fragen*, VI (1955); Sir Samuel Hoare, 'Appeasement: Explosion of the Myth', *The Spectator*, 24th May 1957; John R Hubbard, 'How Franco Financed His War', *Journal of Modern History*, XXV, No 4 (December 1953); William Koren, Jr, 'Britain's Economic Recovery', *Foreign Policy Reports*, XI, Nos 11, 12 (31st July 1935, 14th August 1935); Charles L Mowat, 'Baldwin Restored?" *Journal of Modern History*, XXVII (June 1955); A Snejdarek, 'The Participation of the Sudeten-German Nazis in the Munich Tragedy', *Historica*, I (1959); George Woodbridge, 'Review', *Political Science Quarterly*, LXXVII, No 2 (June 1962).

Index